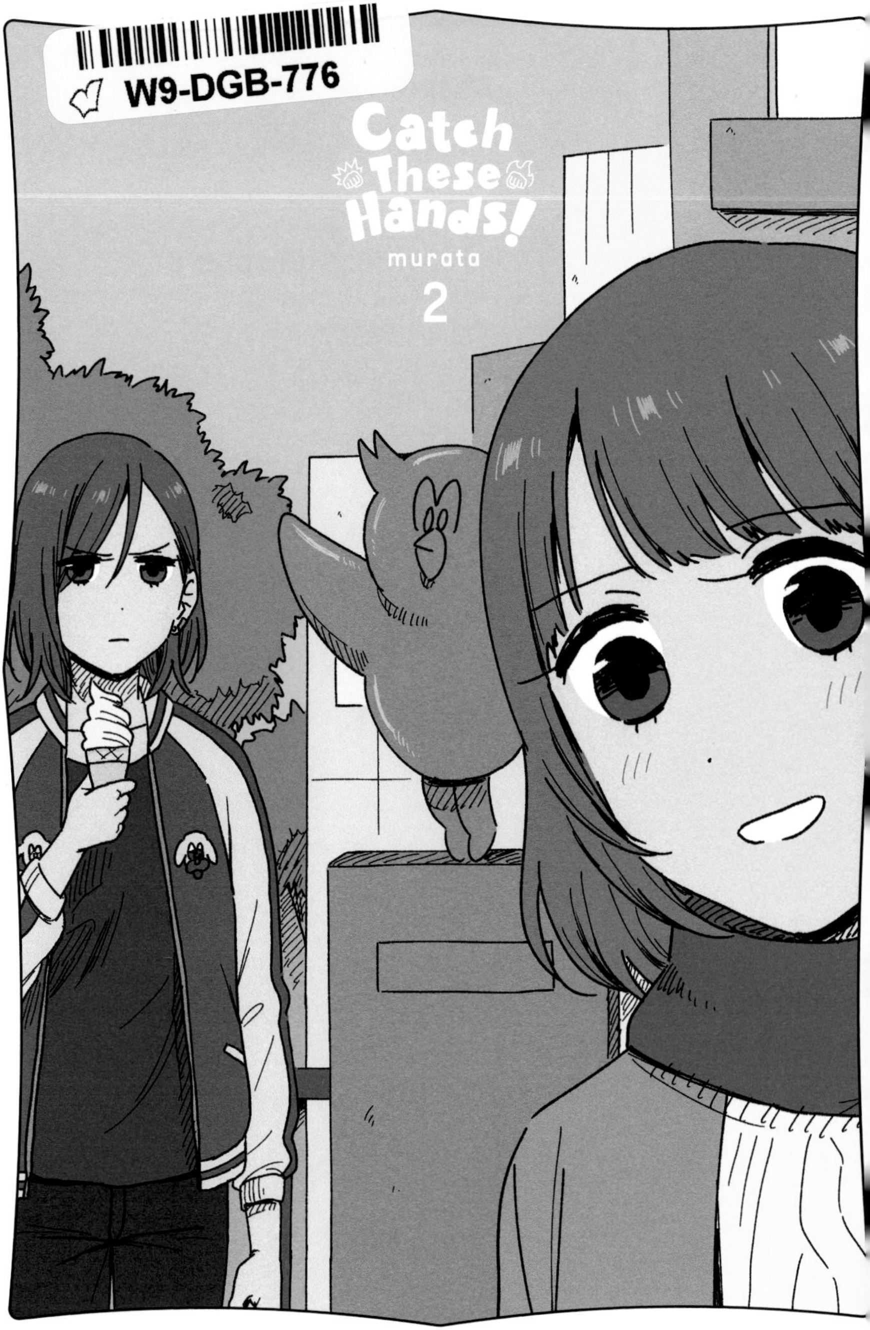
Catch These Hands!
murata
2

Contents

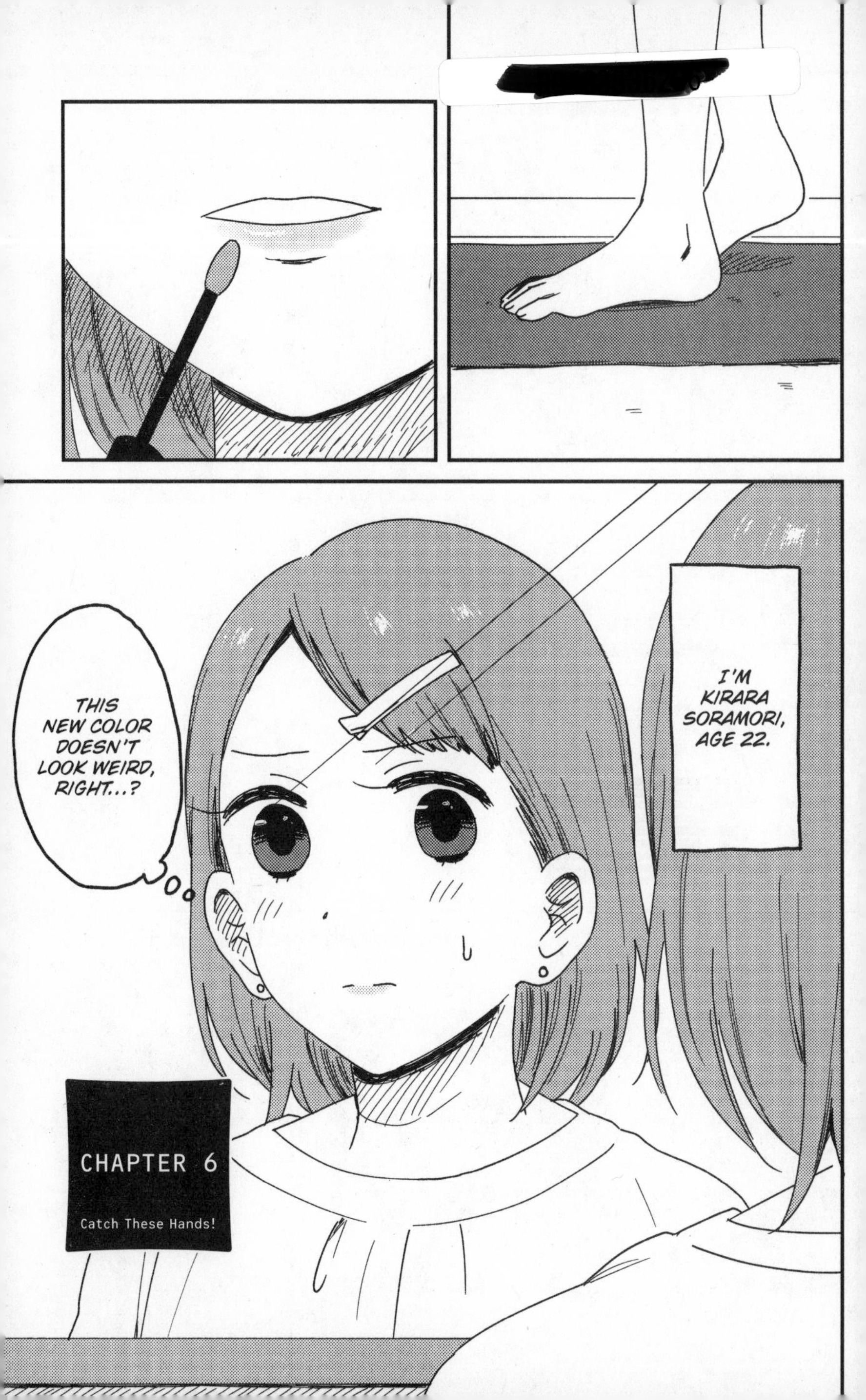
[redacted]
I'M KIRARA SORAMORI, AGE 22.
THIS NEW COLOR DOESN'T LOOK WEIRD, RIGHT...?
CHAPTER 6
Catch These Hands!

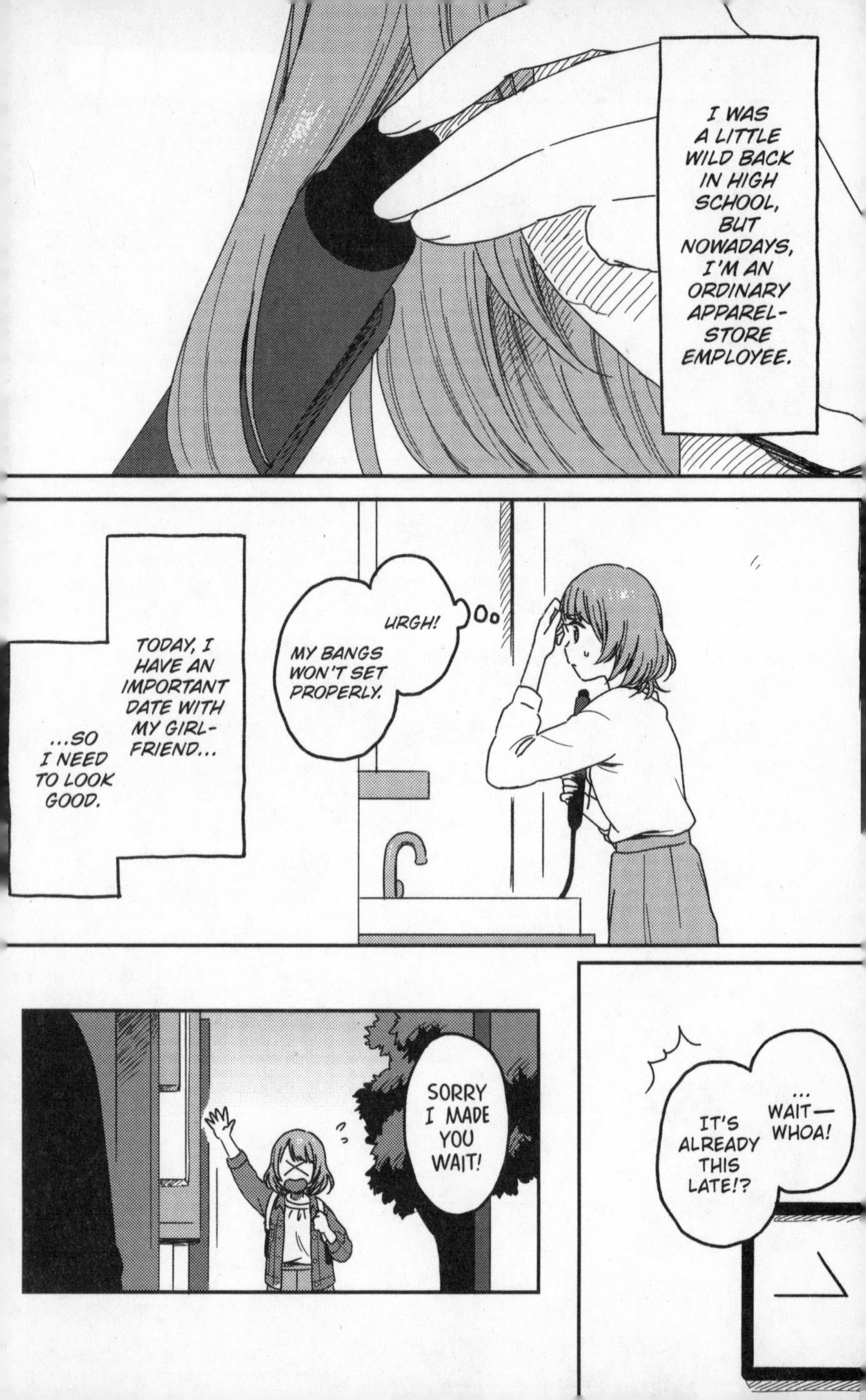
I WAS A LITTLE WILD BACK IN HIGH SCHOOL, BUT NOWADAYS, I'M AN ORDINARY APPAREL-STORE EMPLOYEE.
URGH! MY BANGS WON'T SET PROPERLY.
TODAY, I HAVE AN IMPORTANT DATE WITH MY GIRLFRIEND...
...SO I NEED TO LOOK GOOD.
...WAIT— WHOA!
IT'S ALREADY THIS LATE!?
SORRY I MADE YOU WAIT!

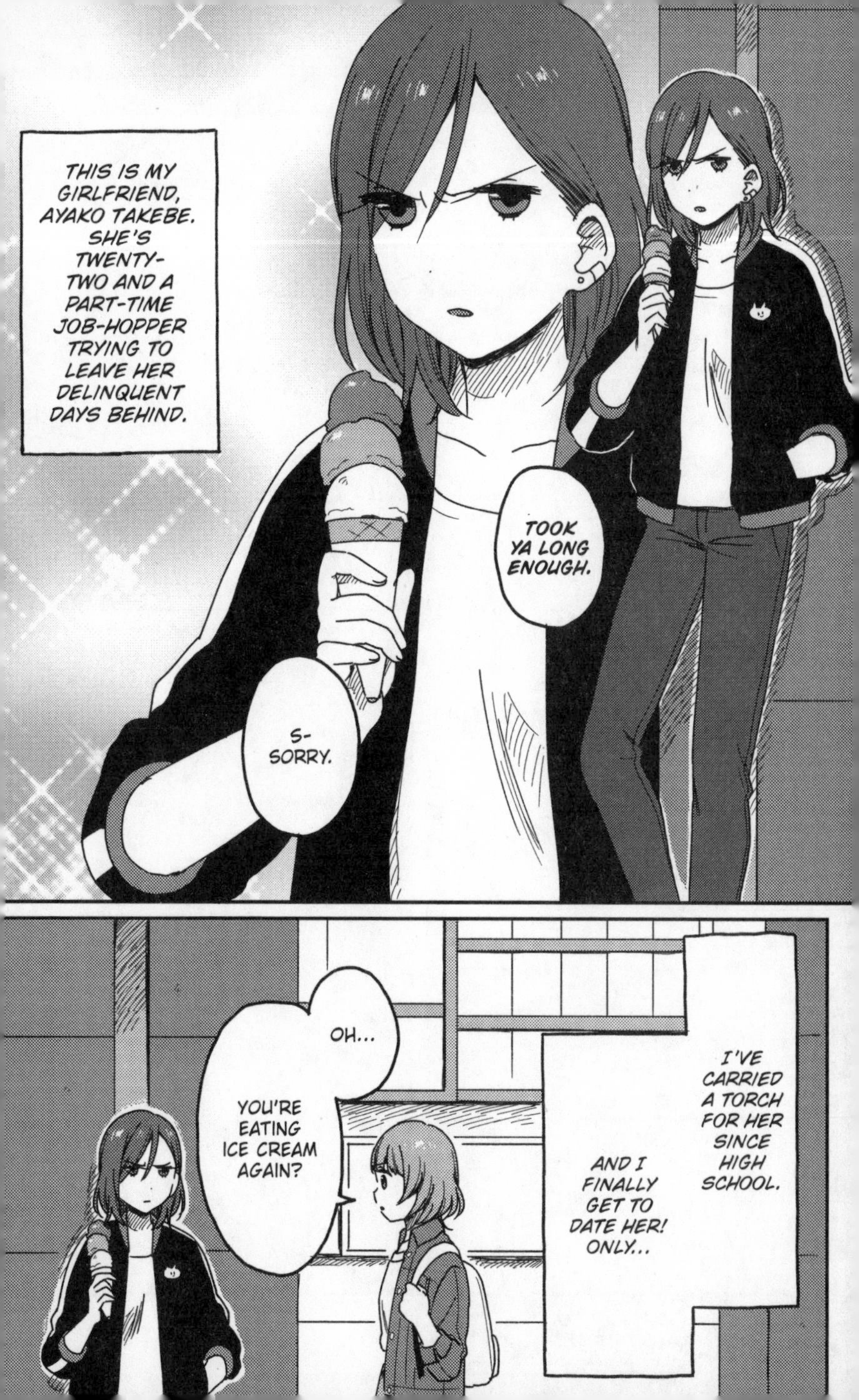
THIS IS MY GIRLFRIEND, AYAKO TAKEBE. SHE'S TWENTY-TWO AND A PART-TIME JOB-HOPPER TRYING TO LEAVE HER DELINQUENT DAYS BEHIND.
TOOK YA LONG ENOUGH.
S-SORRY.
I'VE CARRIED A TORCH FOR HER SINCE HIGH SCHOOL.
AND I FINALLY GET TO DATE HER! ONLY...
OH...
YOU'RE EATING ICE CREAM AGAIN?

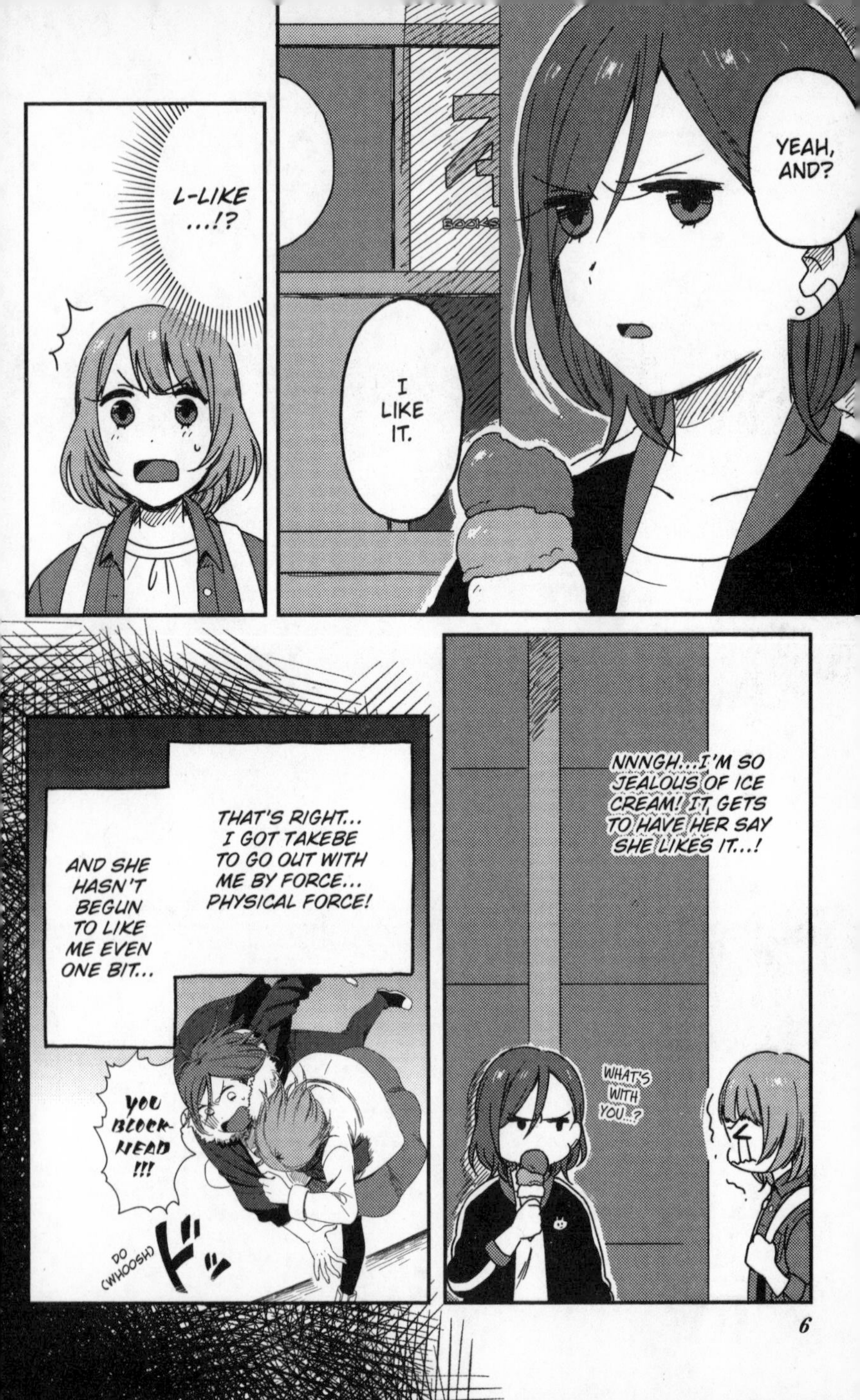
YEAH, AND?
BOOKS
I LIKE IT.
L-LIKE ...!?
NNNGH...I'M SO JEALOUS OF ICE CREAM! IT GETS TO HAVE HER SAY SHE LIKES IT...!
WHAT'S WITH YOU...?
THAT'S RIGHT... I GOT TAKEBE TO GO OUT WITH ME BY FORCE... PHYSICAL FORCE!
AND SHE HASN'T BEGUN TO LIKE ME EVEN ONE BIT...
YOU BLOCKHEAD !!!
ドッ
DO (WHOOSH)

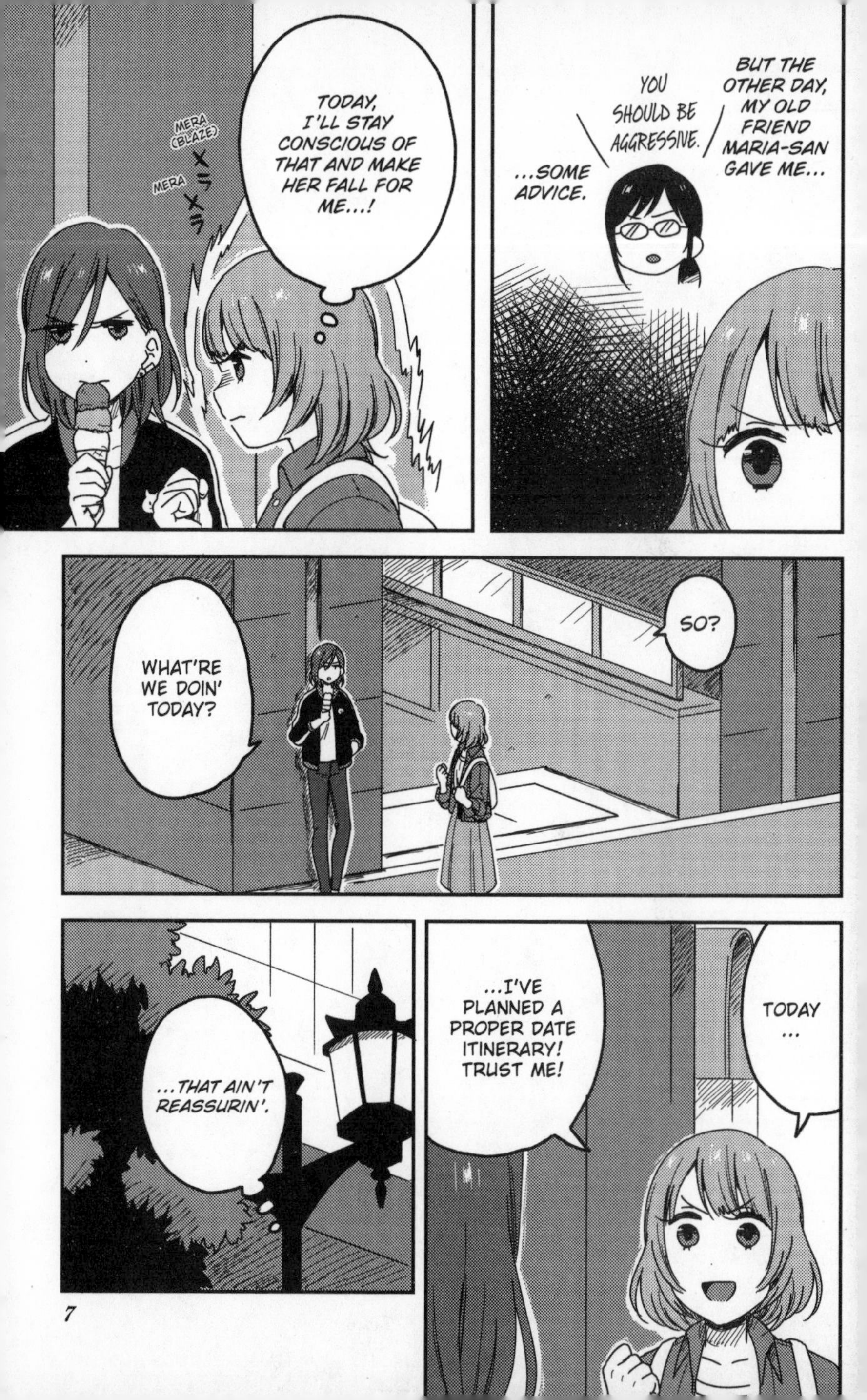
BUT THE OTHER DAY, MY OLD FRIEND MARIA-SAN GAVE ME...
YOU SHOULD BE AGGRESSIVE.
...SOME ADVICE.
TODAY, I'LL STAY CONSCIOUS OF THAT AND MAKE HER FALL FOR ME...!
MERA (BLAZE)
MERA
SO?
WHAT'RE WE DOIN' TODAY?
TODAY...
...I'VE PLANNED A PROPER DATE ITINERARY! TRUST ME!
...THAT AIN'T REASSURIN'.

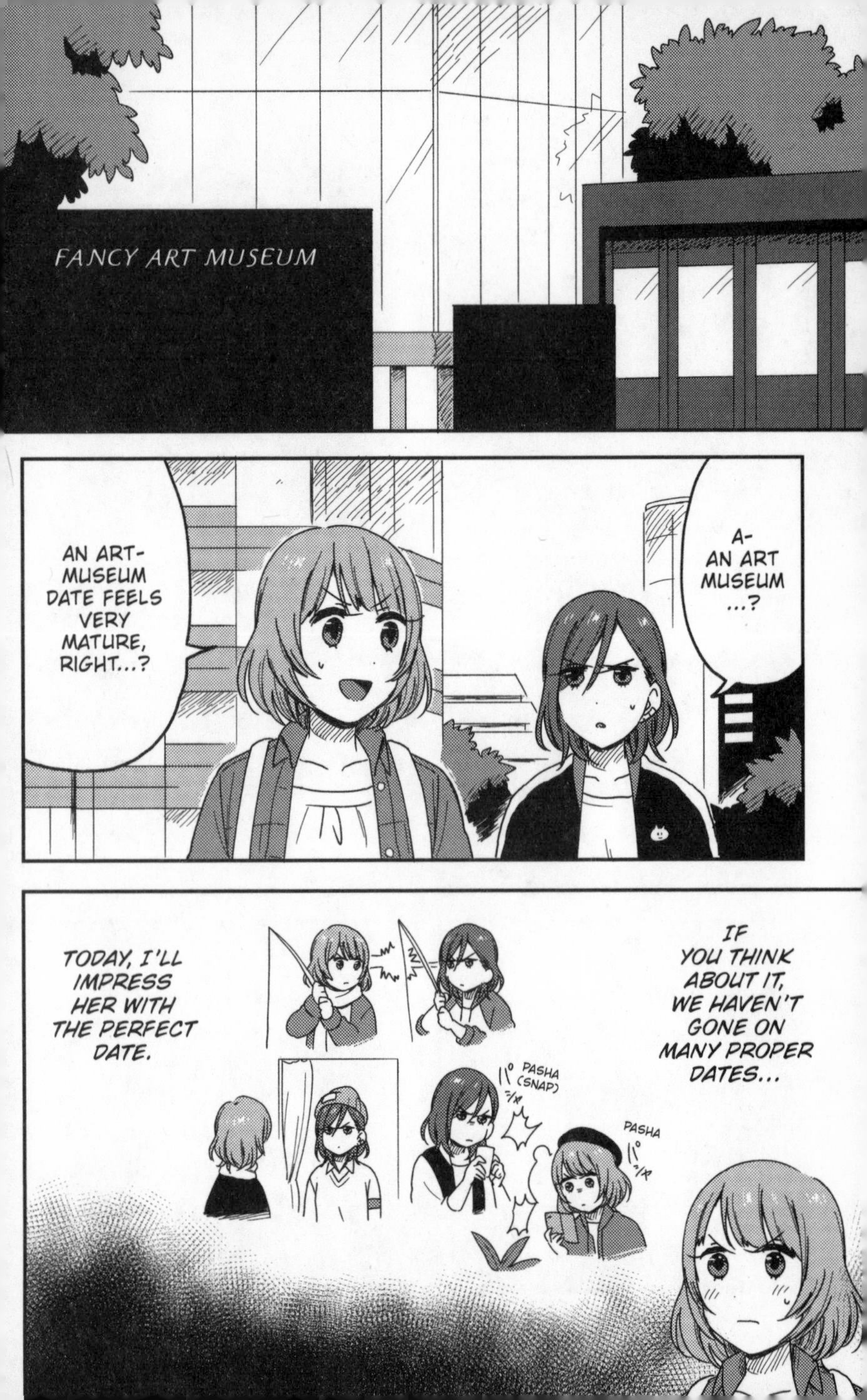
FANCY ART MUSEUM
A- AN ART MUSEUM ...?
AN ART-MUSEUM DATE FEELS VERY MATURE, RIGHT...?
IF YOU THINK ABOUT IT, WE HAVEN'T GONE ON MANY PROPER DATES...
TODAY, I'LL IMPRESS HER WITH THE PERFECT DATE.
PASHA (SNAP)
PASHA

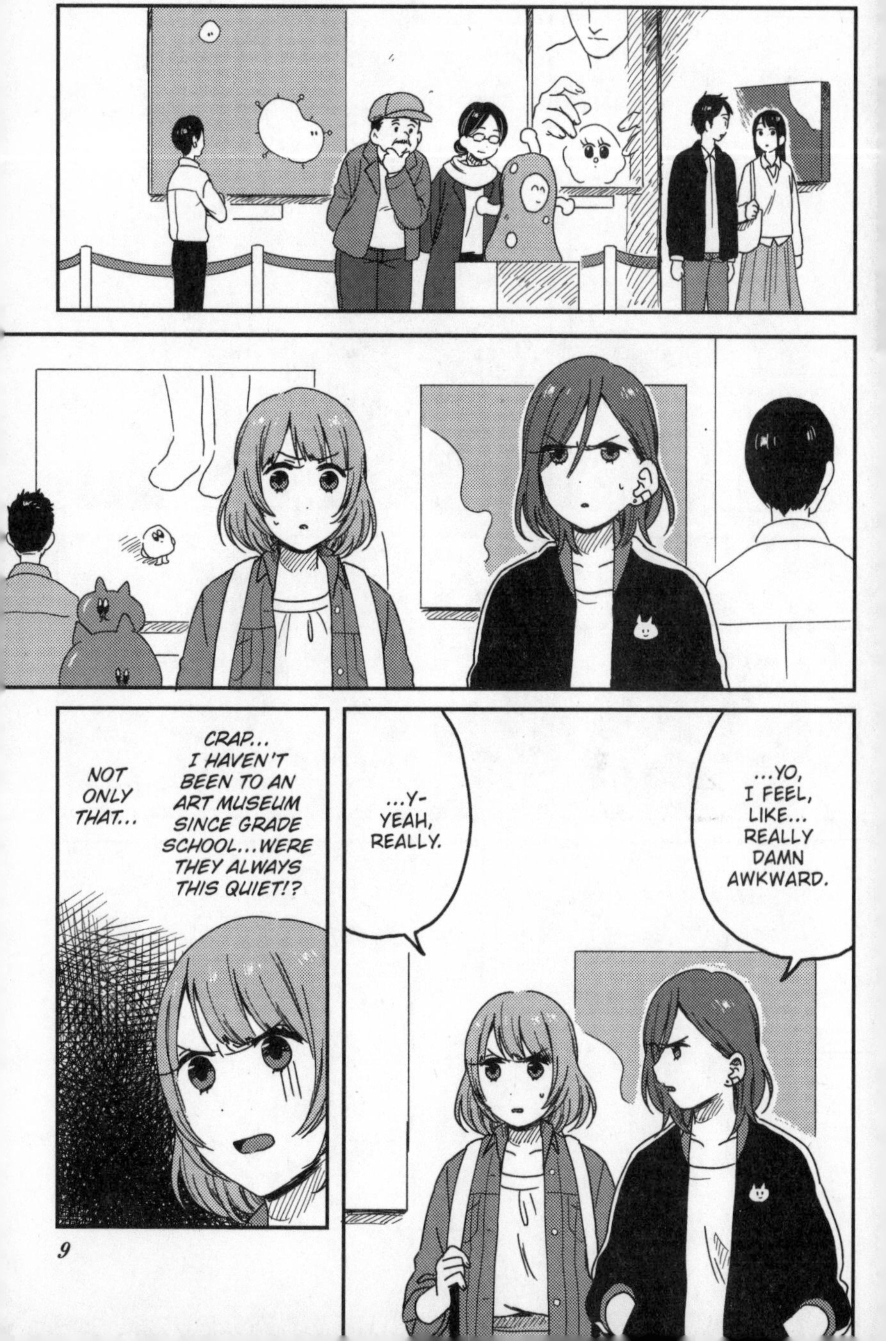
...YO, I FEEL, LIKE... REALLY DAMN AWKWARD.
...Y-YEAH, REALLY.
CRAP... I HAVEN'T BEEN TO AN ART MUSEUM SINCE GRADE SCHOOL...WERE THEY ALWAYS THIS QUIET!?
NOT ONLY THAT...

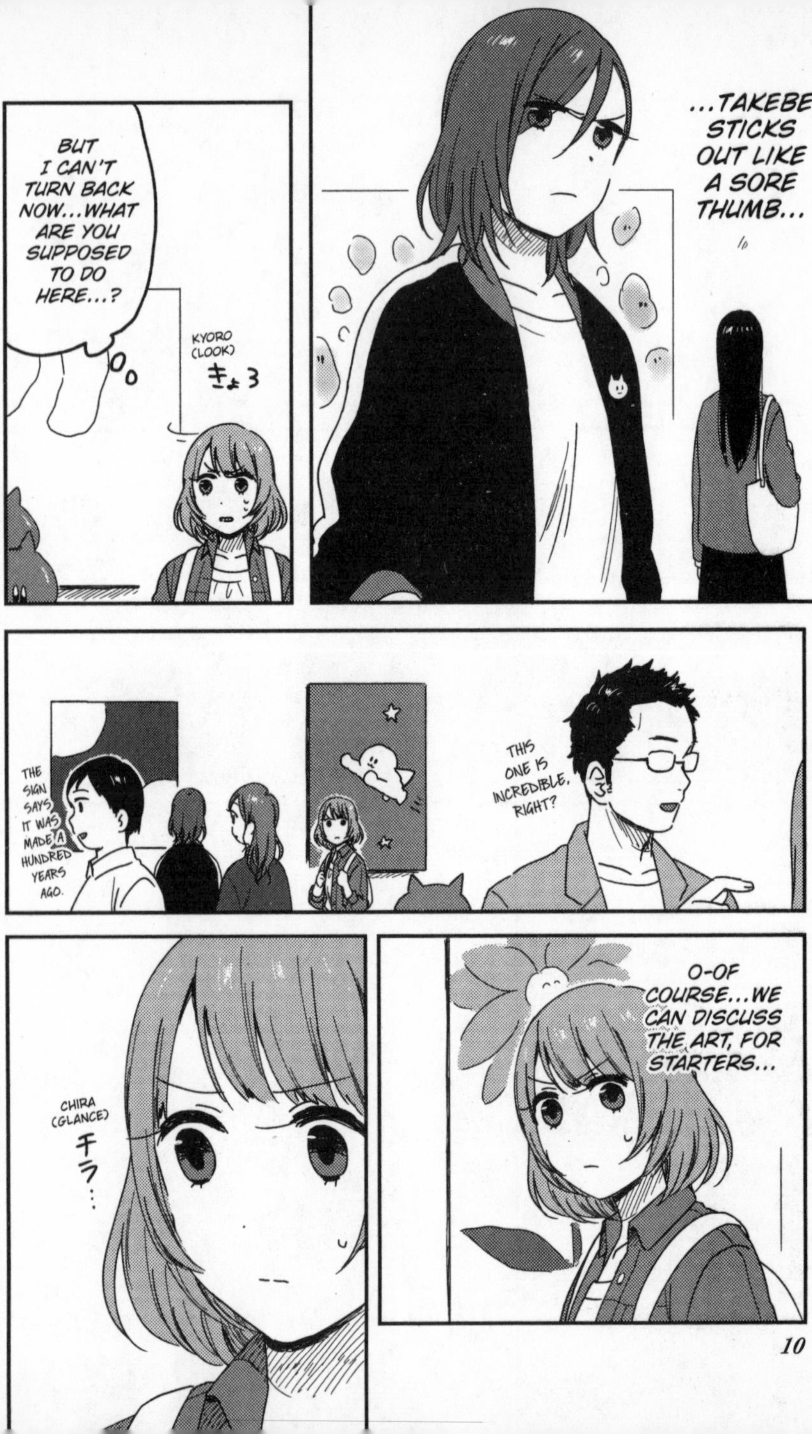
...TAKEBE STICKS OUT LIKE A SORE THUMB...
BUT I CAN'T TURN BACK NOW...WHAT ARE YOU SUPPOSED TO DO HERE...?
KYORO (LOOK)
きょろ
THIS ONE IS INCREDIBLE, RIGHT?
THE SIGN SAYS IT WAS MADE A HUNDRED YEARS AGO.
O-OF COURSE...WE CAN DISCUSS THE ART, FOR STARTERS...
CHIRA (GLANCE)
チラ...

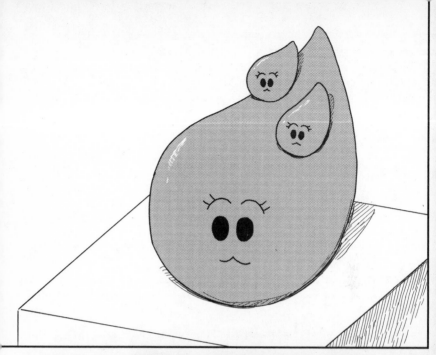

...WH- WHAT THE HECK IS IT...?

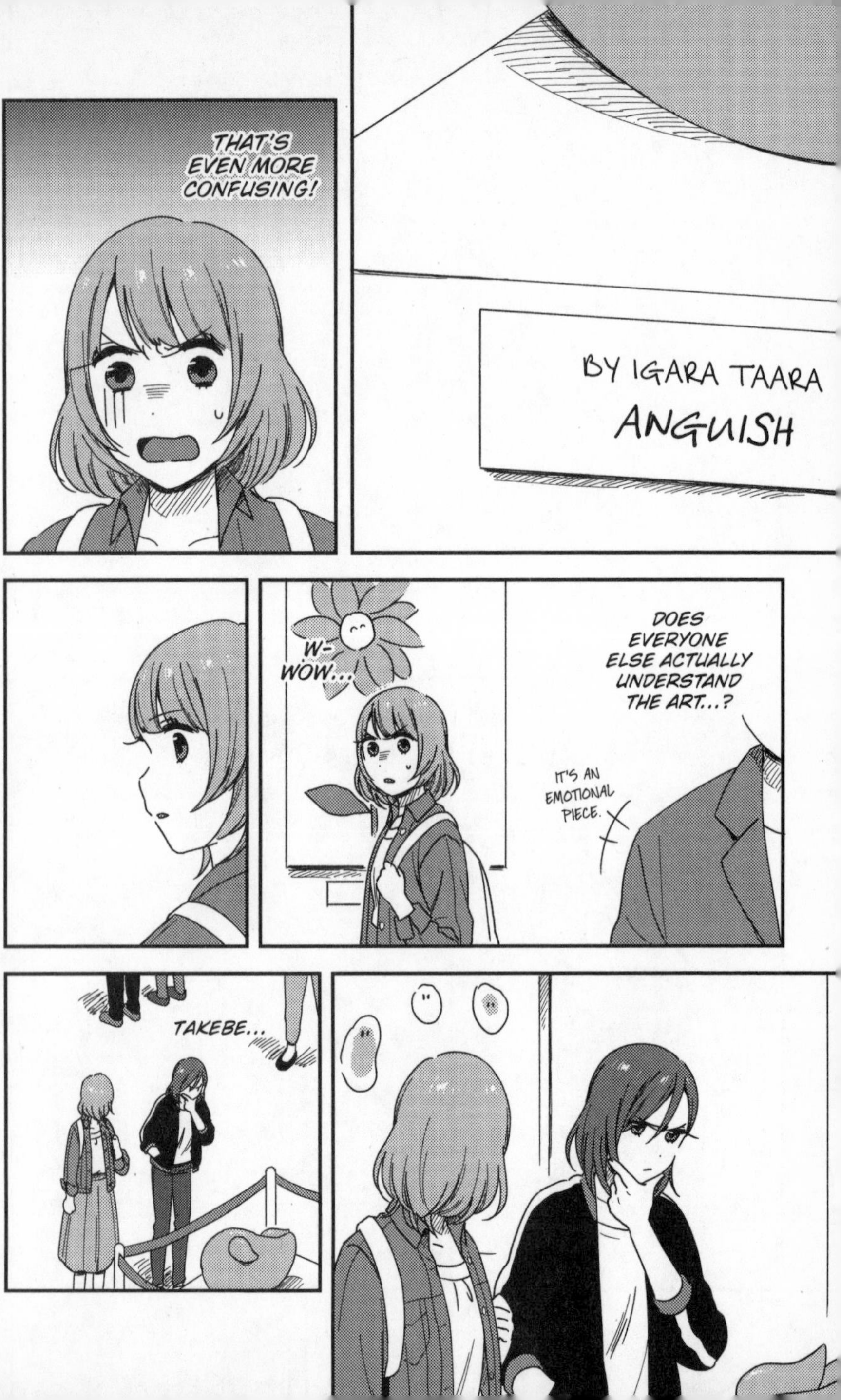
BY IGARA TAARA
ANGUISH
THAT'S EVEN MORE CONFUSING!
DOES EVERYONE ELSE ACTUALLY UNDERSTAND THE ART...?
W-WOW...
IT'S AN EMOTIONAL PIECE.
TAKEBE...

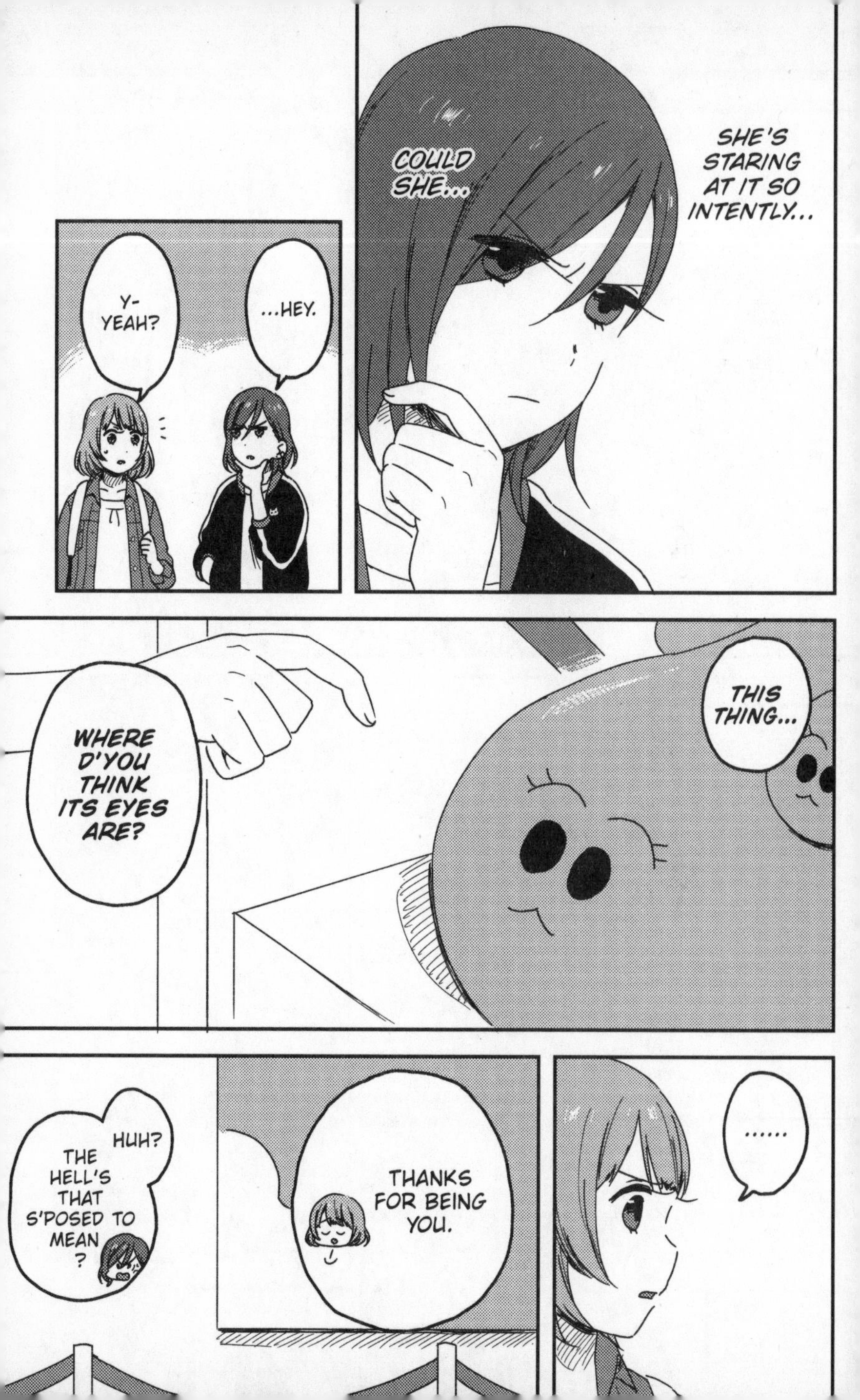
SHE'S STARING AT IT SO INTENTLY...
COULD SHE...
...HEY.
Y-YEAH?
THIS THING...
WHERE D'YOU THINK ITS EYES ARE?
......
THANKS FOR BEING YOU.
HUH? THE HELL'S THAT S'POSED TO MEAN?

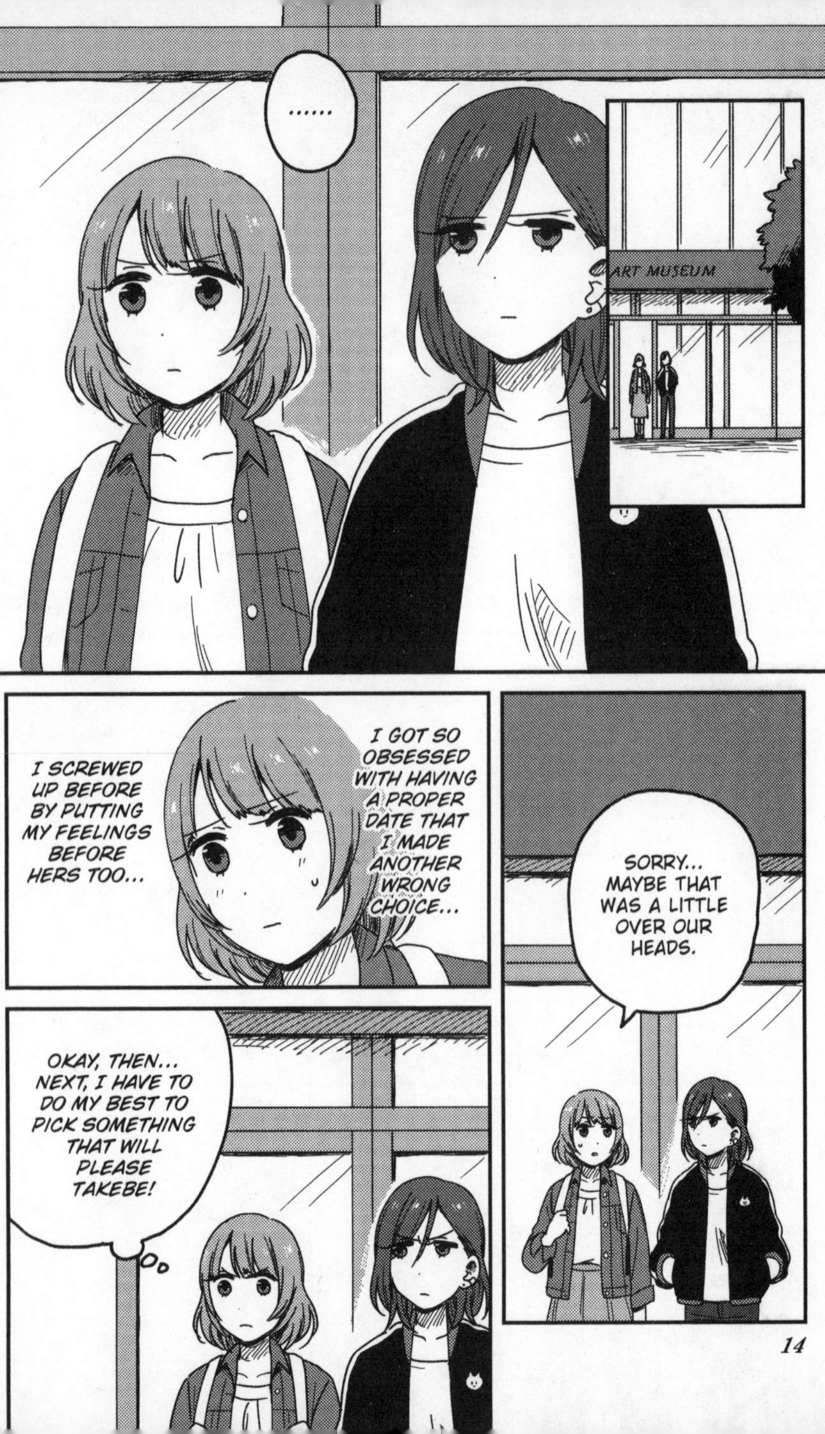
ART MUSEUM
......
SORRY... MAYBE THAT WAS A LITTLE OVER OUR HEADS.
I GOT SO OBSESSED WITH HAVING A PROPER DATE THAT I MADE ANOTHER WRONG CHOICE...
I SCREWED UP BEFORE BY PUTTING MY FEELINGS BEFORE HERS TOO...
OKAY, THEN... NEXT, I HAVE TO DO MY BEST TO PICK SOMETHING THAT WILL PLEASE TAKEBE!

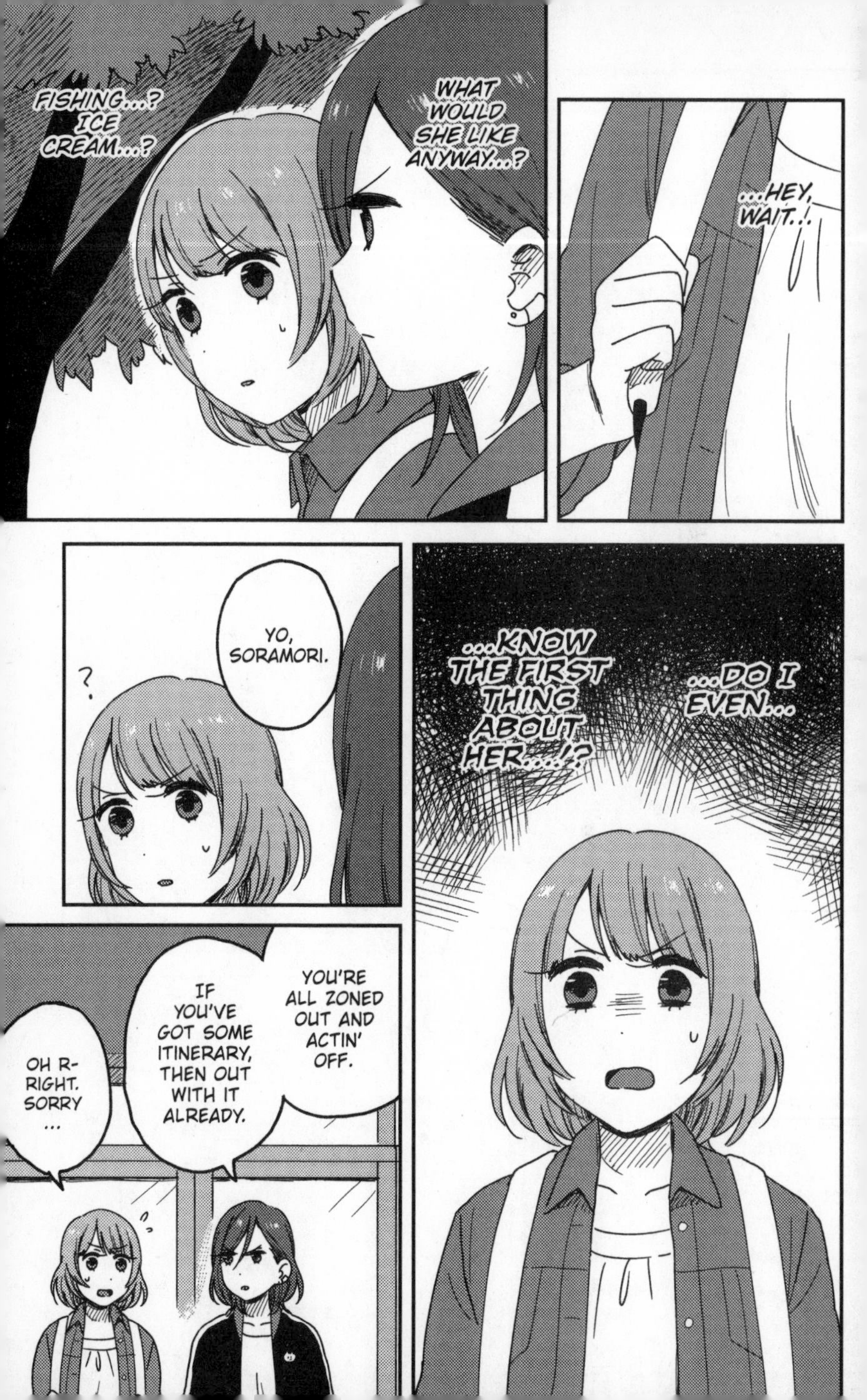
...HEY, WAIT..!
WHAT WOULD SHE LIKE ANYWAY...?
FISHING...? ICE CREAM...?
...DO I EVEN...
...KNOW THE FIRST THING ABOUT HER...!?
YO, SORAMORI.
?
YOU'RE ALL ZONED OUT AND ACTIN' OFF.
IF YOU'VE GOT SOME ITINERARY, THEN OUT WITH IT ALREADY.
OH R-RIGHT. SORRY...

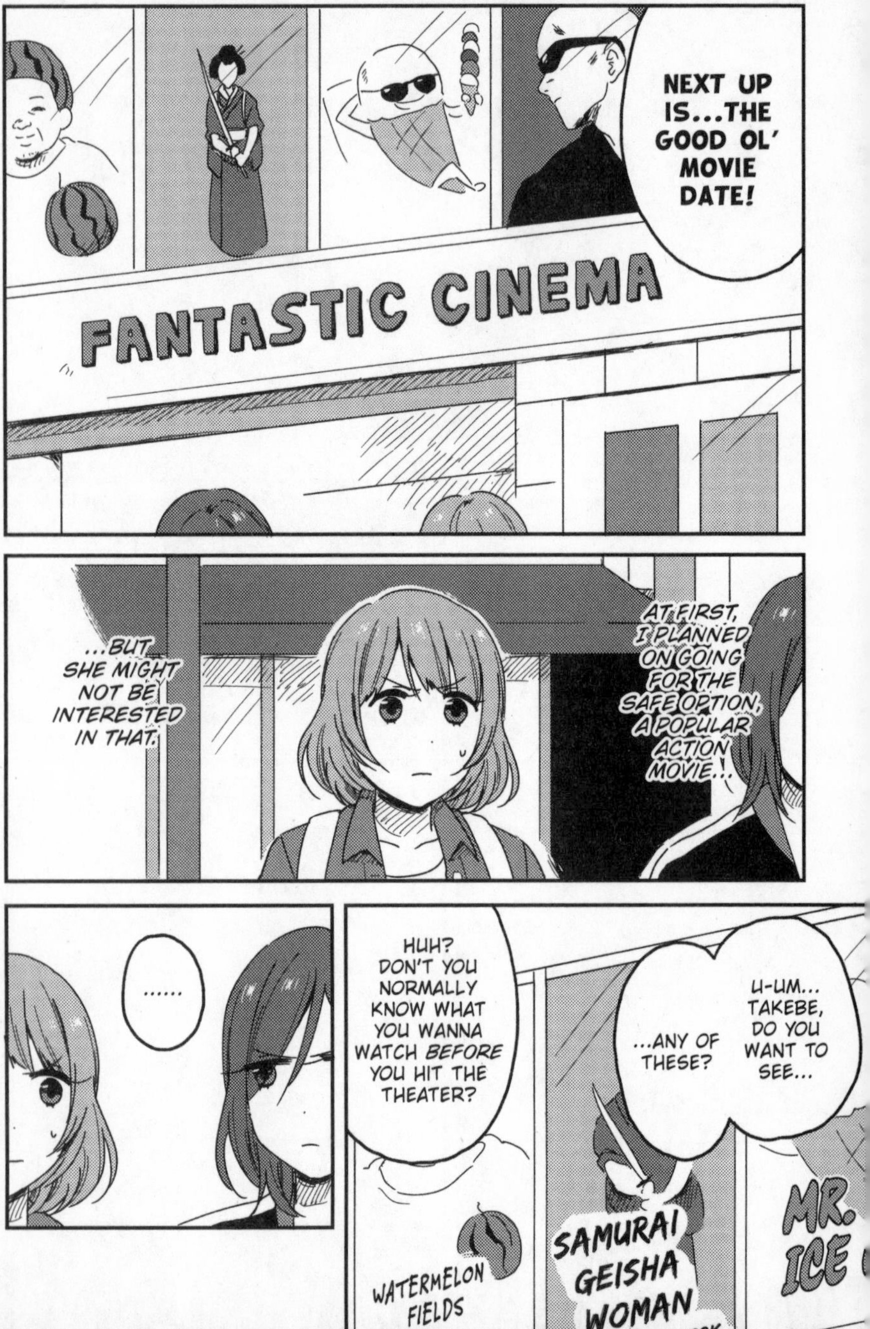
NEXT UP IS...THE GOOD OL' MOVIE DATE!
FANTASTIC CINEMA
AT FIRST, I PLANNED ON GOING FOR THE SAFE OPTION, A POPULAR ACTION MOVIE...
...BUT SHE MIGHT NOT BE INTERESTED IN THAT.
U-UM... TAKEBE, DO YOU WANT TO SEE...
...ANY OF THESE?
HUH? DON'T YOU NORMALLY KNOW WHAT YOU WANNA WATCH *BEFORE* YOU HIT THE THEATER?
MR. ICE
SAMURAI GEISHA WOMAN
WATERMELON FIELDS
......

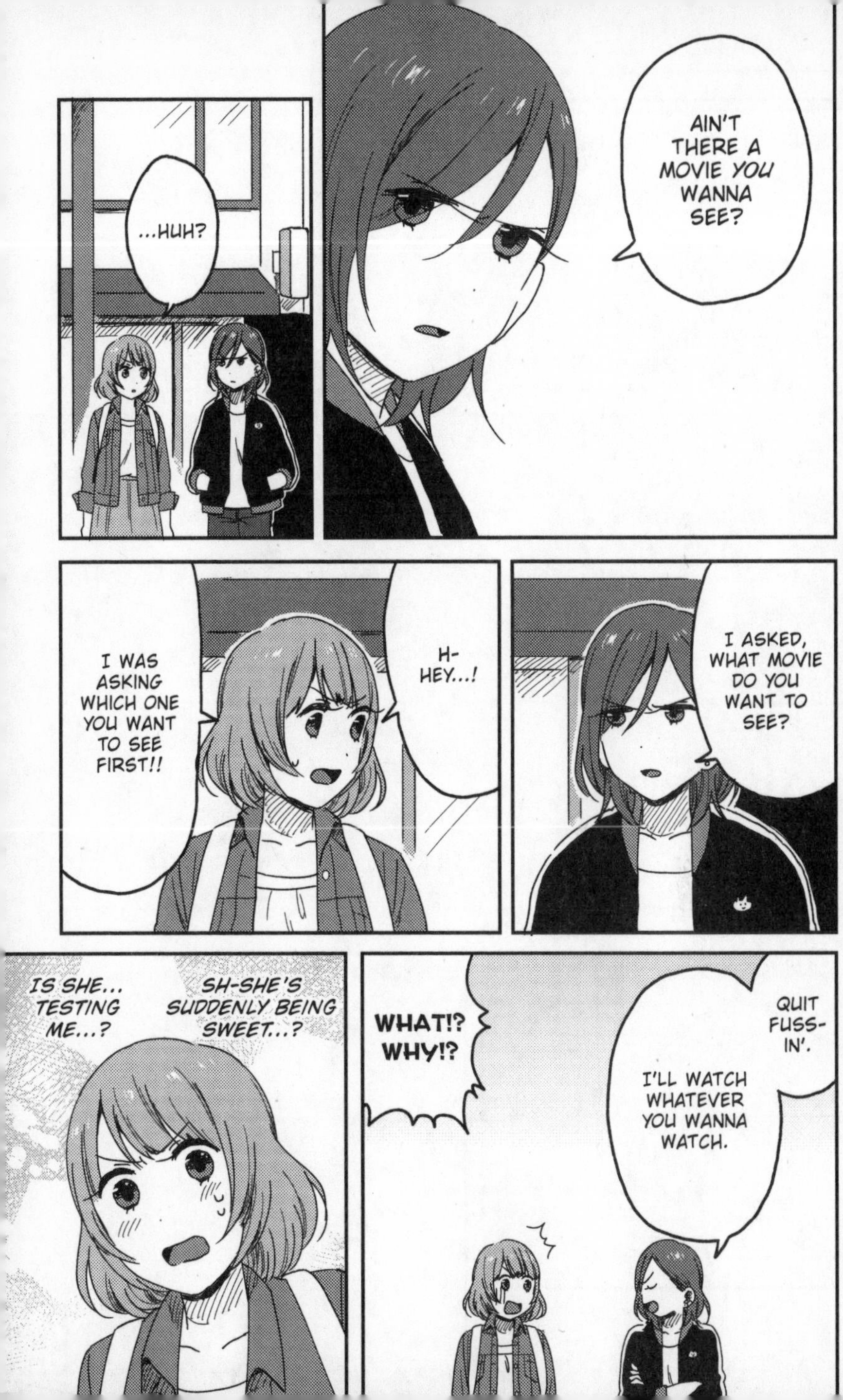
AIN'T THERE A MOVIE *YOU* WANNA SEE?
...HUH?
I ASKED, WHAT MOVIE DO YOU WANT TO SEE?
H-HEY...!
I WAS ASKING WHICH ONE YOU WANT TO SEE FIRST!!
QUIT FUSS-IN'.
I'LL WATCH WHATEVER YOU WANNA WATCH.
WHAT!? WHY!?
SH-SHE'S SUDDENLY BEING SWEET...?
IS SHE... TESTING ME...?

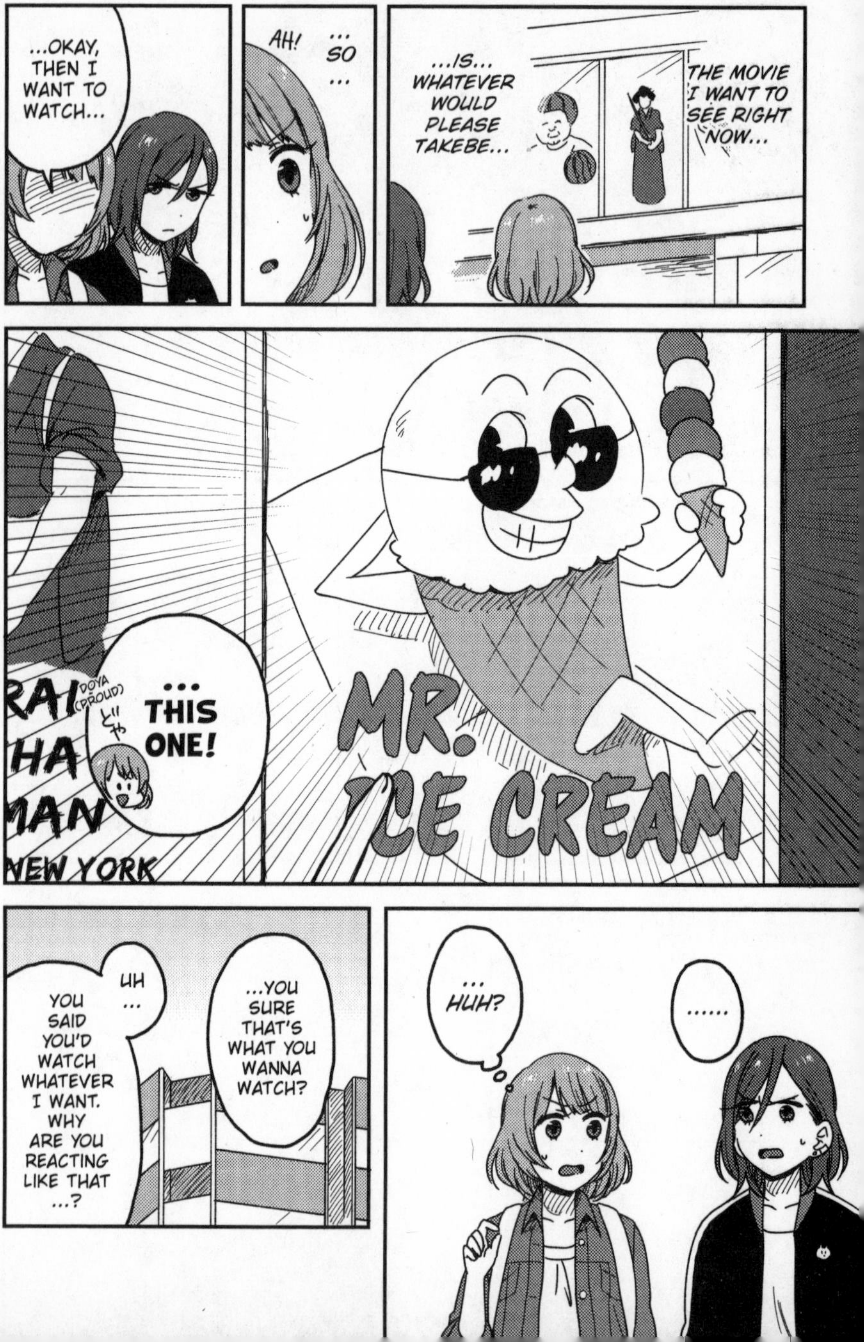
THE MOVIE I WANT TO SEE RIGHT NOW...
...IS... WHATEVER WOULD PLEASE TAKEBE...
... SO ...
AH!
...OKAY, THEN I WANT TO WATCH...
... THIS ONE!
DOYA (PROUD) どや
MR. ICE CREAM
RAI
HA
MAN
NEW YORK
......
... HUH?
...YOU SURE THAT'S WHAT YOU WANNA WATCH?
UH ...
YOU SAID YOU'D WATCH WHATEVER I WANT. WHY ARE YOU REACTING LIKE THAT ...?

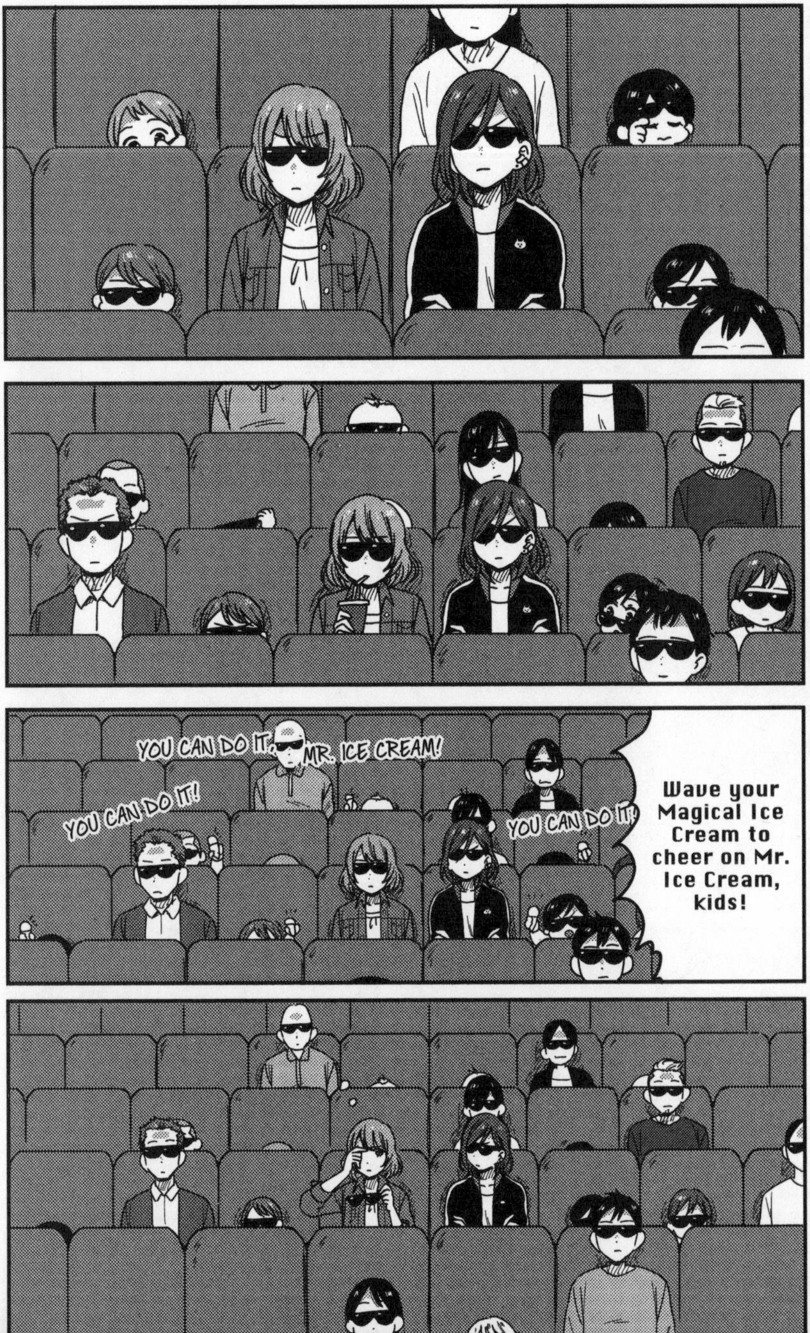
Wave your Magical Ice Cream to cheer on Mr. Ice Cream, kids!
YOU CAN DO IT!
YOU CAN DO IT, MR. ICE CREAM!
YOU CAN DO IT!

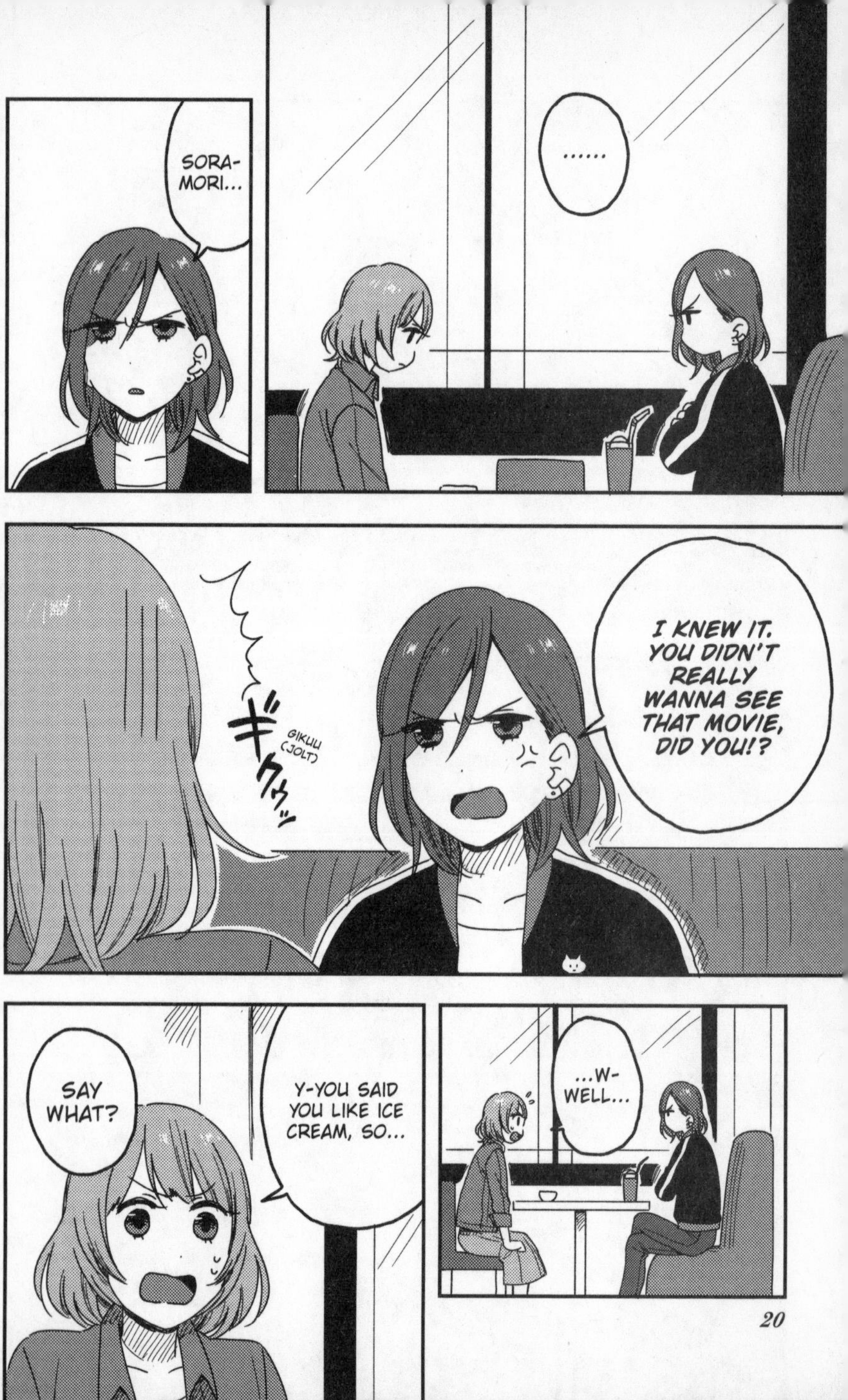

......
SORA-MORI...
I KNEW IT. YOU DIDN'T REALLY WANNA SEE THAT MOVIE, DID YOU!?
ギクゥッ
GIKUU (JOLT)
...W-WELL...
Y-YOU SAID YOU LIKE ICE CREAM, SO...
SAY WHAT?

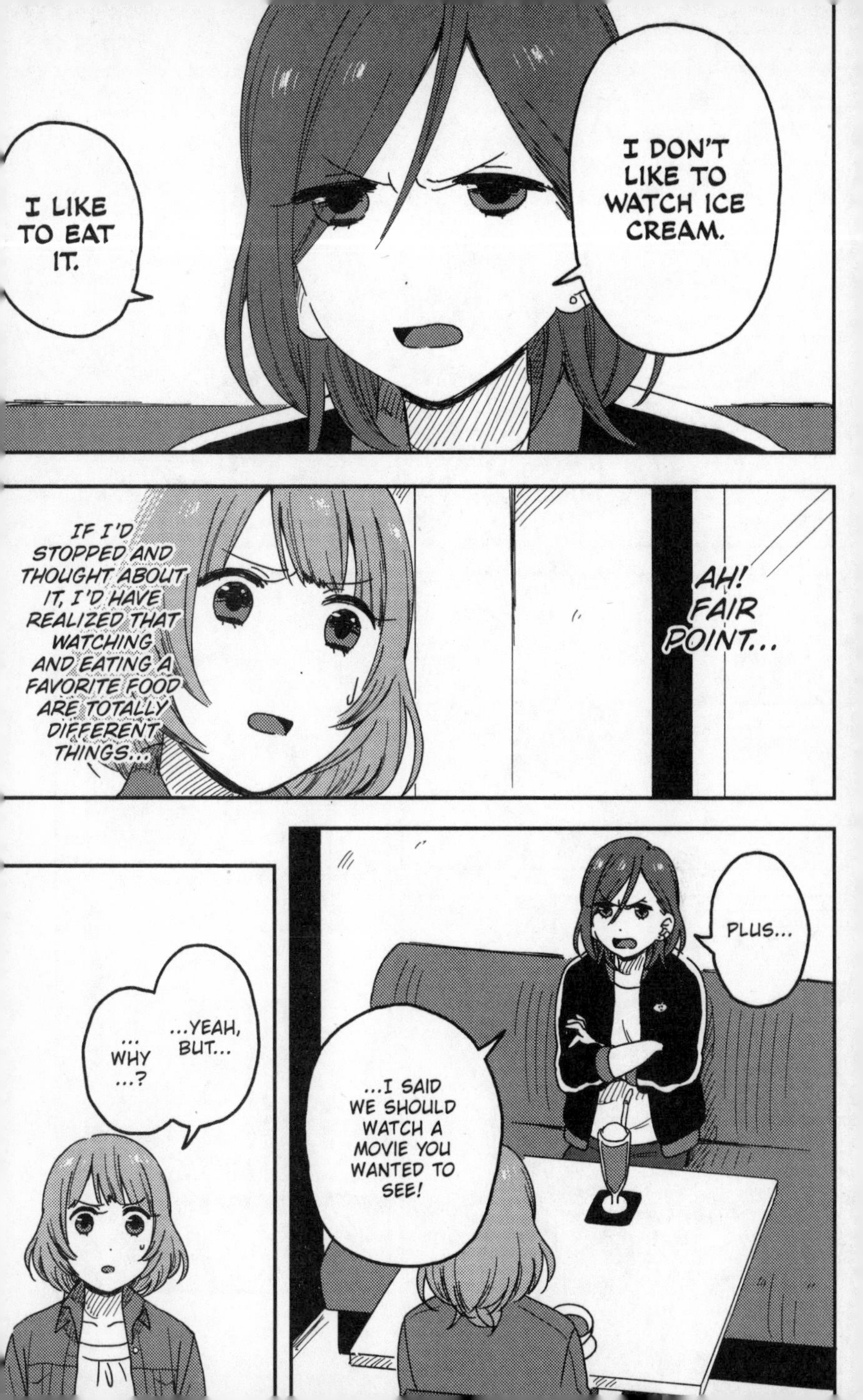
I DON'T LIKE TO WATCH ICE CREAM.
I LIKE TO EAT IT.
AH! FAIR POINT...
IF I'D STOPPED AND THOUGHT ABOUT IT, I'D HAVE REALIZED THAT WATCHING AND EATING A FAVORITE FOOD ARE TOTALLY DIFFERENT THINGS...
PLUS...
...I SAID WE SHOULD WATCH A MOVIE YOU WANTED TO SEE!
...YEAH, BUT...
...WHY...?

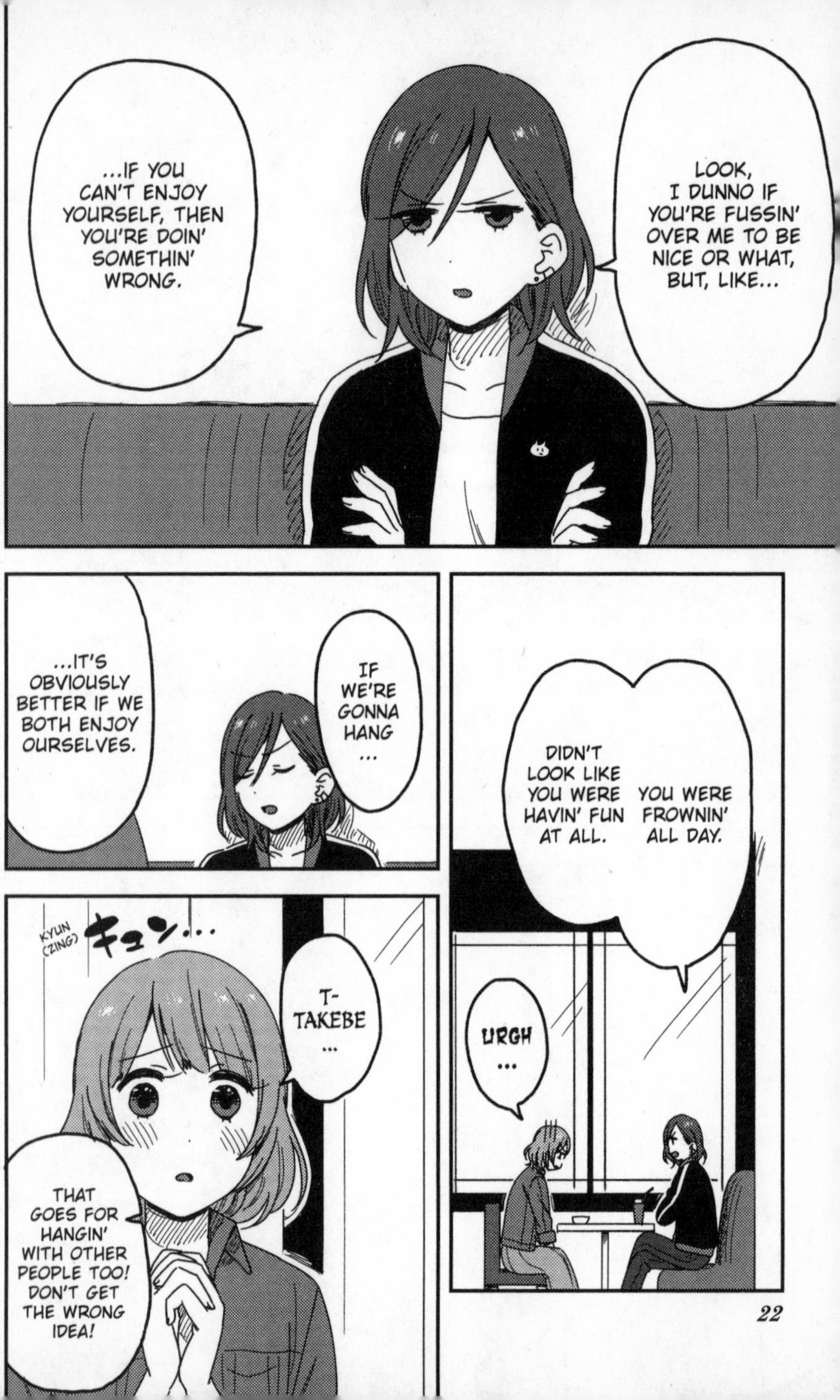
LOOK, I DUNNO IF YOU'RE FUSSIN' OVER ME TO BE NICE OR WHAT, BUT, LIKE...
...IF YOU CAN'T ENJOY YOURSELF, THEN YOU'RE DOIN' SOMETHIN' WRONG.
YOU WERE FROWNIN' ALL DAY.
DIDN'T LOOK LIKE YOU WERE HAVIN' FUN AT ALL.
URGH ...
IF WE'RE GONNA HANG ...
...IT'S OBVIOUSLY BETTER IF WE BOTH ENJOY OURSELVES.
KYUN (ZING) キュン...
T-TAKEBE ...
THAT GOES FOR HANGIN' WITH OTHER PEOPLE TOO! DON'T GET THE WRONG IDEA!

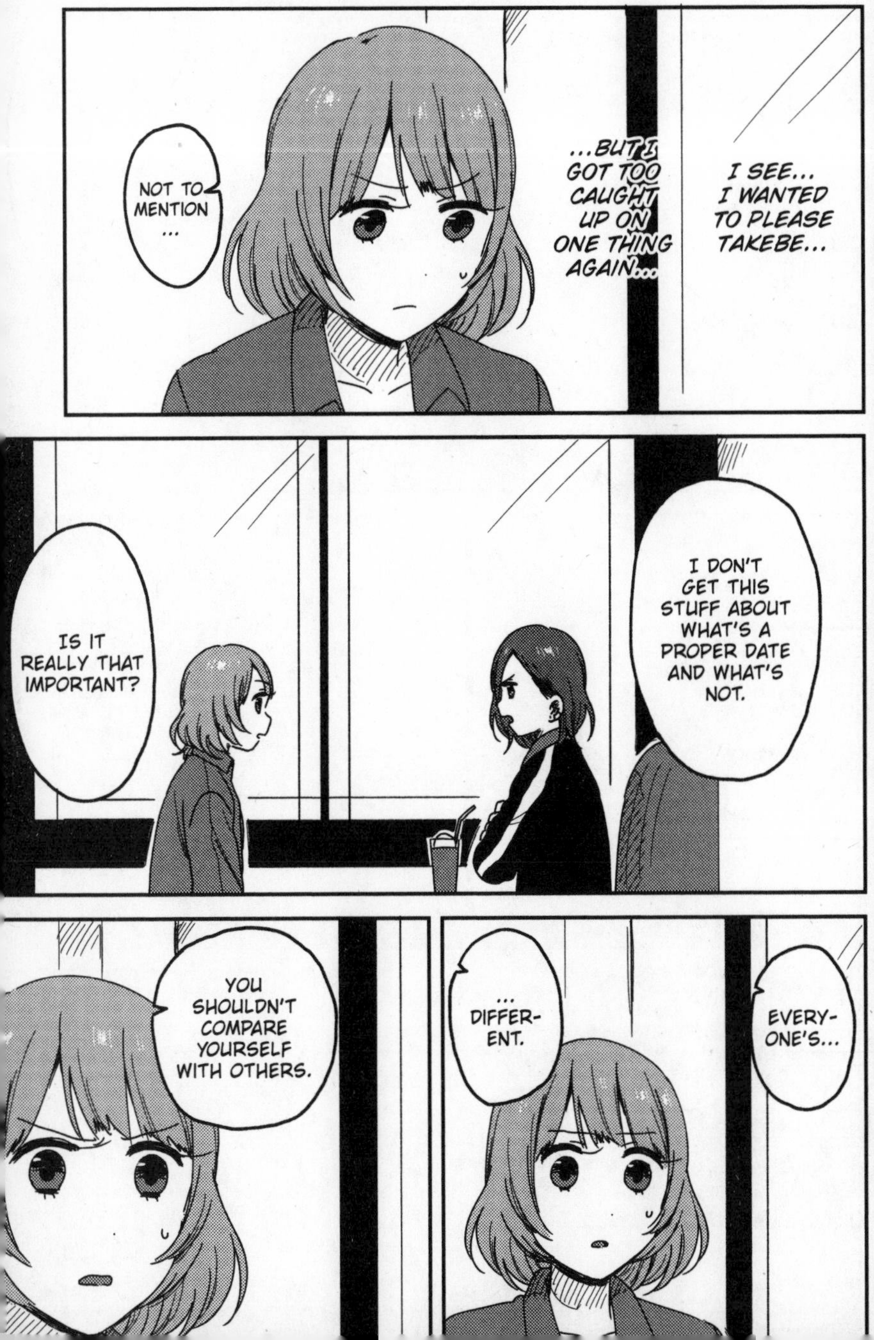
I SEE... I WANTED TO PLEASE TAKEBE...
...BUT I GOT TOO CAUGHT UP ON ONE THING AGAIN...
NOT TO MENTION ...
I DON'T GET THIS STUFF ABOUT WHAT'S A PROPER DATE AND WHAT'S NOT.
IS IT REALLY THAT IMPORTANT?
EVERY-ONE'S...
... DIFFER-ENT.
YOU SHOULDN'T COMPARE YOURSELF WITH OTHERS.

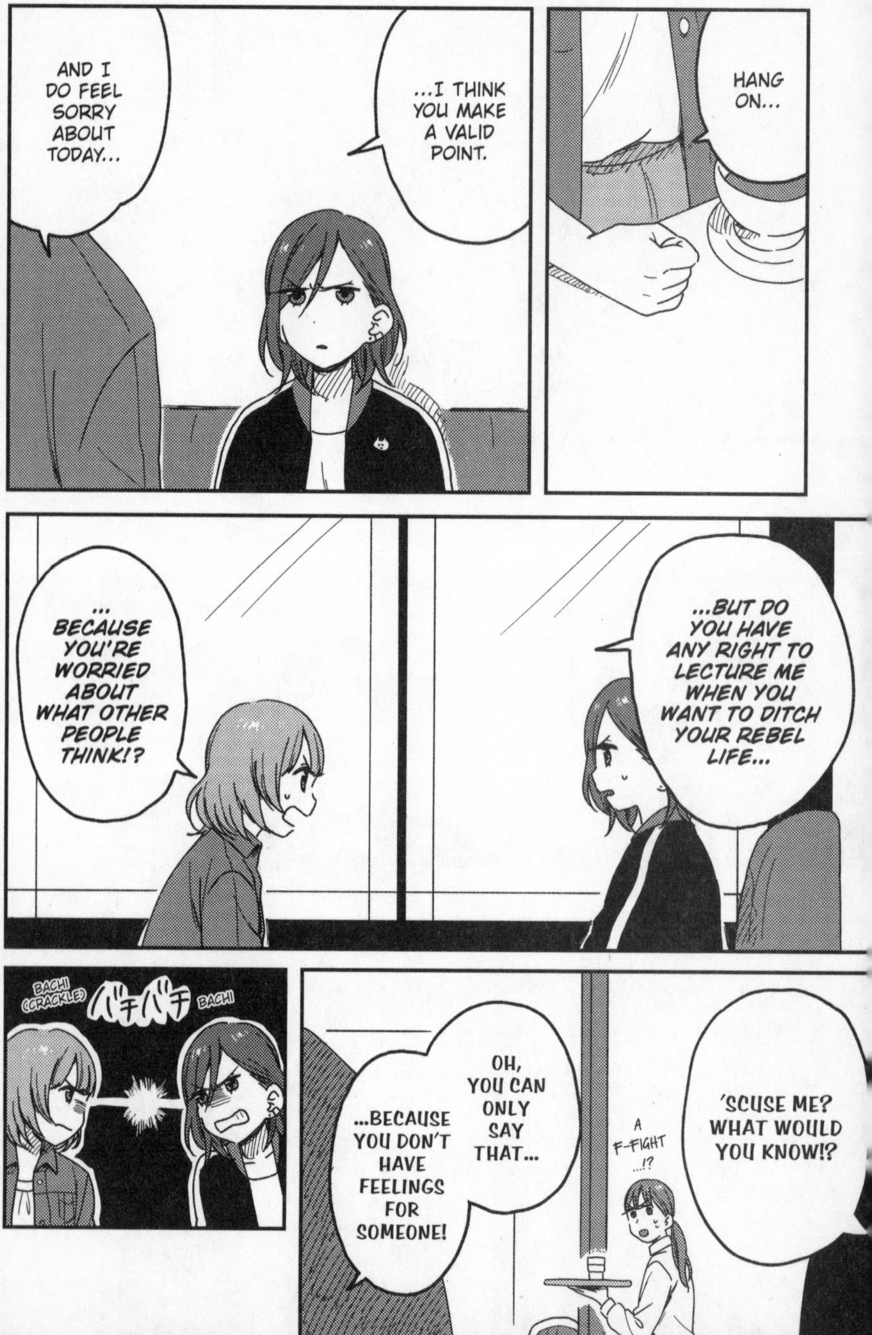
HANG ON...
...I THINK YOU MAKE A VALID POINT.
AND I DO FEEL SORRY ABOUT TODAY...
...BUT DO YOU HAVE ANY RIGHT TO LECTURE ME WHEN YOU WANT TO DITCH YOUR REBEL LIFE...
...BECAUSE YOU'RE WORRIED ABOUT WHAT OTHER PEOPLE THINK!?
'SCUSE ME? WHAT WOULD YOU KNOW!?
A F-FIGHT ...!?
OH, YOU CAN ONLY SAY THAT...
...BECAUSE YOU DON'T HAVE FEELINGS FOR SOMEONE!
BACHI (CRACKLE)
バチバチ
BACHI

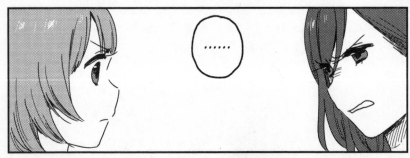

......

PFFT!

SORRY.

AH HA HA!

WHAT'S SO FUNNY? YOU FINALLY LOST YOUR MIND?

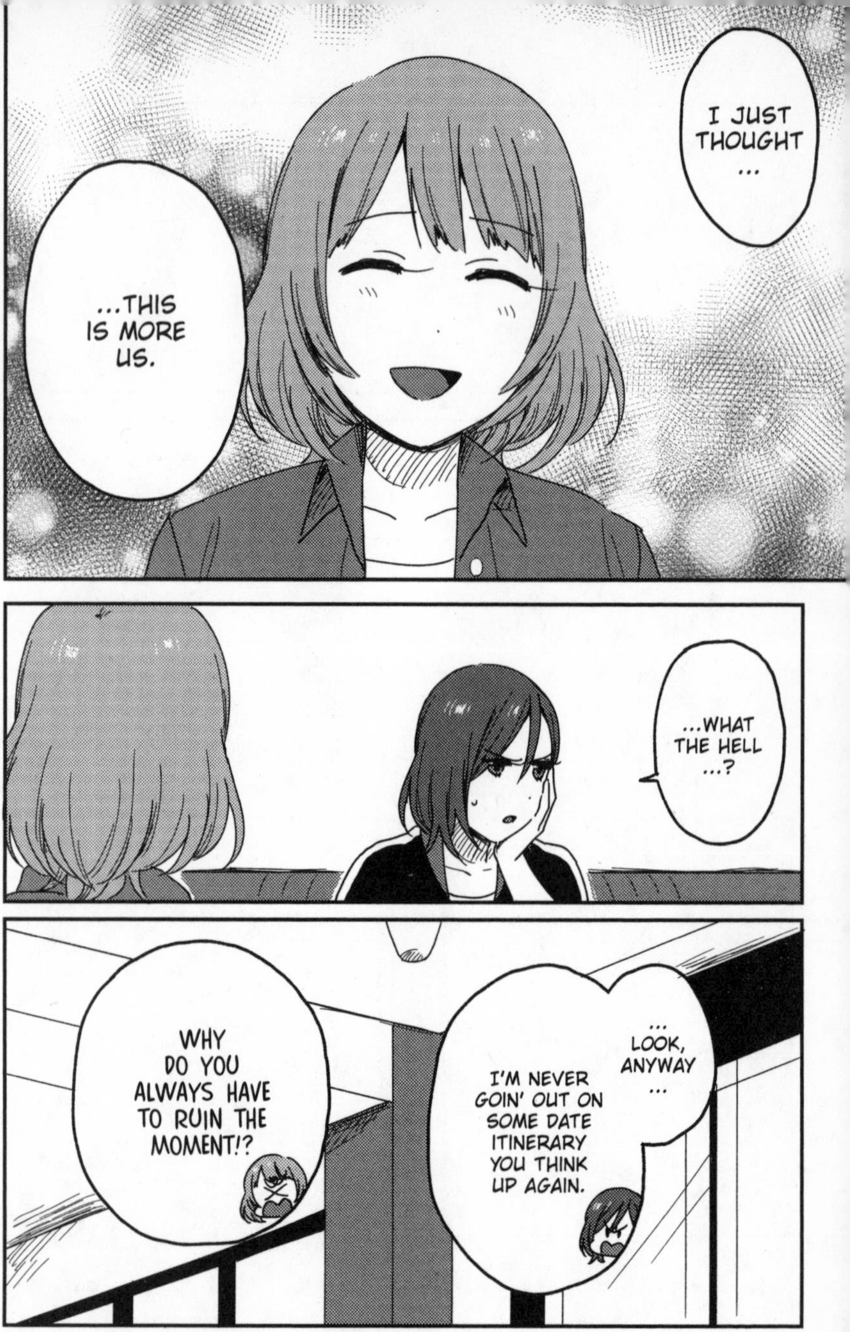
I JUST THOUGHT ...
...THIS IS MORE US.
...WHAT THE HELL ...?
... LOOK, ANYWAY ...
I'M NEVER GOIN' OUT ON SOME DATE ITINERARY YOU THINK UP AGAIN.
WHY DO YOU ALWAYS HAVE TO RUIN THE MOMENT!?

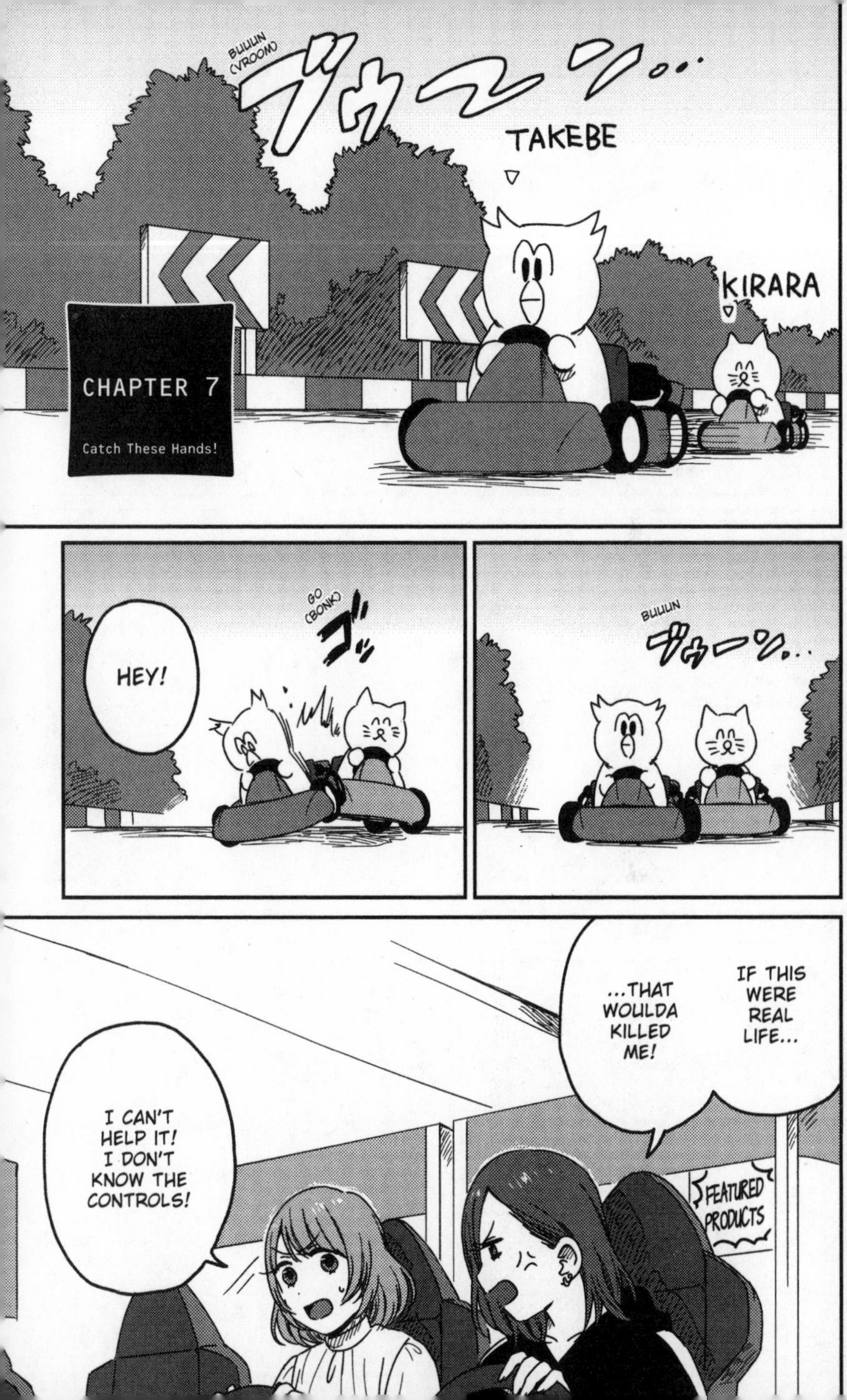
BUUUN (VROOM)
TAKEBE
KIRARA
CHAPTER 7
Catch These Hands!
BUUUN
GO (BONK)
HEY!
IF THIS WERE REAL LIFE...
...THAT WOULDA KILLED ME!
FEATURED PRODUCTS
I CAN'T HELP IT! I DON'T KNOW THE CONTROLS!

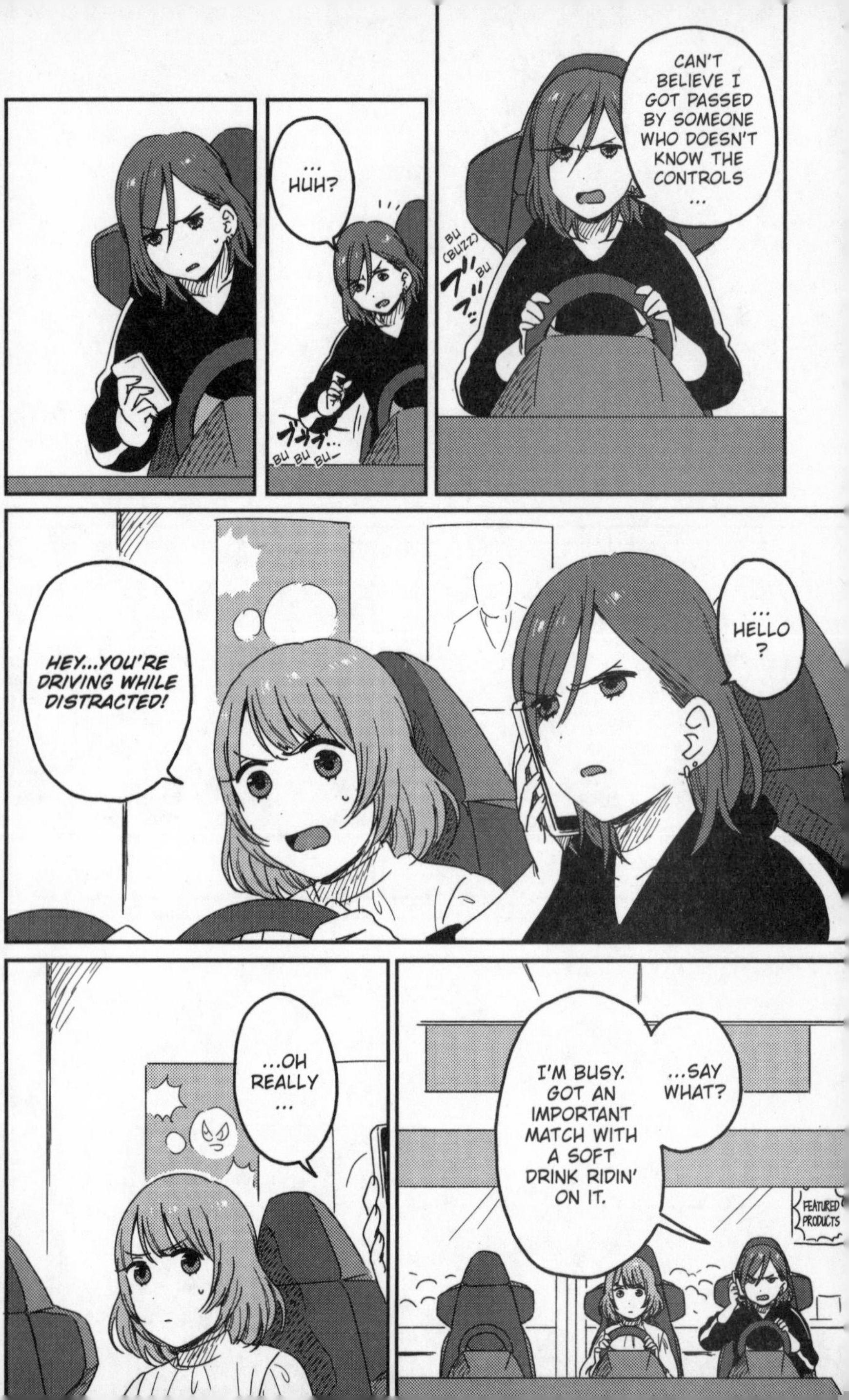
CAN'T BELIEVE I GOT PASSED BY SOMEONE WHO DOESN'T KNOW THE CONTROLS ...
BU (BUZZ) BU
... HUH?
BU BU BU—
... HELLO ?
HEY...YOU'RE DRIVING WHILE DISTRACTED!
...SAY WHAT?
I'M BUSY. GOT AN IMPORTANT MATCH WITH A SOFT DRINK RIDIN' ON IT.
FEATURED PRODUCTS
...OH REALLY ...

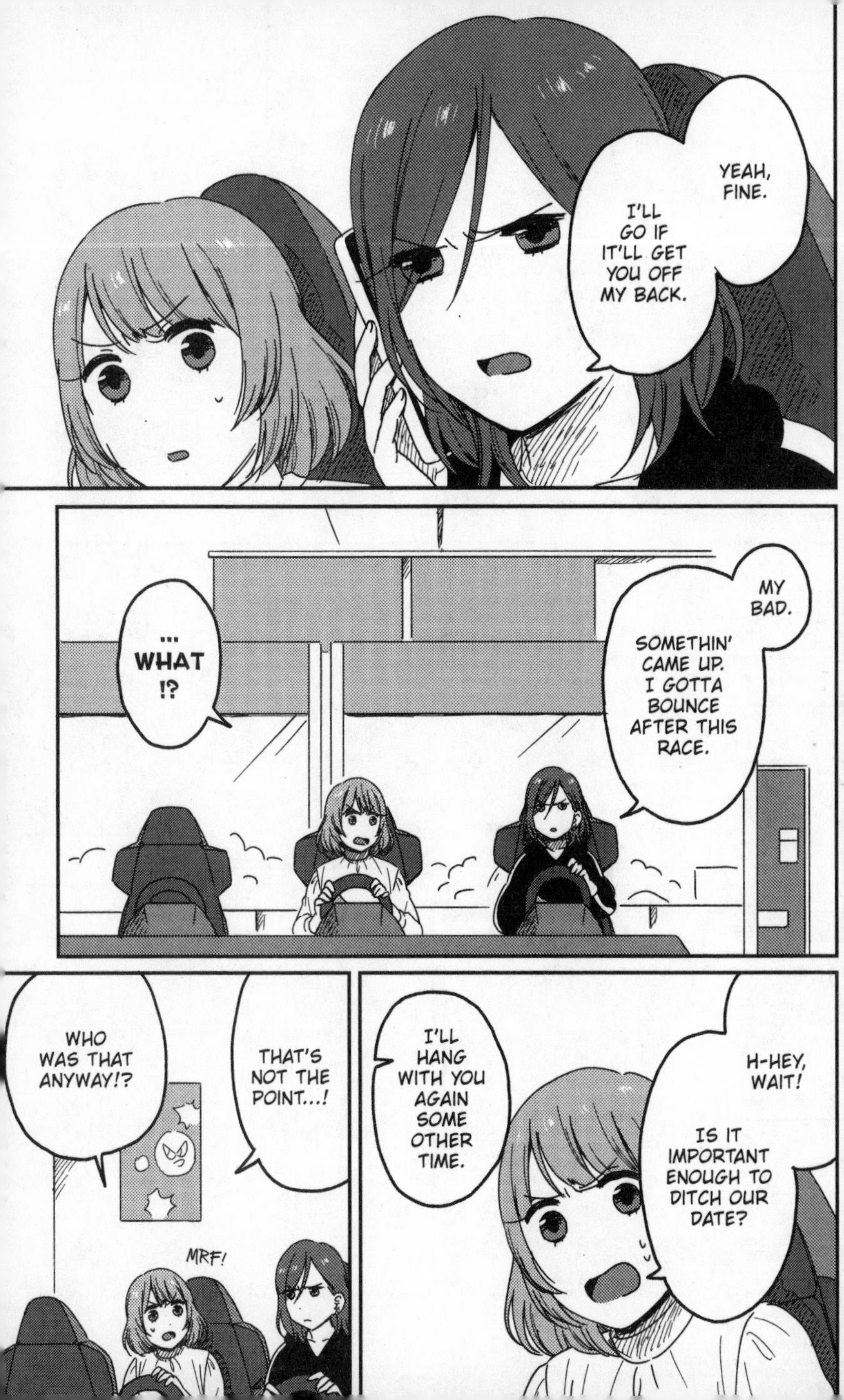
YEAH, FINE.
I'LL GO IF IT'LL GET YOU OFF MY BACK.
MY BAD.
SOMETHIN' CAME UP. I GOTTA BOUNCE AFTER THIS RACE.
...WHAT!?
H-HEY, WAIT!
IS IT IMPORTANT ENOUGH TO DITCH OUR DATE?
I'LL HANG WITH YOU AGAIN SOME OTHER TIME.
THAT'S NOT THE POINT...!
WHO WAS THAT ANYWAY!?
MRF!

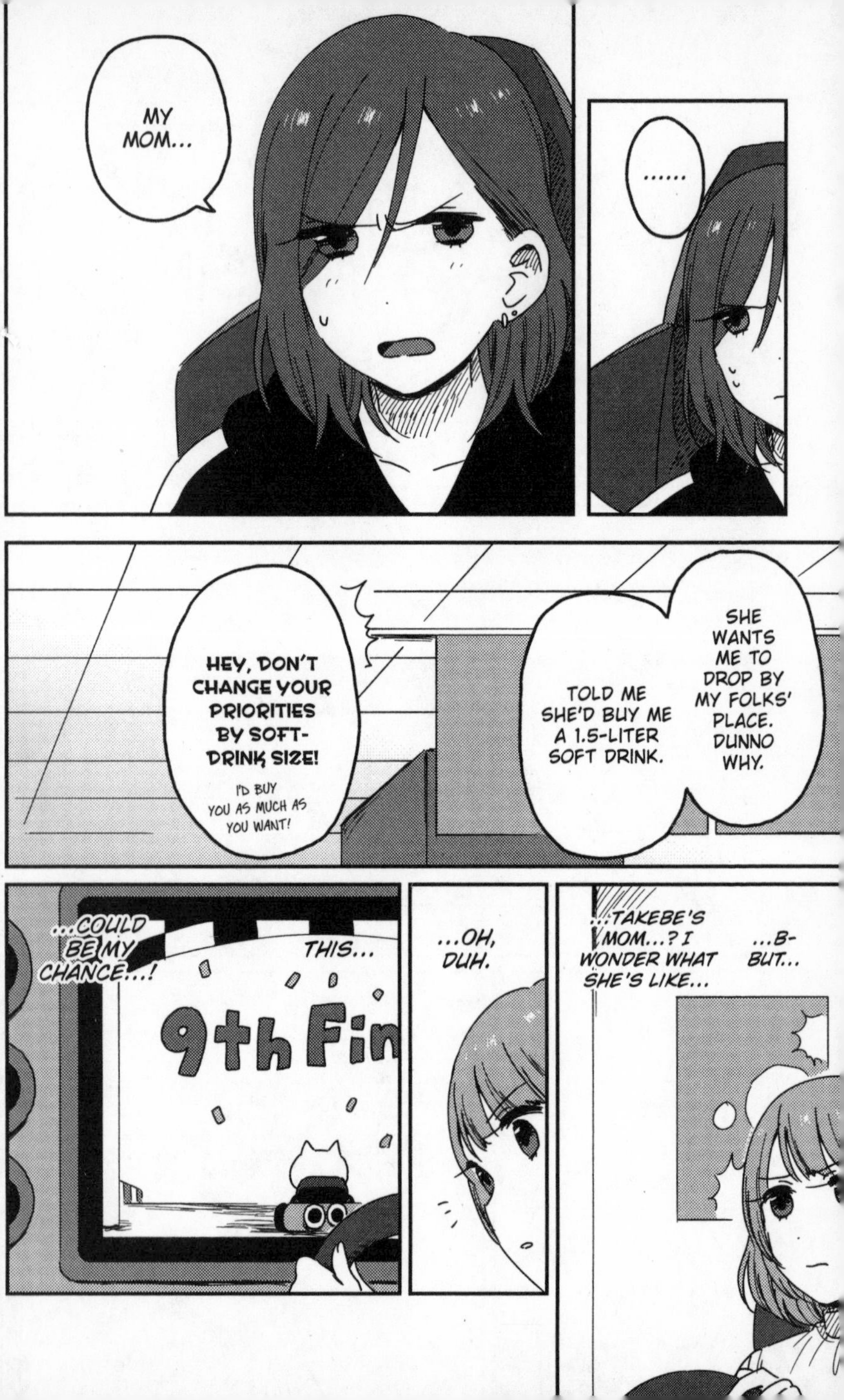
......
MY MOM...
SHE WANTS ME TO DROP BY MY FOLKS' PLACE. DUNNO WHY.
TOLD ME SHE'D BUY ME A 1.5-LITER SOFT DRINK.
HEY, DON'T CHANGE YOUR PRIORITIES BY SOFT-DRINK SIZE!
I'D BUY YOU AS MUCH AS YOU WANT!
...B-BUT...
...TAKEBE'S MOM...? I WONDER WHAT SHE'S LIKE...
...OH, DUH.
THIS...
...COULD BE MY CHANCE...!
9th Fin

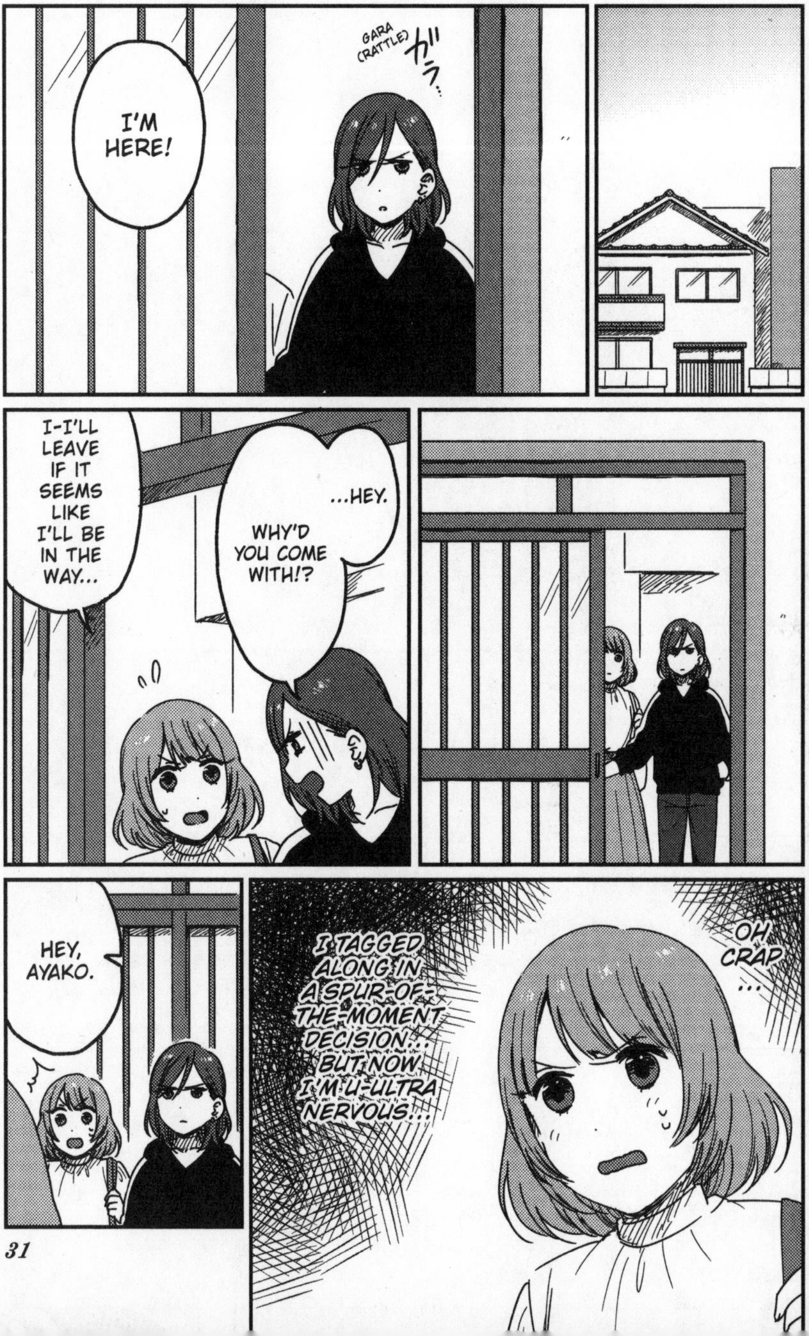
GARA (RATTLE)
I'M HERE!
...HEY. WHY'D YOU COME WITH!?
I-I'LL LEAVE IF IT SEEMS LIKE I'LL BE IN THE WAY...
OH CRAP...
I TAGGED ALONG IN A SPUR-OF-THE-MOMENT DECISION... BUT NOW I'M U-ULTRA NERVOUS...
HEY, AYAKO.

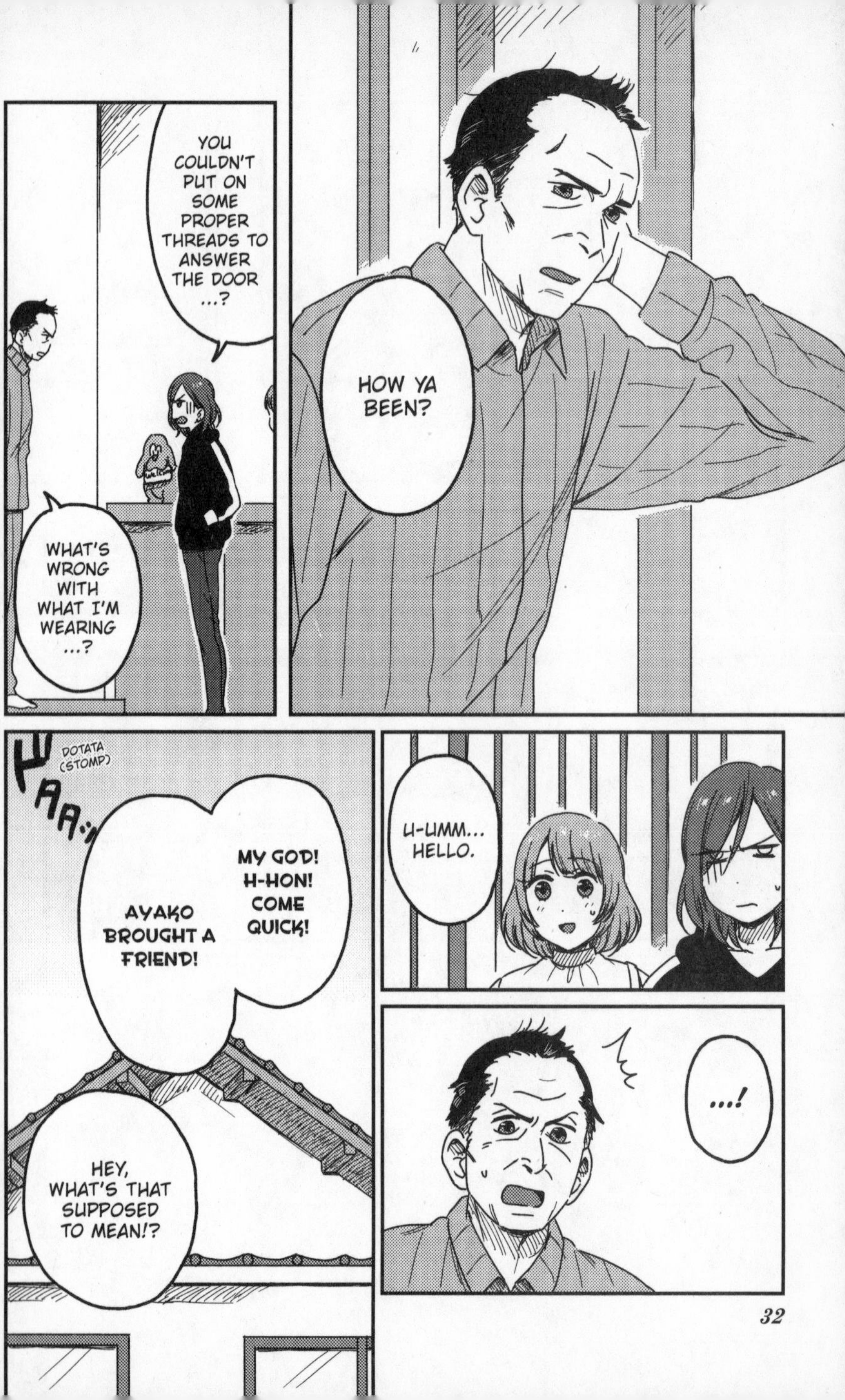

HOW YA BEEN?
YOU COULDN'T PUT ON SOME PROPER THREADS TO ANSWER THE DOOR ...?
WHAT'S WRONG WITH WHAT I'M WEARING ...?
U-UMM... HELLO.
...!
DOTATA (STOMP)
MY GOD! H-HON! COME QUICK!
AYAKO BROUGHT A FRIEND!
HEY, WHAT'S THAT SUPPOSED TO MEAN!?

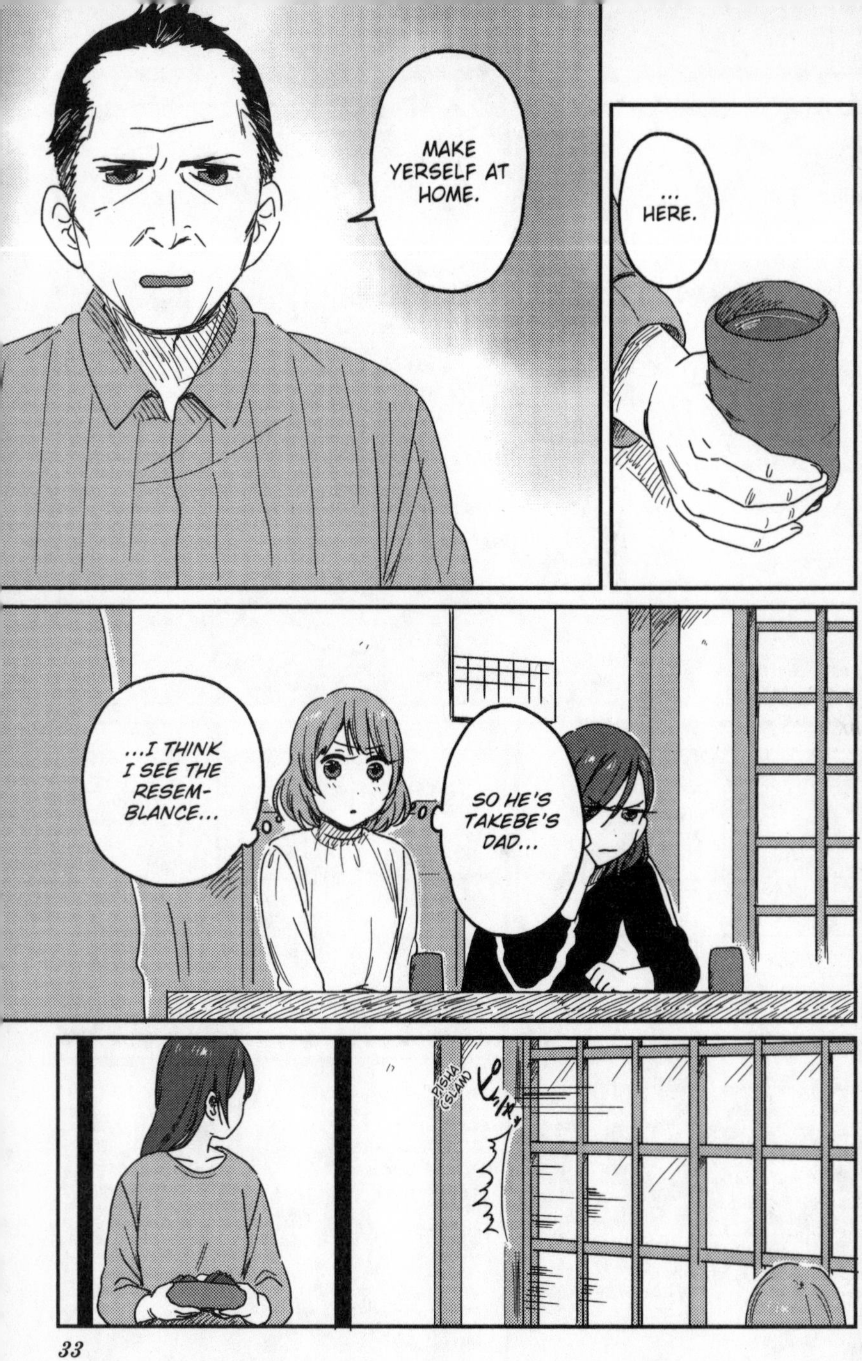
... HERE.
MAKE YERSELF AT HOME.
SO HE'S TAKEBE'S DAD...
...I THINK I SEE THE RESEM-BLANCE...
PISHA (SLAM)

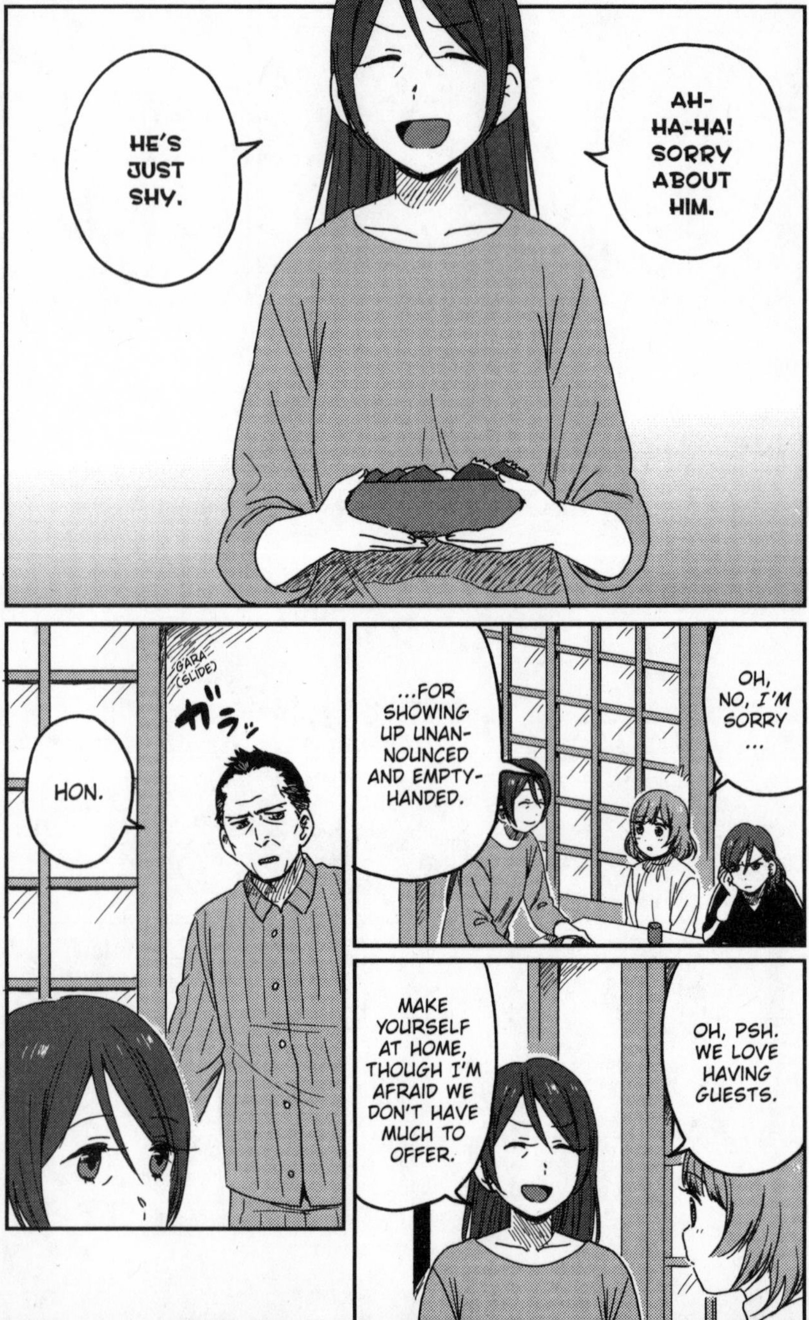
AH-HA-HA! SORRY ABOUT HIM.
HE'S JUST SHY.
OH, NO, I'M SORRY...
...FOR SHOWING UP UNANNOUNCED AND EMPTY-HANDED.
OH, PSH. WE LOVE HAVING GUESTS.
MAKE YOURSELF AT HOME, THOUGH I'M AFRAID WE DON'T HAVE MUCH TO OFFER.
GARA (SLIDE)
ガラッ
HON.

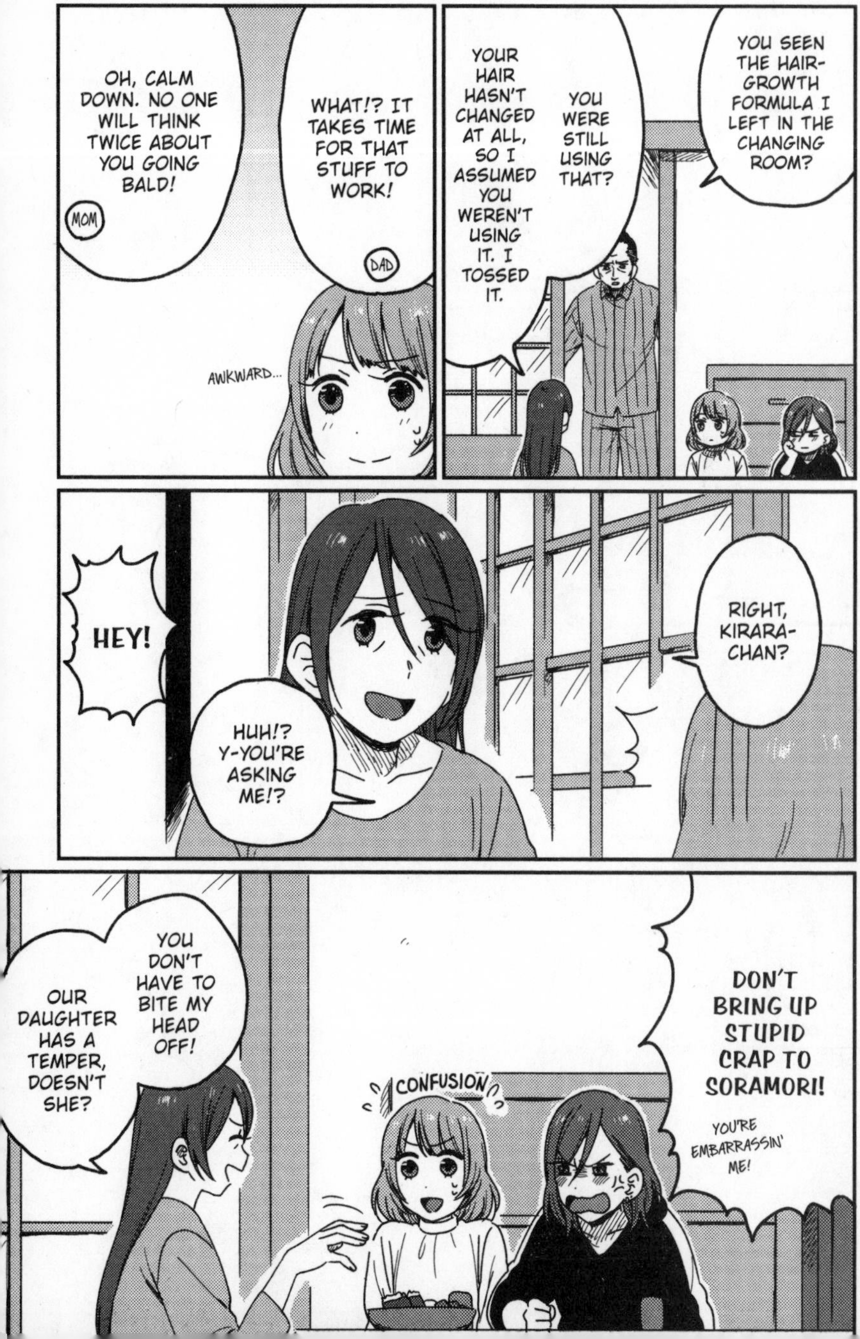
YOU SEEN THE HAIR-GROWTH FORMULA I LEFT IN THE CHANGING ROOM?
YOU WERE STILL USING THAT?
YOUR HAIR HASN'T CHANGED AT ALL, SO I ASSUMED YOU WEREN'T USING IT. I TOSSED IT.
WHAT!? IT TAKES TIME FOR THAT STUFF TO WORK!
DAD
OH, CALM DOWN. NO ONE WILL THINK TWICE ABOUT YOU GOING BALD!
MOM
AWKWARD...
RIGHT, KIRARA-CHAN?
HUH!? Y-YOU'RE ASKING ME!?
HEY!
DON'T BRING UP STUPID CRAP TO SORAMORI!
YOU'RE EMBARRASSIN' ME!
CONFUSION
YOU DON'T HAVE TO BITE MY HEAD OFF!
OUR DAUGHTER HAS A TEMPER, DOESN'T SHE?

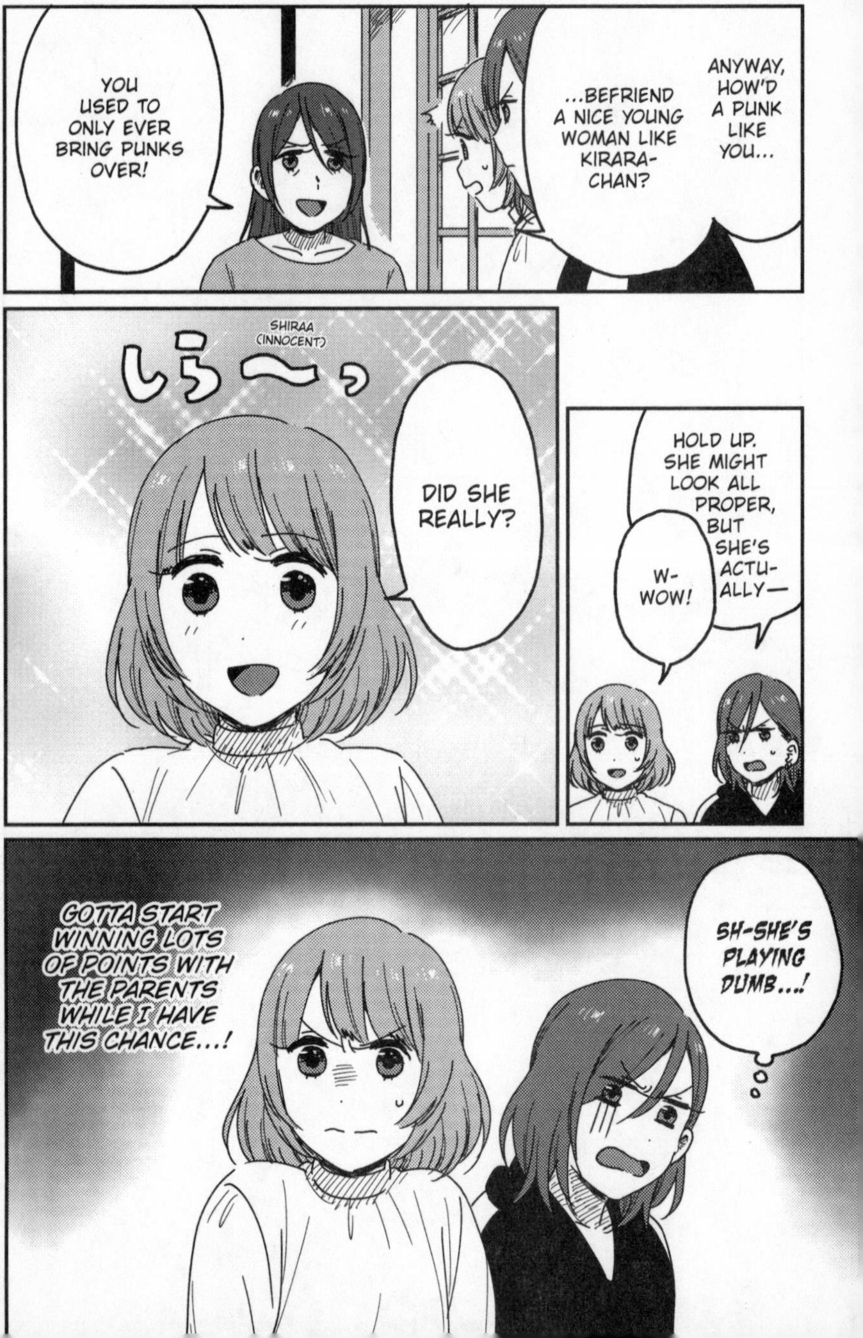
ANYWAY, HOW'D A PUNK LIKE YOU...
...BEFRIEND A NICE YOUNG WOMAN LIKE KIRARA-CHAN?
YOU USED TO ONLY EVER BRING PUNKS OVER!
HOLD UP. SHE MIGHT LOOK ALL PROPER, BUT SHE'S ACTU-ALLY—
W-WOW!
DID SHE REALLY?
しら〜っ
SHIRAA (INNOCENT)
SH-SHE'S PLAYING DUMB...!
GOTTA START WINNING LOTS OF POINTS WITH THE PARENTS WHILE I HAVE THIS CHANCE...!

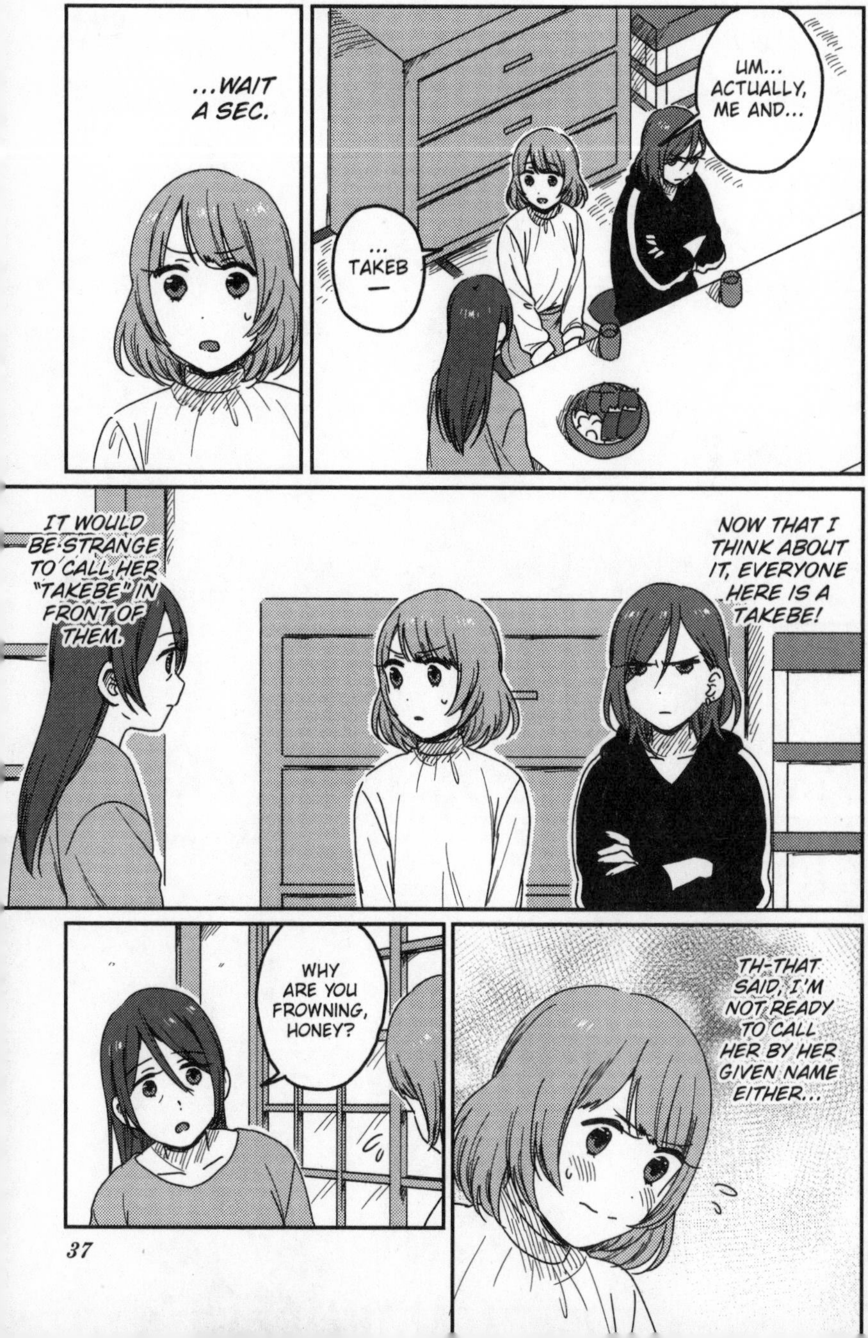
UM... ACTUALLY, ME AND...
... TAKEB—
...WAIT A SEC.
NOW THAT I THINK ABOUT IT, EVERYONE HERE IS A TAKEBE!
IT WOULD BE STRANGE TO CALL HER "TAKEBE" IN FRONT OF THEM.
TH-THAT SAID, I'M NOT READY TO CALL HER BY HER GIVEN NAME EITHER...
WHY ARE YOU FROWNING, HONEY?

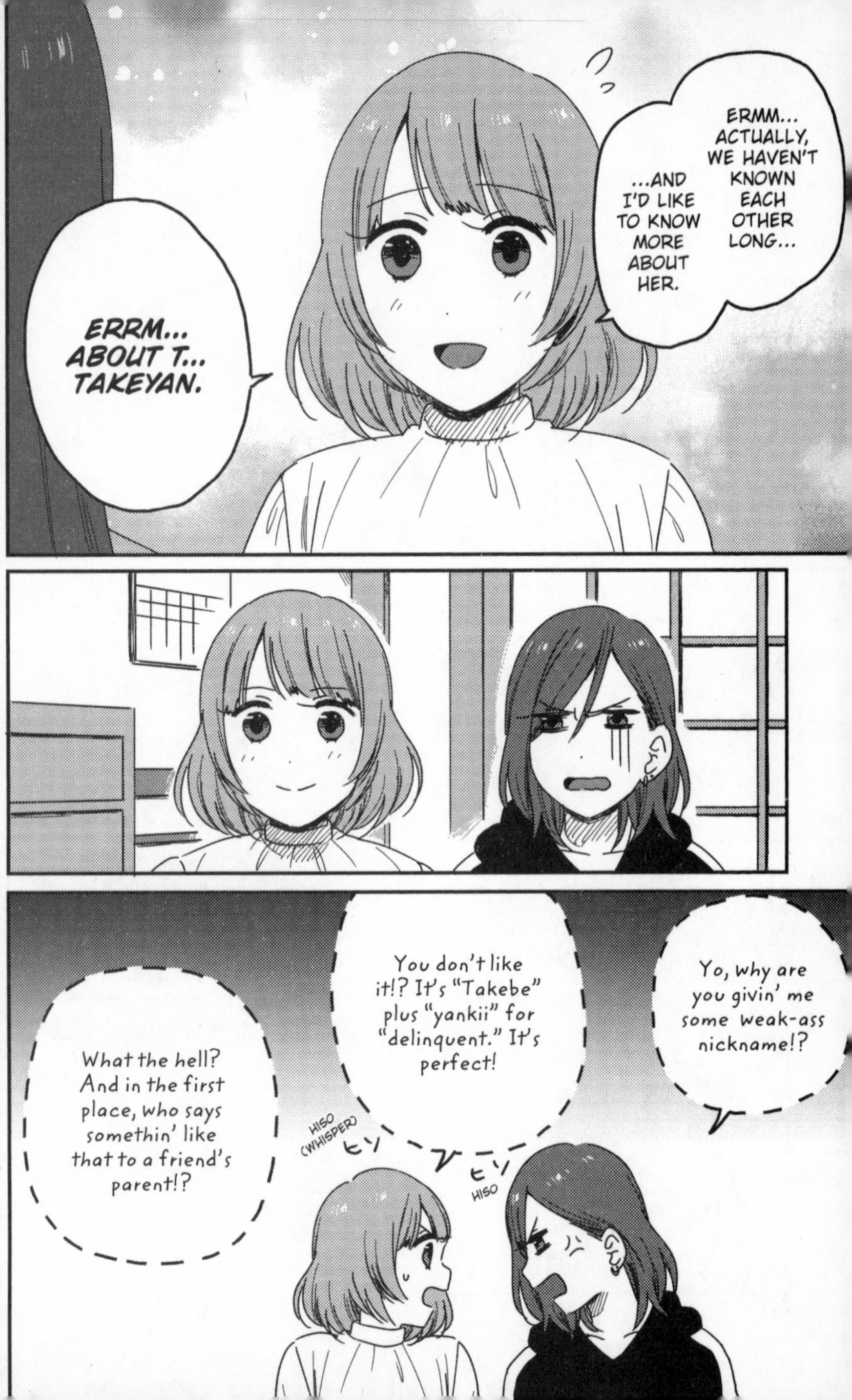
ERMM... ACTUALLY, WE HAVEN'T KNOWN EACH OTHER LONG...
...AND I'D LIKE TO KNOW MORE ABOUT HER.
ERRM... ABOUT T... TAKEYAN.
Yo, why are you givin' me some weak-ass nickname!?
You don't like it!? It's "Takebe" plus "yankii" for "delinquent." It's perfect!
HISO
HISO (WHISPER)
What the hell? And in the first place, who says somethin' like that to a friend's parent!?

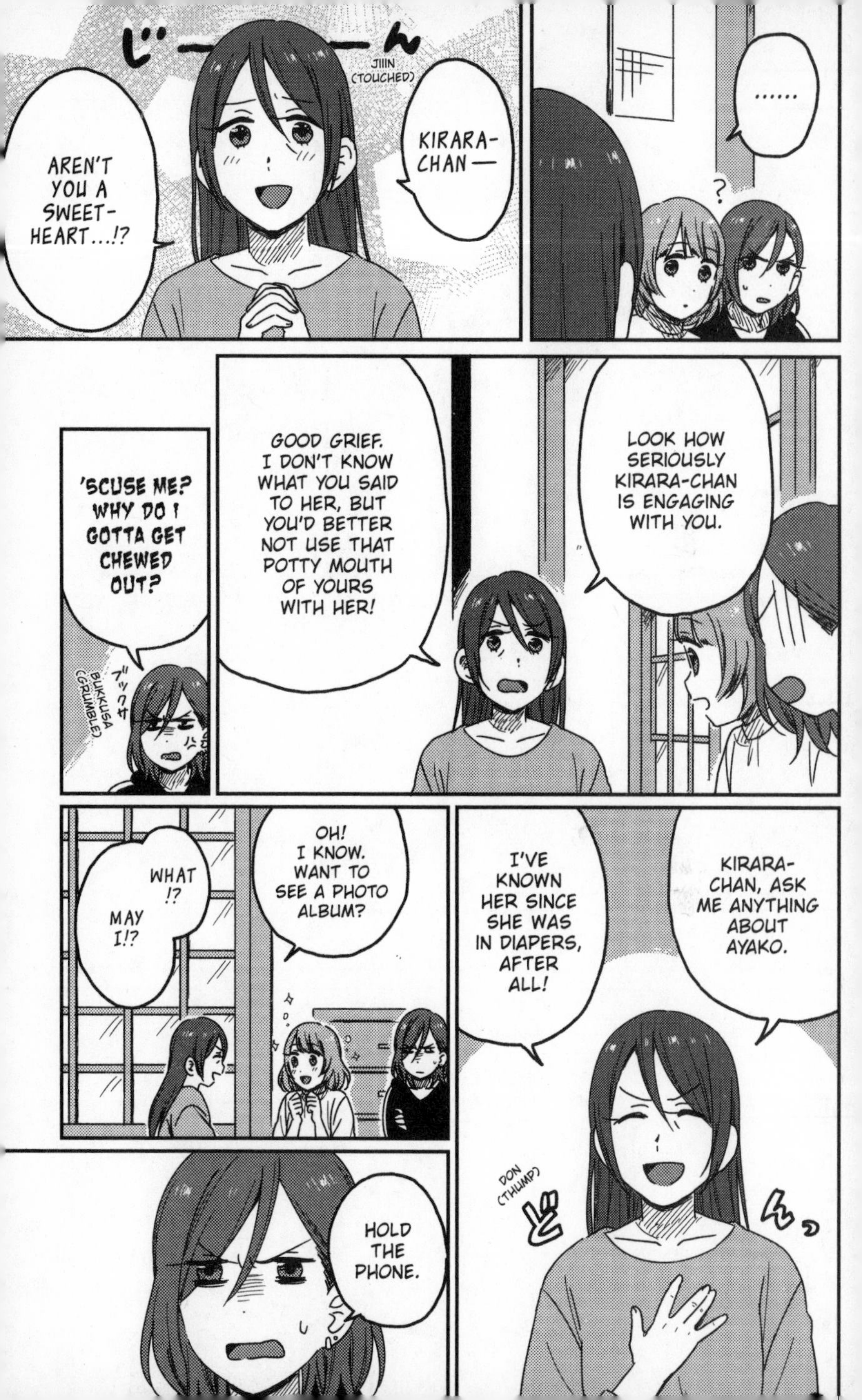

......
?
じーーん
JIIN (TOUCHED)
KIRARA-CHAN—
AREN'T YOU A SWEET-HEART...!?
LOOK HOW SERIOUSLY KIRARA-CHAN IS ENGAGING WITH YOU.
GOOD GRIEF. I DON'T KNOW WHAT YOU SAID TO HER, BUT YOU'D BETTER NOT USE THAT POTTY MOUTH OF YOURS WITH HER!
'SCUSE ME? WHY DO I GOTTA GET CHEWED OUT?
ブックサ
BUKKUSA (GRUMBLE)
KIRARA-CHAN, ASK ME ANYTHING ABOUT AYAKO.
I'VE KNOWN HER SINCE SHE WAS IN DIAPERS, AFTER ALL!
どんっ
DON (THUMP)
OH! I KNOW. WANT TO SEE A PHOTO ALBUM?
WHAT!? MAY I!?
HOLD THE PHONE.

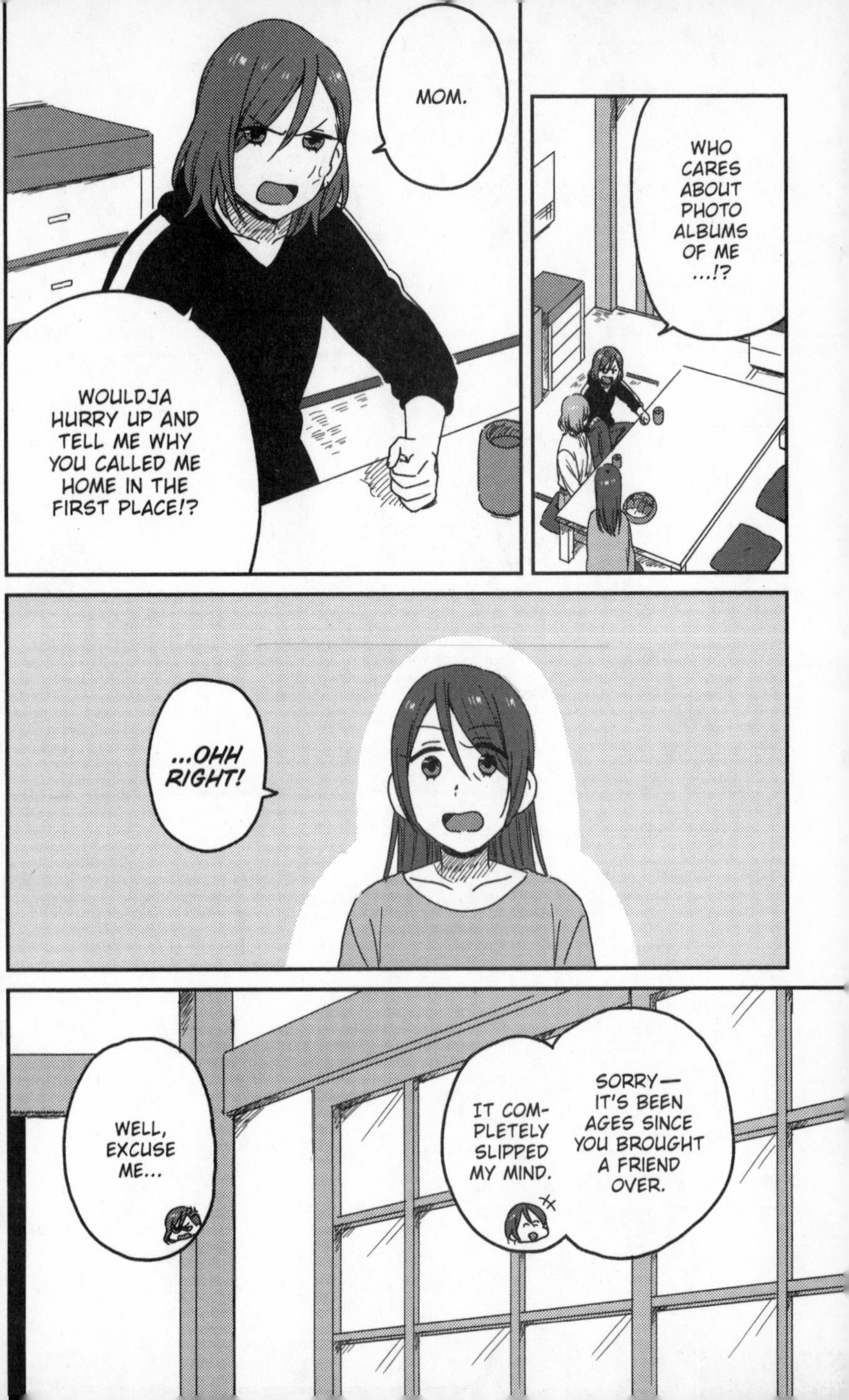
WHO CARES ABOUT PHOTO ALBUMS OF ME ...!?
MOM.
WOULDJA HURRY UP AND TELL ME WHY YOU CALLED ME HOME IN THE FIRST PLACE!?
...OHH RIGHT!
SORRY— IT'S BEEN AGES SINCE YOU BROUGHT A FRIEND OVER.
IT COM- PLETELY SLIPPED MY MIND.
WELL, EXCUSE ME...

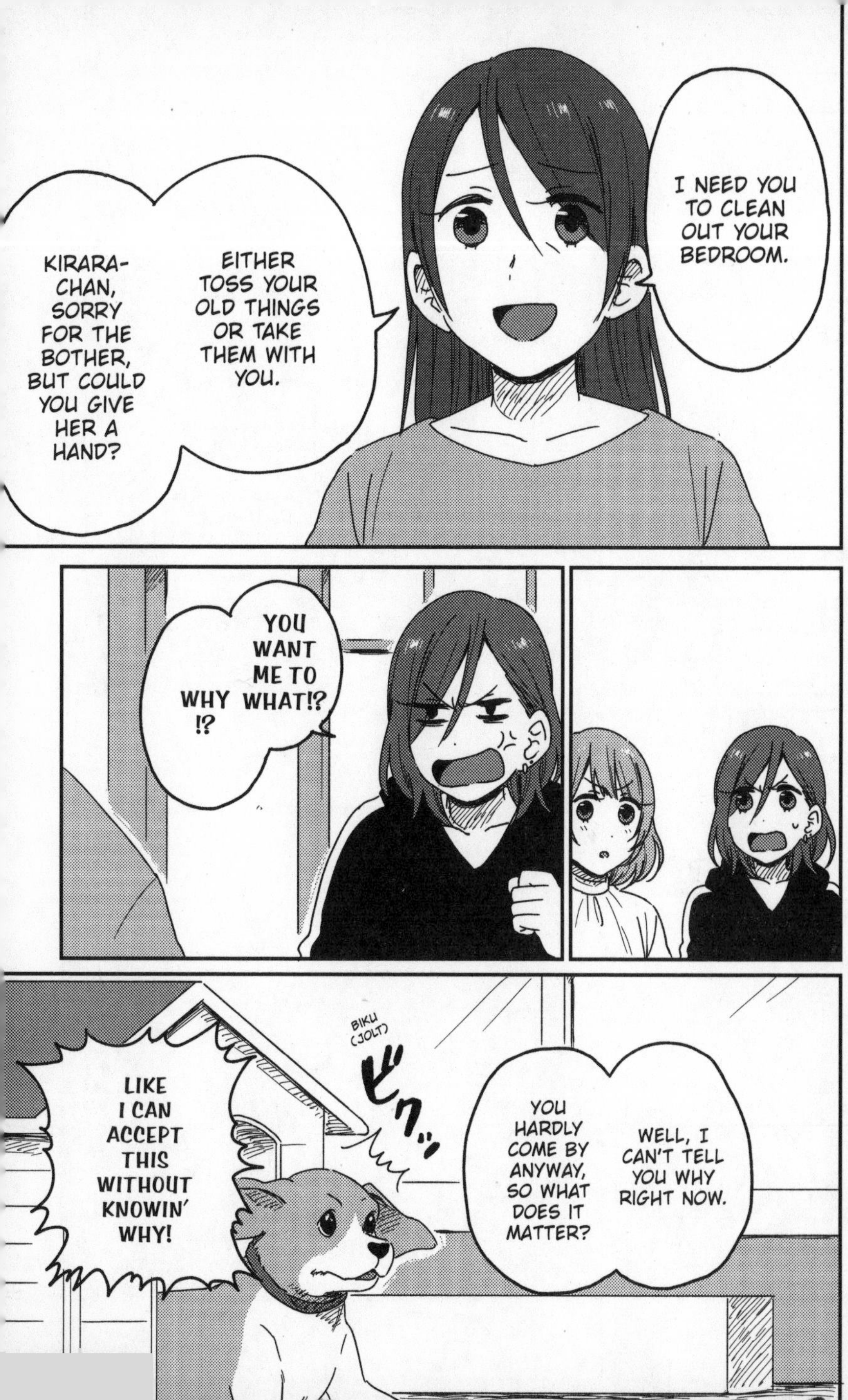
I NEED YOU TO CLEAN OUT YOUR BEDROOM.
EITHER TOSS YOUR OLD THINGS OR TAKE THEM WITH YOU.
KIRARA-CHAN, SORRY FOR THE BOTHER, BUT COULD YOU GIVE HER A HAND?
YOU WANT ME TO WHAT!?
WHY!?
WELL, I CAN'T TELL YOU WHY RIGHT NOW.
YOU HARDLY COME BY ANYWAY, SO WHAT DOES IT MATTER?
ビクッ
BIKU (JOLT)
LIKE I CAN ACCEPT THIS WITHOUT KNOWIN' WHY!

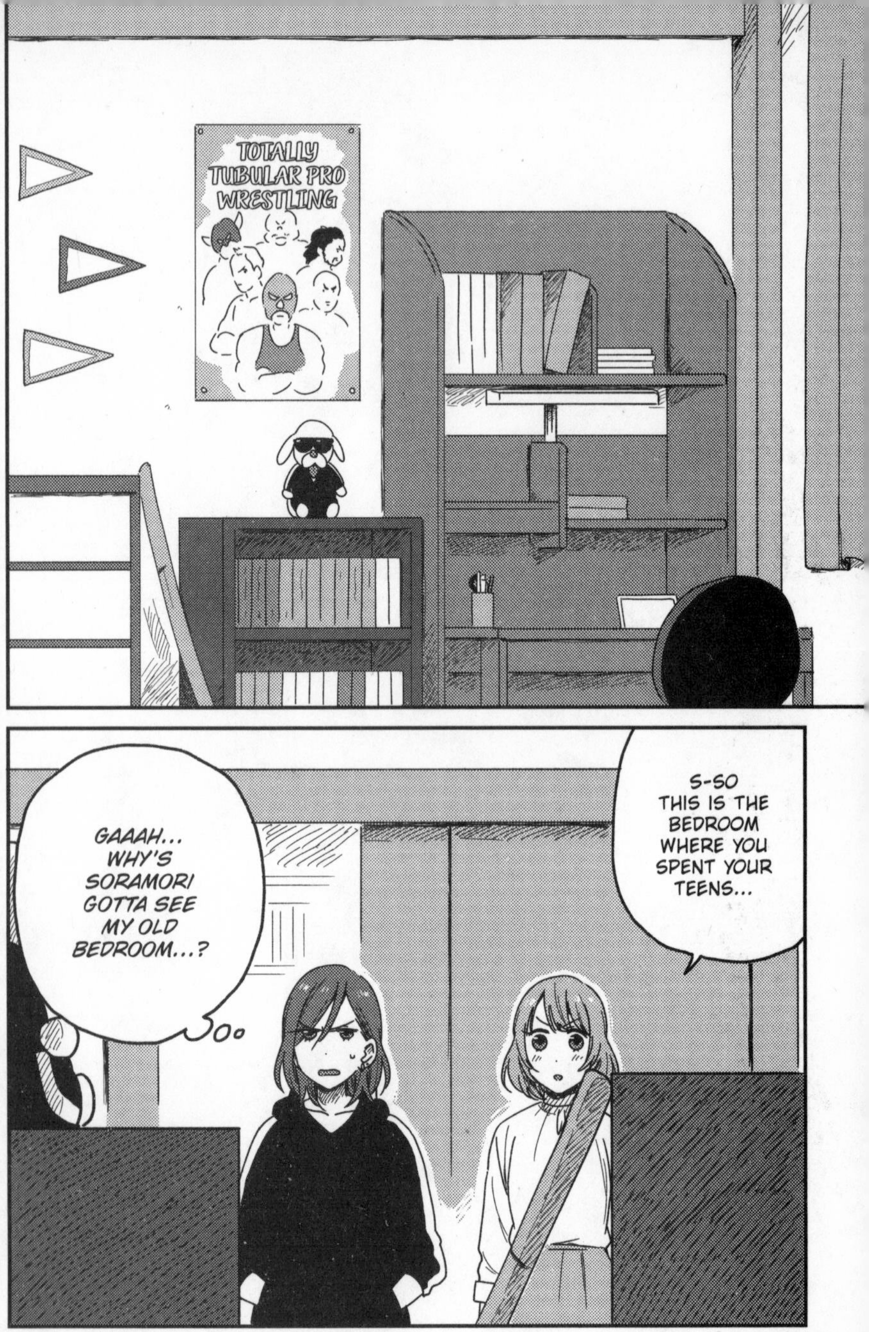
TOTALLY TUBULAR PRO WRESTLING
S-SO THIS IS THE BEDROOM WHERE YOU SPENT YOUR TEENS...
GAAAH... WHY'S SORAMORI GOTTA SEE MY OLD BEDROOM...?

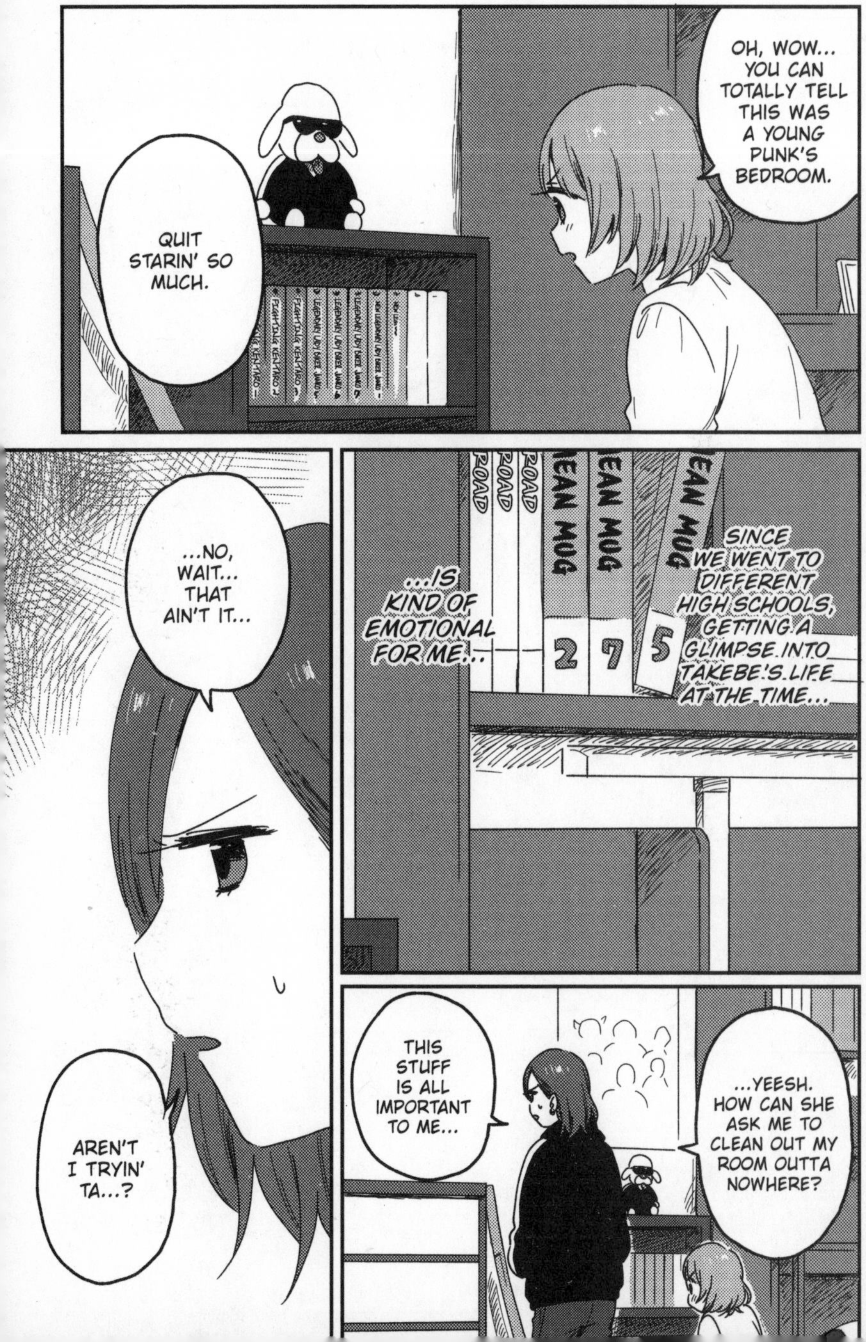
OH, WOW... YOU CAN TOTALLY TELL THIS WAS A YOUNG PUNK'S BEDROOM.
QUIT STARIN' SO MUCH.
SINCE WE WENT TO DIFFERENT HIGH SCHOOLS, GETTING A GLIMPSE INTO TAKEBE'S LIFE AT THE TIME...
...IS KIND OF EMOTIONAL FOR ME...
...YEESH. HOW CAN SHE ASK ME TO CLEAN OUT MY ROOM OUTTA NOWHERE?
THIS STUFF IS ALL IMPORTANT TO ME...
...NO, WAIT... THAT AIN'T IT...
AREN'T I TRYIN' TA...?

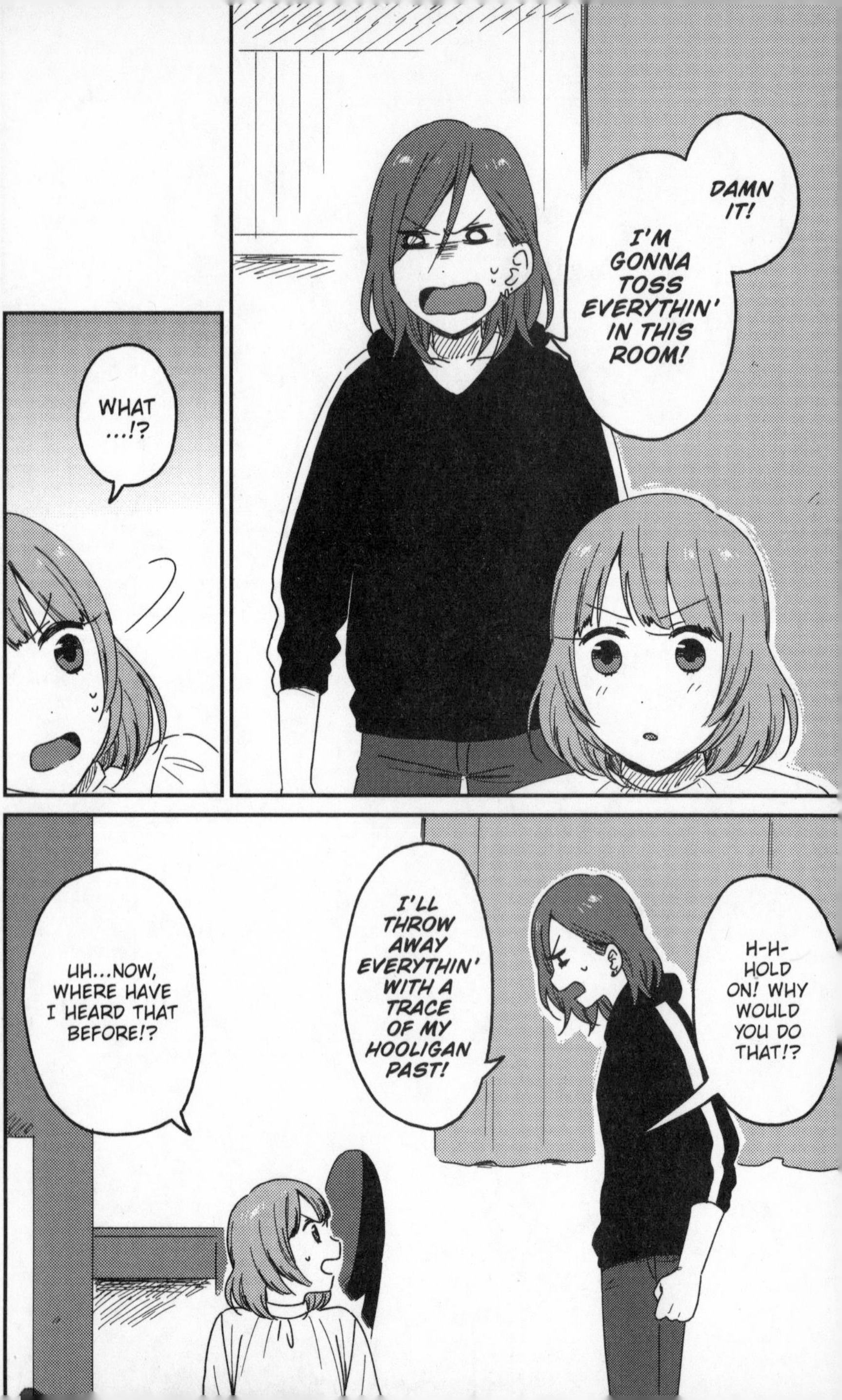
DAMN IT!
I'M GONNA TOSS EVERYTHIN' IN THIS ROOM!
WHAT ...!?
H-H-HOLD ON! WHY WOULD YOU DO THAT!?
I'LL THROW AWAY EVERYTHIN' WITH A TRACE OF MY HOOLIGAN PAST!
UH...NOW, WHERE HAVE I HEARD THAT BEFORE!?

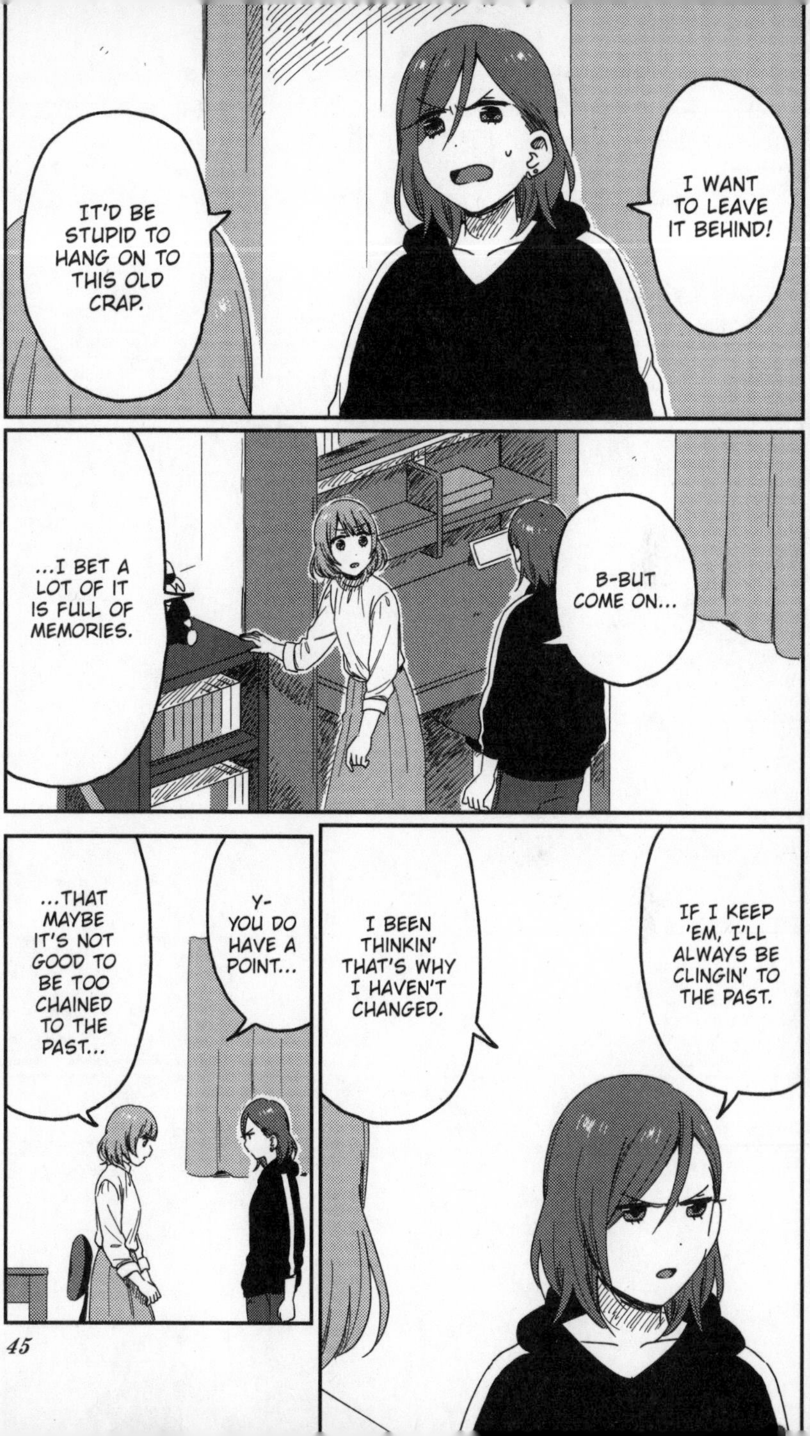
I WANT TO LEAVE IT BEHIND!
IT'D BE STUPID TO HANG ON TO THIS OLD CRAP.
B-BUT COME ON...
...I BET A LOT OF IT IS FULL OF MEMORIES.
IF I KEEP 'EM, I'LL ALWAYS BE CLINGIN' TO THE PAST.
I BEEN THINKIN' THAT'S WHY I HAVEN'T CHANGED.
Y-YOU DO HAVE A POINT...
...THAT MAYBE IT'S NOT GOOD TO BE TOO CHAINED TO THE PAST...

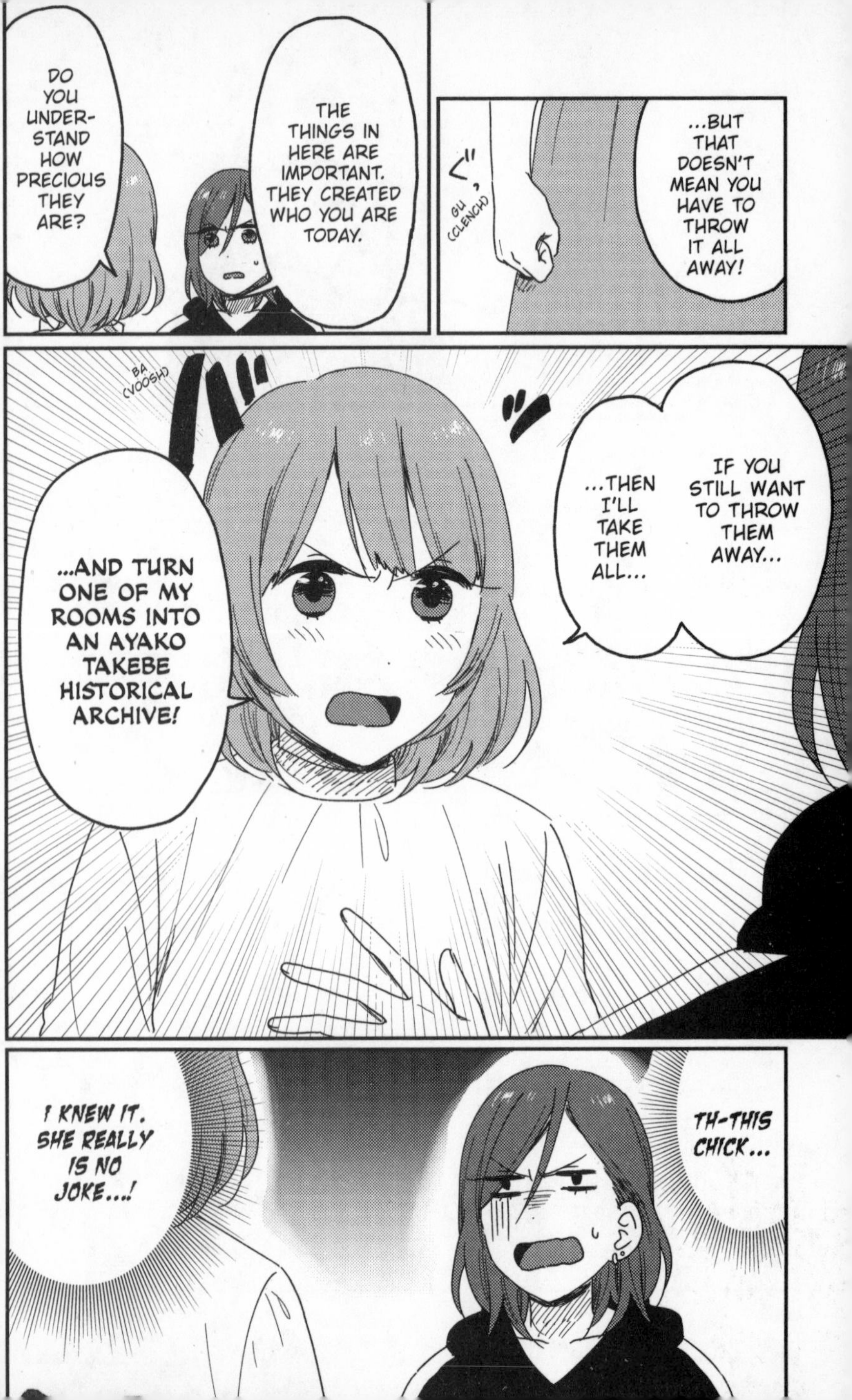

...BUT THAT DOESN'T MEAN YOU HAVE TO THROW IT ALL AWAY!
GU (CLENCH)
THE THINGS IN HERE ARE IMPORTANT. THEY CREATED WHO YOU ARE TODAY.
DO YOU UNDER-STAND HOW PRECIOUS THEY ARE?
BA (VOOSH)
IF YOU STILL WANT TO THROW THEM AWAY...
...THEN I'LL TAKE THEM ALL...
...AND TURN ONE OF MY ROOMS INTO AN AYAKO TAKEBE HISTORICAL ARCHIVE!
TH-THIS CHICK...
I KNEW IT. SHE REALLY IS NO JOKE...!

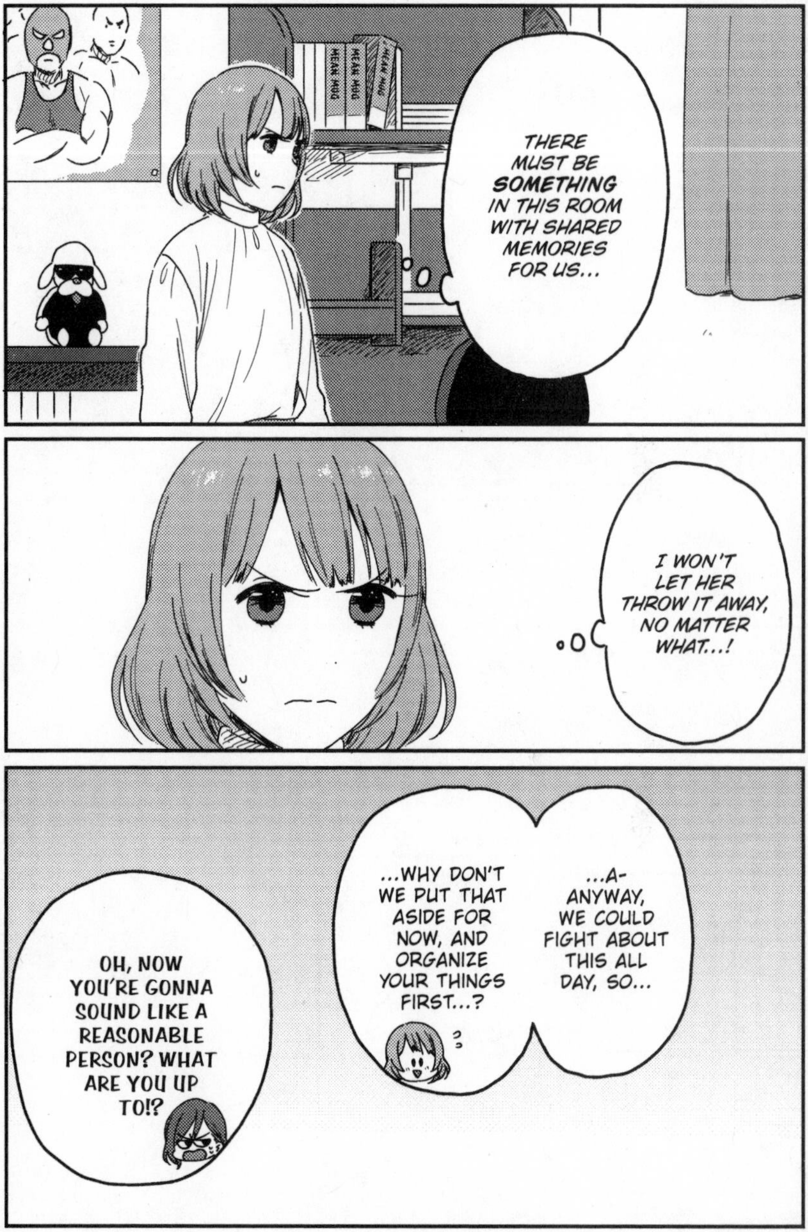
MEAN MUG
MEAN MUG
MEAN MUG
THERE MUST BE **SOMETHING** IN THIS ROOM WITH SHARED MEMORIES FOR US...
I WON'T LET HER THROW IT AWAY, NO MATTER WHAT...!
...A- ANYWAY, WE COULD FIGHT ABOUT THIS ALL DAY, SO...
...WHY DON'T WE PUT THAT ASIDE FOR NOW, AND ORGANIZE YOUR THINGS FIRST...?
OH, NOW YOU'RE GONNA SOUND LIKE A REASONABLE PERSON? WHAT ARE YOU UP TO!?

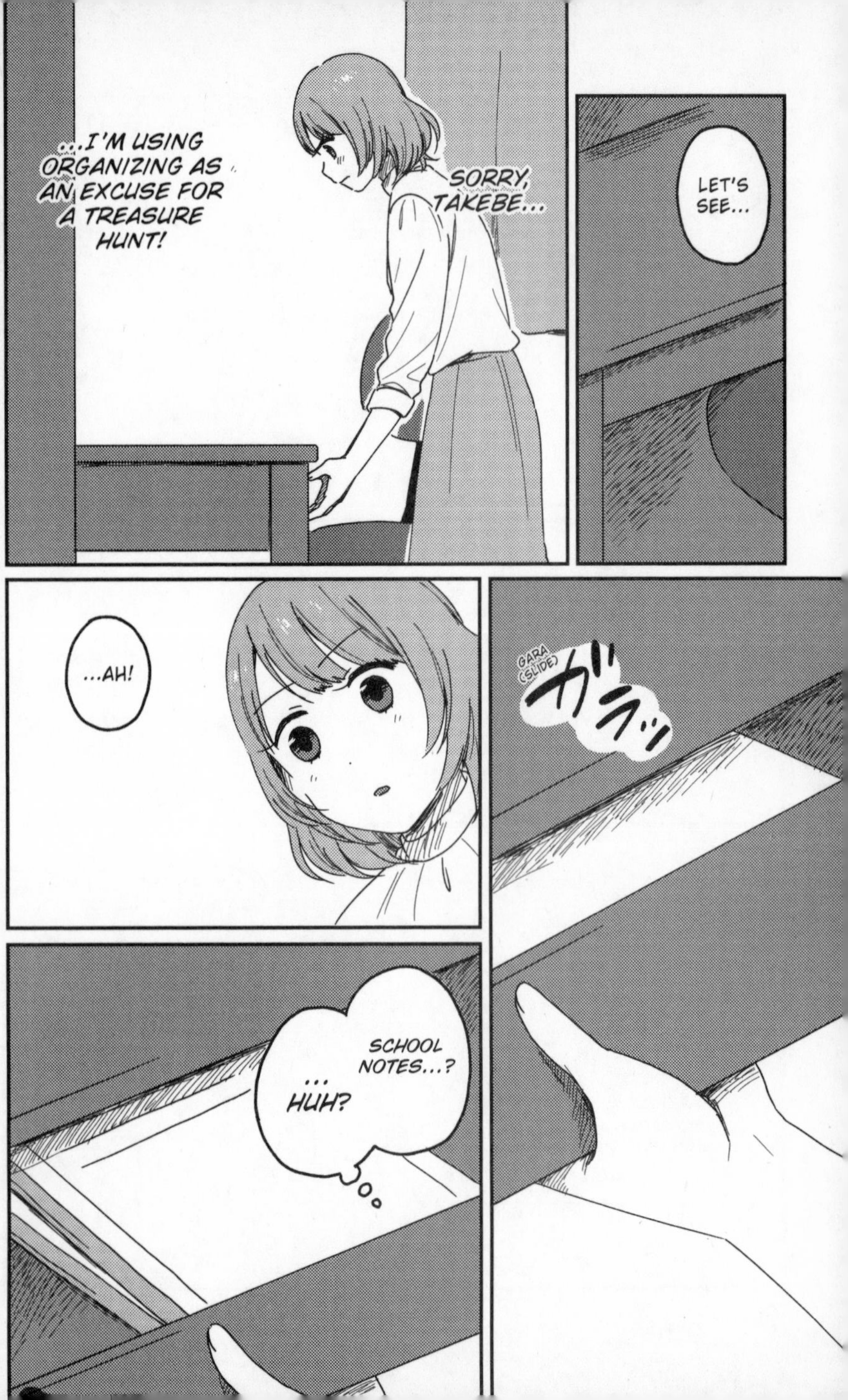
LET'S SEE...
SORRY, TAKEBE...
...I'M USING ORGANIZING AS AN EXCUSE FOR A TREASURE HUNT!
GARA (SLIDE)
...AH!
SCHOOL NOTES...? ... HUH?

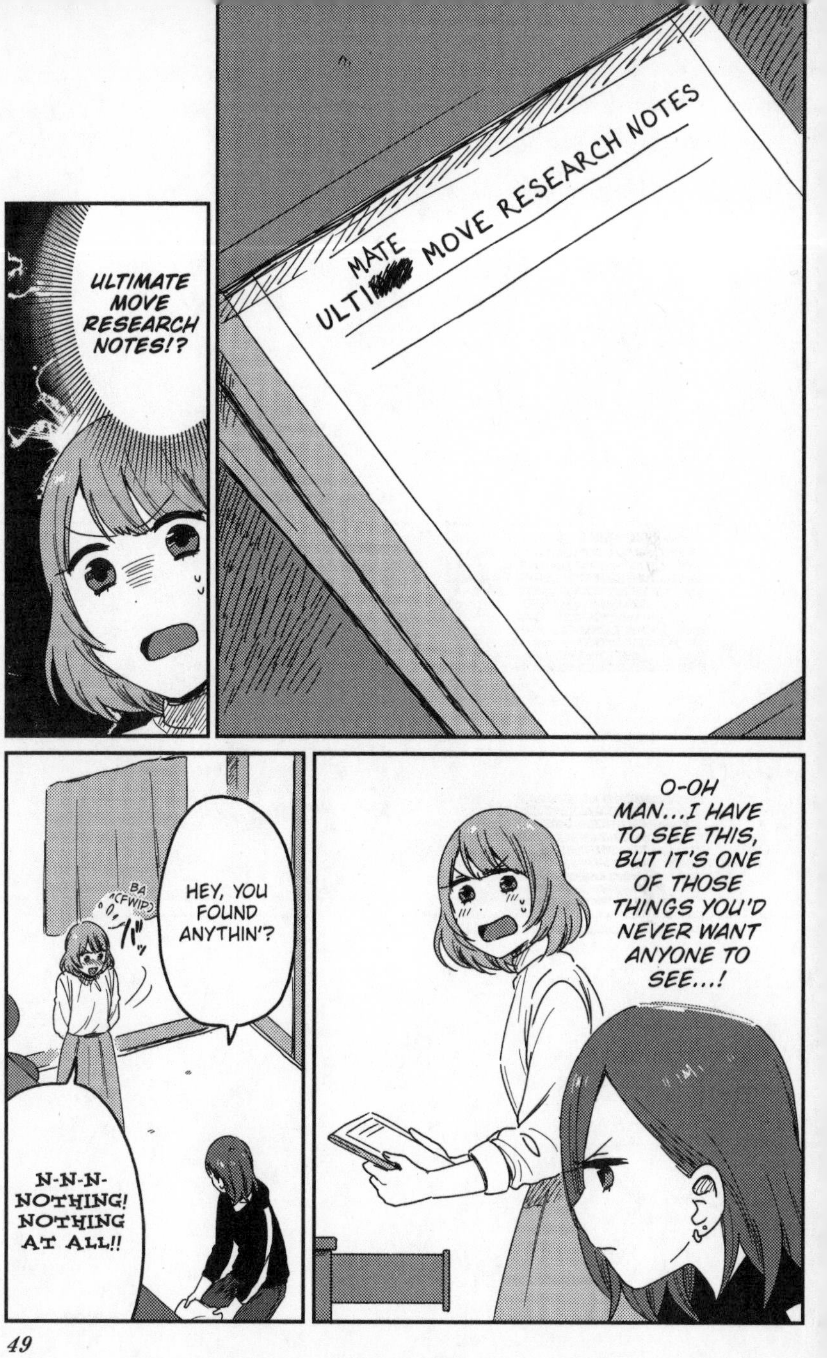
MATE
ULTI MOVE RESEARCH NOTES
ULTIMATE MOVE RESEARCH NOTES!?
O-OH MAN...I HAVE TO SEE THIS, BUT IT'S ONE OF THOSE THINGS YOU'D NEVER WANT ANYONE TO SEE...!
HEY, YOU FOUND ANYTHIN'?
BA (FWIP)
N-N-N-NOTHING! NOTHING AT ALL!!

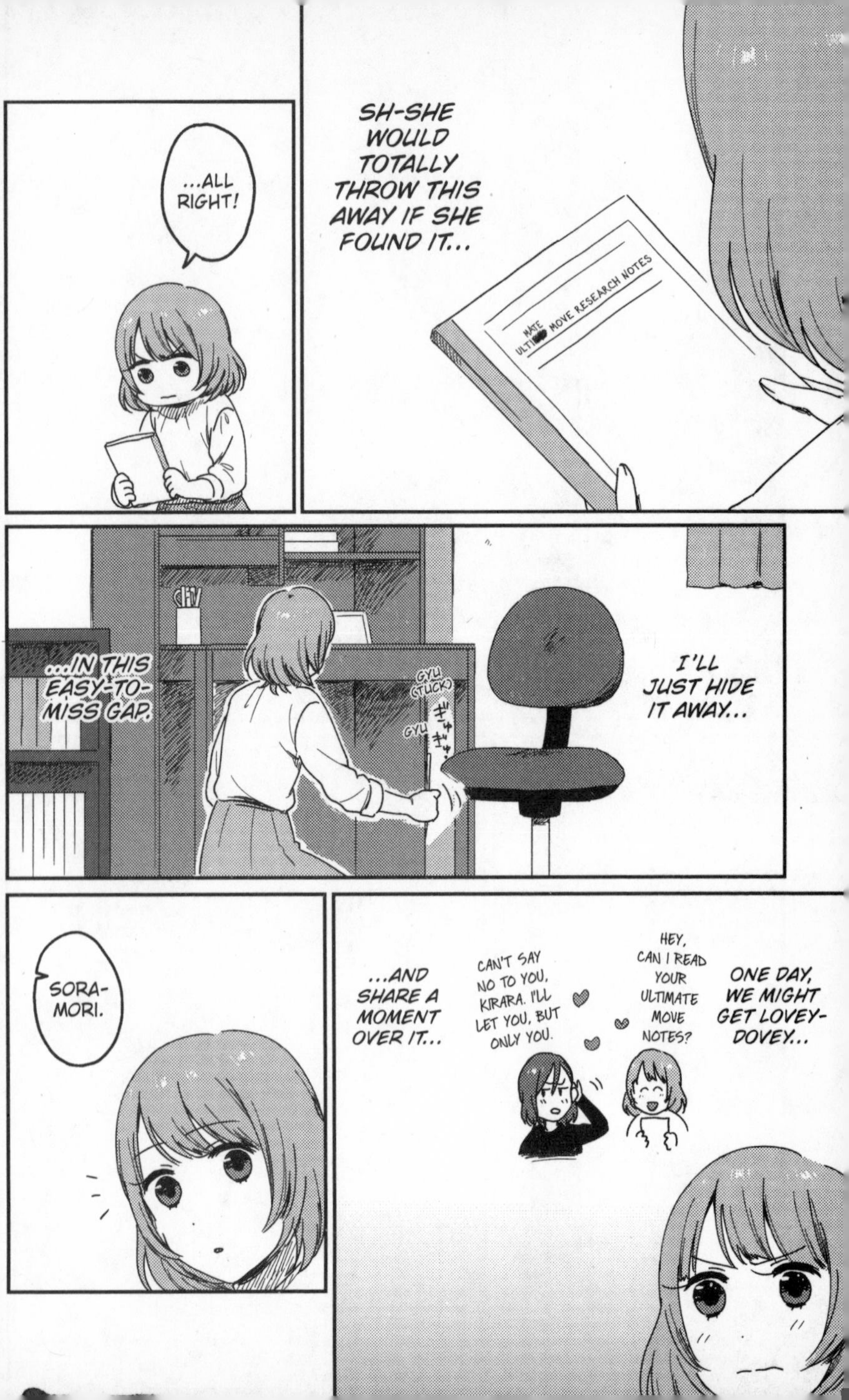
SH-SHE WOULD TOTALLY THROW THIS AWAY IF SHE FOUND IT...
ULTIMATE MOVE RESEARCH NOTES
...ALL RIGHT!
I'LL JUST HIDE IT AWAY...
GYU (TUCK)
ギュ
GYU
ギュッ
...IN THIS EASY-TO-MISS GAP.
ONE DAY, WE MIGHT GET LOVEY-DOVEY...
HEY, CAN I READ YOUR ULTIMATE MOVE NOTES?
CAN'T SAY NO TO YOU, KIRARA. I'LL LET YOU, BUT ONLY YOU.
...AND SHARE A MOMENT OVER IT...
SORA-MORI.

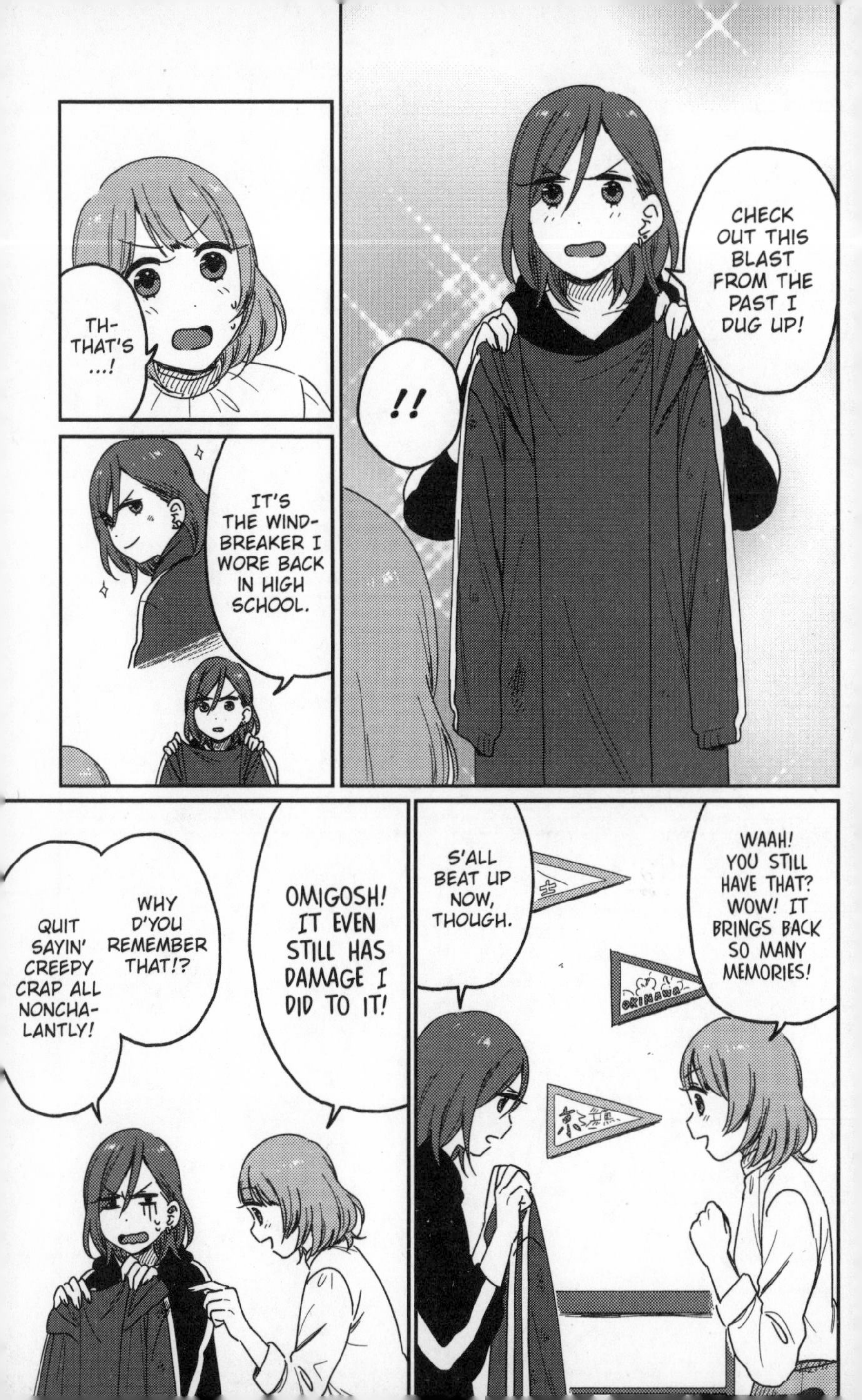
CHECK OUT THIS BLAST FROM THE PAST I DUG UP!
!!
TH-THAT'S ...!
IT'S THE WIND-BREAKER I WORE BACK IN HIGH SCHOOL.
WAAH! YOU STILL HAVE THAT? WOW! IT BRINGS BACK SO MANY MEMORIES!
S'ALL BEAT UP NOW, THOUGH.
OKINAWA
OMIGOSH! IT EVEN STILL HAS DAMAGE I DID TO IT!
WHY D'YOU REMEMBER THAT!?
QUIT SAYIN' CREEPY CRAP ALL NONCHA-LANTLY!

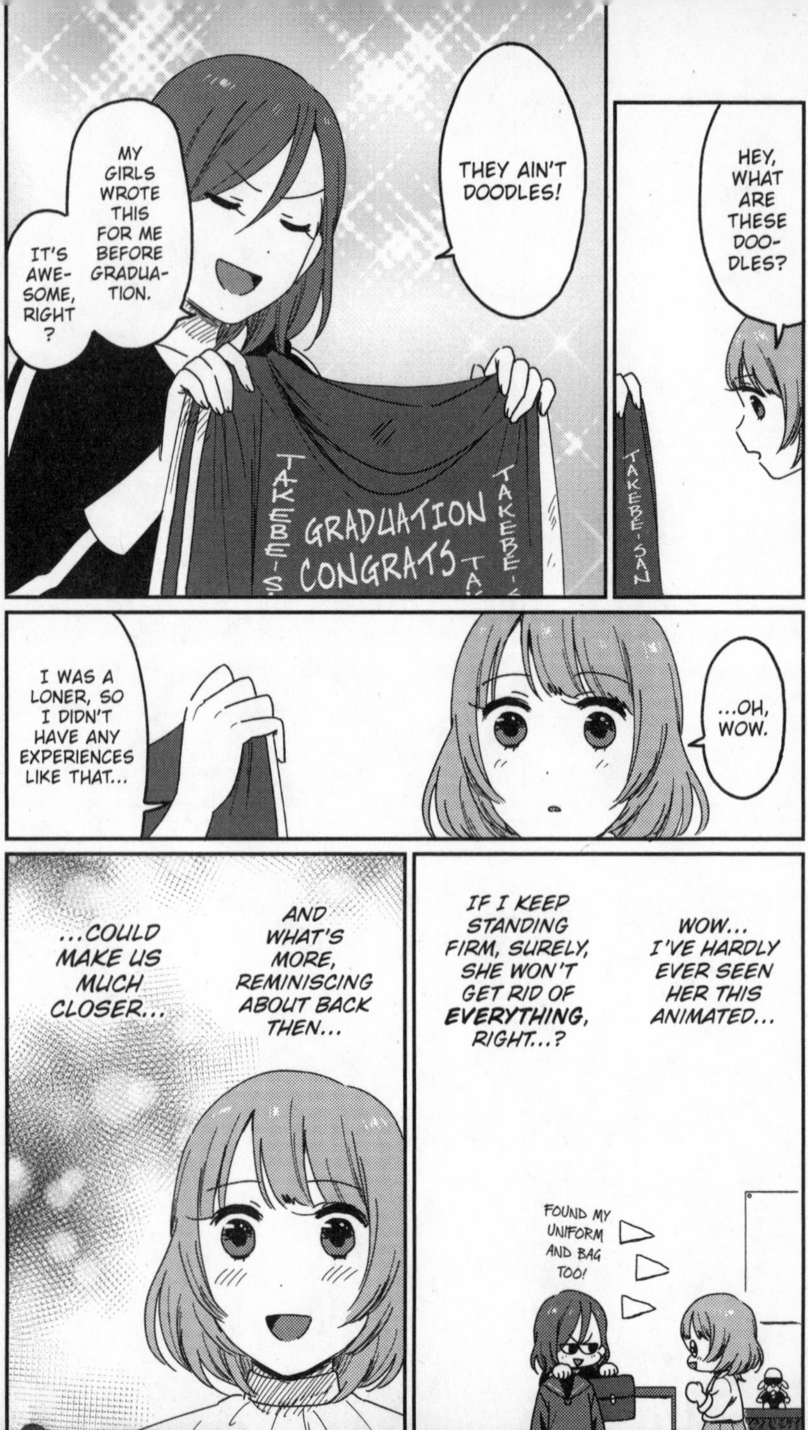

HEY, WHAT ARE THESE DOO-DLES?
TAKEBE-SAN
THEY AIN'T DOODLES!
MY GIRLS WROTE THIS FOR ME BEFORE GRADUA-TION.
IT'S AWE-SOME, RIGHT?
GRADUATION CONGRATS
...OH, WOW.
I WAS A LONER, SO I DIDN'T HAVE ANY EXPERIENCES LIKE THAT...
WOW... I'VE HARDLY EVER SEEN HER THIS ANIMATED...
IF I KEEP STANDING FIRM, SURELY, SHE WON'T GET RID OF **EVERYTHING**, RIGHT...?
FOUND MY UNIFORM AND BAG TOO!
AND WHAT'S MORE, REMINISCING ABOUT BACK THEN...
...COULD MAKE US MUCH CLOSER...

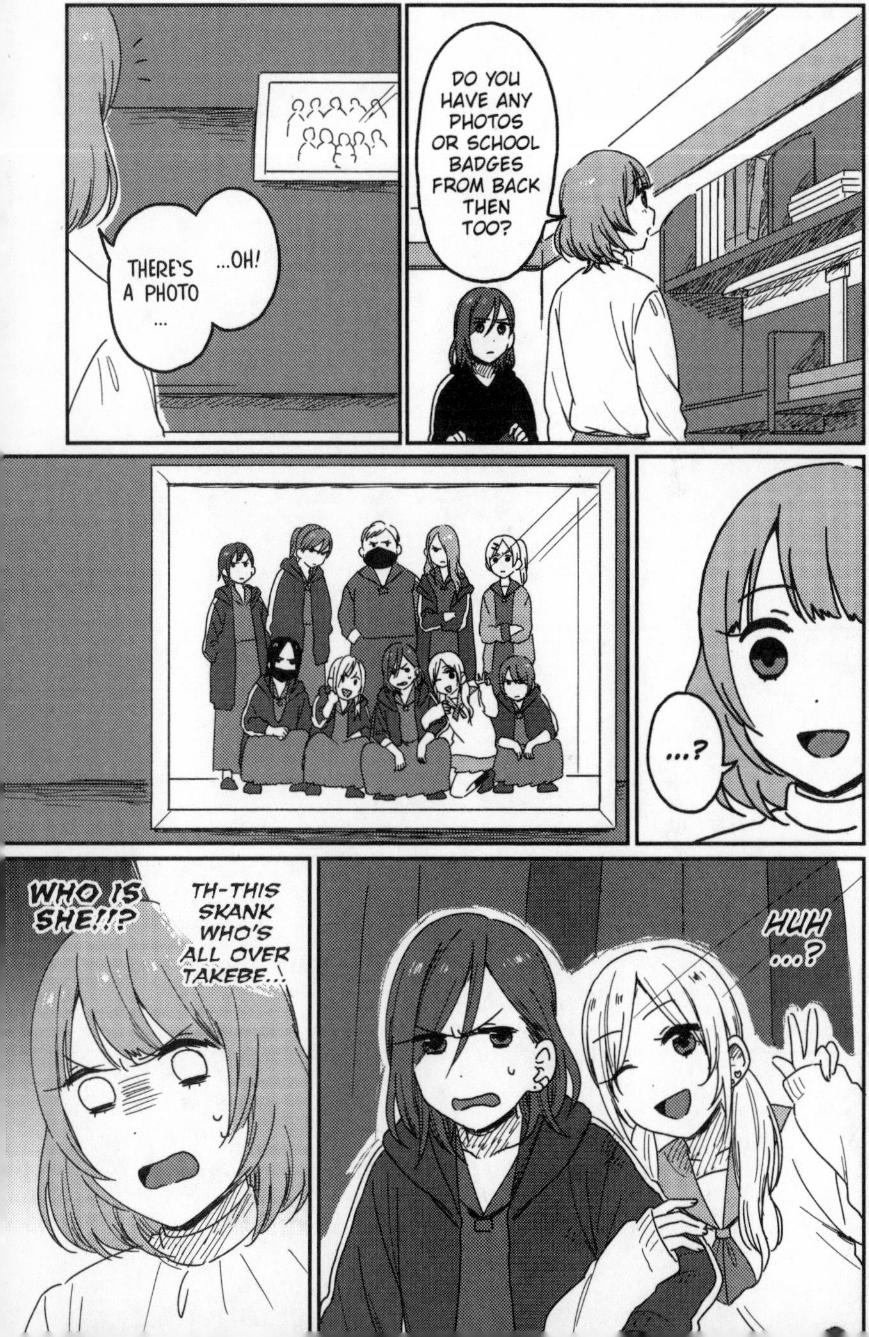
DO YOU HAVE ANY PHOTOS OR SCHOOL BADGES FROM BACK THEN TOO?
...OH!
THERE'S A PHOTO ...
...?
HUH ...?
TH-THIS SKANK WHO'S ALL OVER TAKEBE...
WHO IS SHE!!?

Catch These Hands!

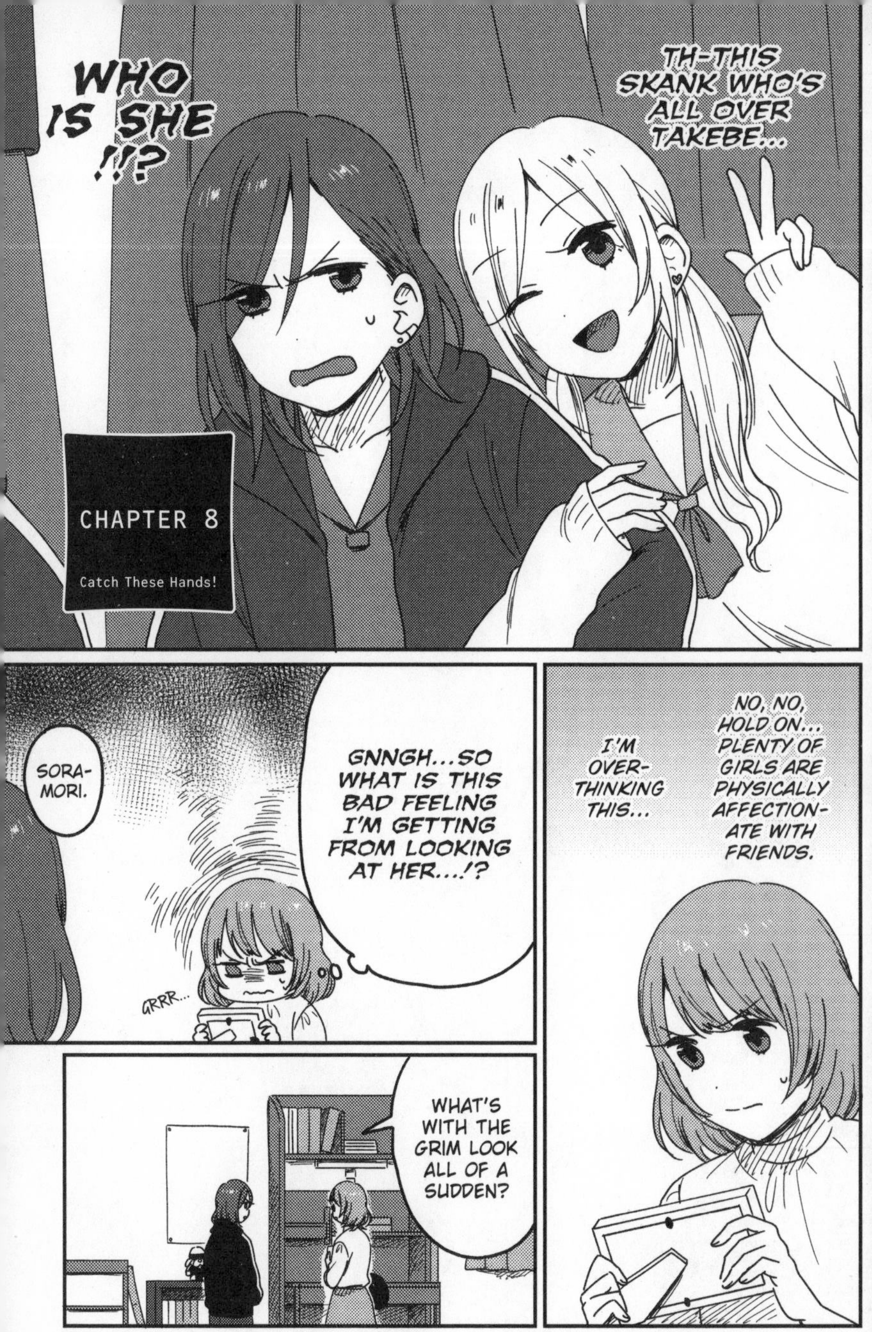
TH-THIS SKANK WHO'S ALL OVER TAKEBE...
WHO IS SHE!!?
CHAPTER 8
Catch These Hands!
NO, NO, HOLD ON... PLENTY OF GIRLS ARE PHYSICALLY AFFECTION-ATE WITH FRIENDS.
I'M OVER-THINKING THIS...
GNNGH...SO WHAT IS THIS BAD FEELING I'M GETTING FROM LOOKING AT HER...!?
SORA-MORI.
GRRR...
WHAT'S WITH THE GRIM LOOK ALL OF A SUDDEN?

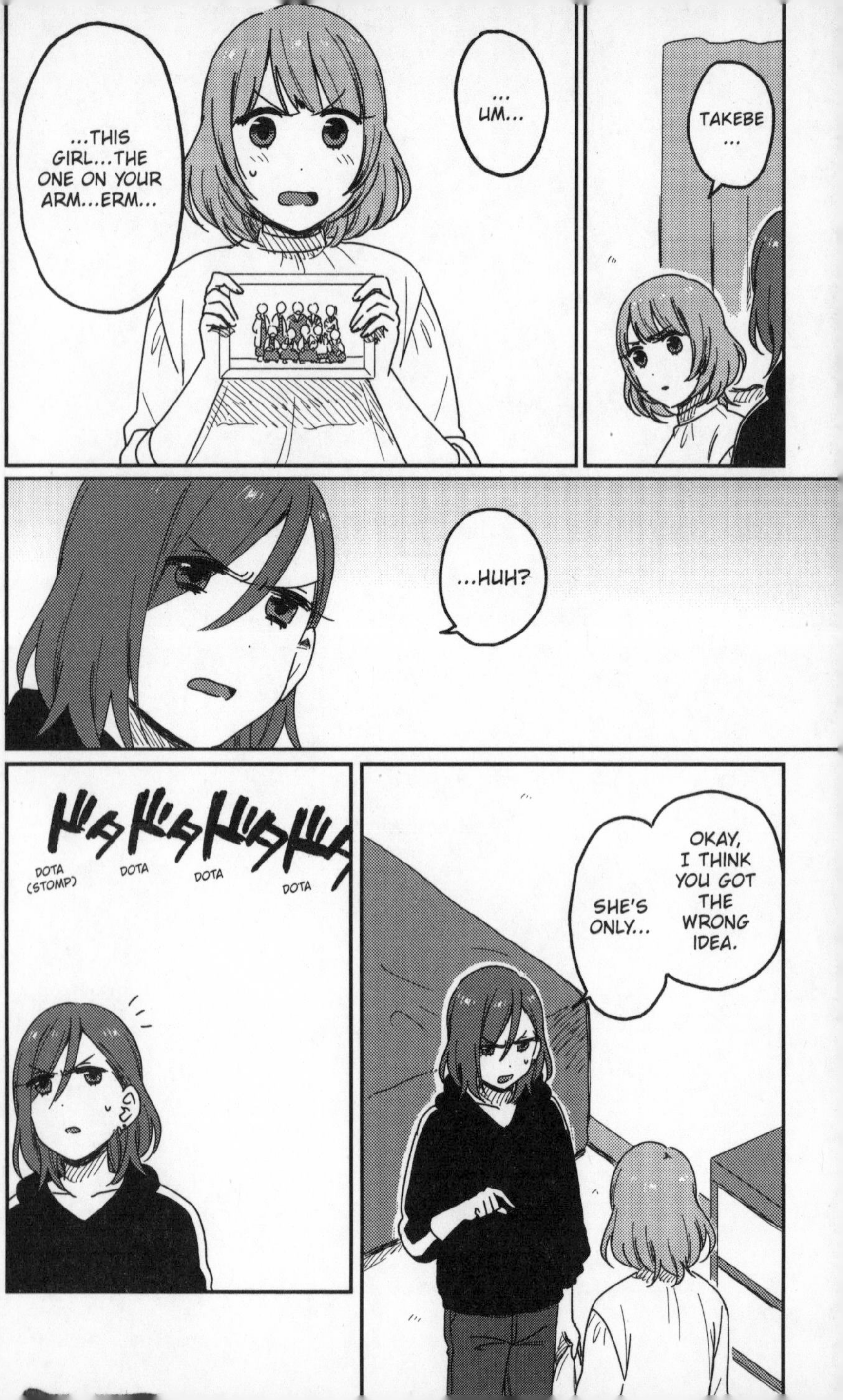
TAKEBE ...
... UM...
...THIS GIRL...THE ONE ON YOUR ARM...ERM...
...HUH?
OKAY, I THINK YOU GOT THE WRONG IDEA.
SHE'S ONLY...
DOTA (STOMP)
DOTA
DOTA
DOTA

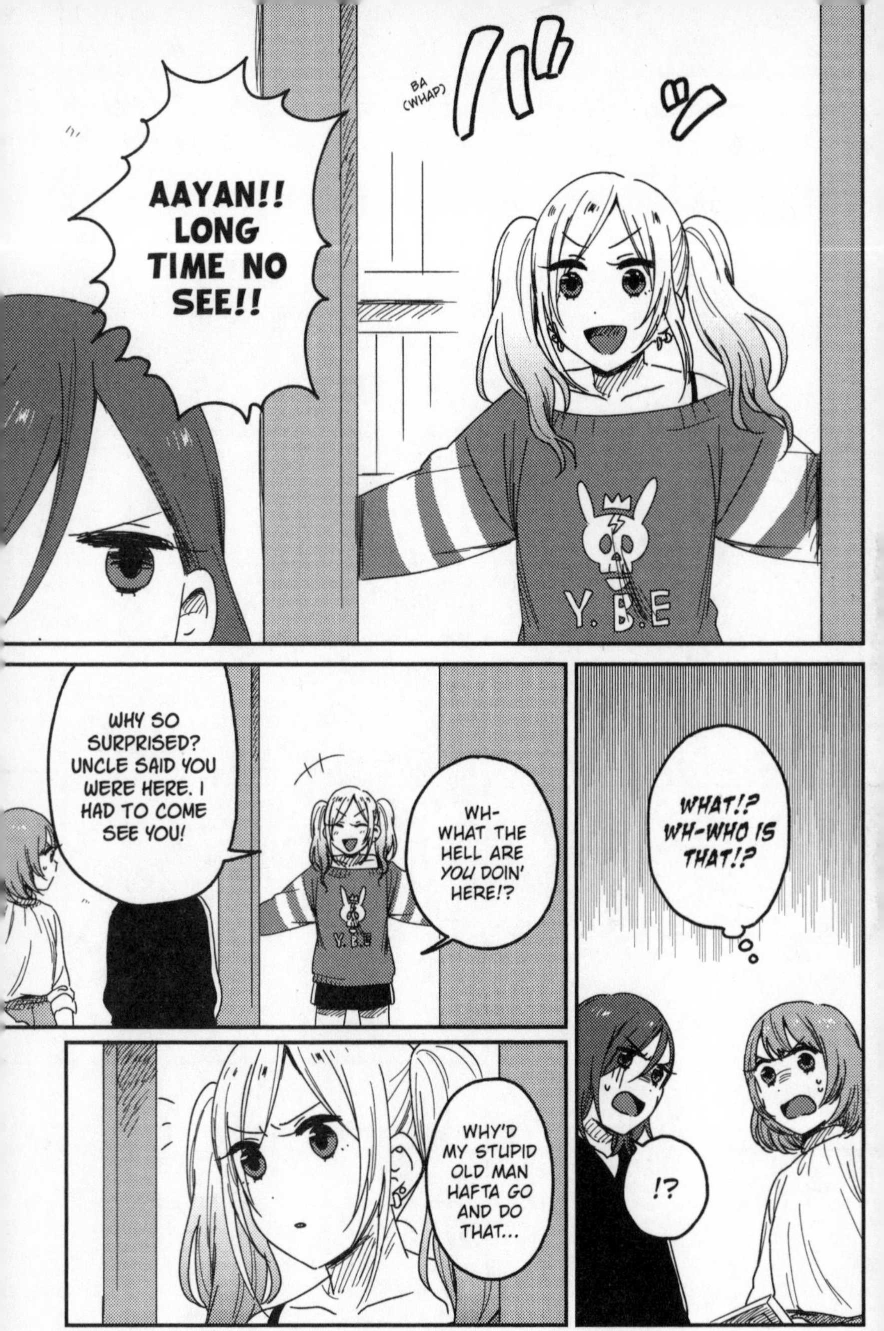

BA (WHAP)
AAYAN!! LONG TIME NO SEE!!
WHAT!? WH-WHO IS THAT!?
!?
WH- WHAT THE HELL ARE YOU DOIN' HERE!?
WHY SO SURPRISED? UNCLE SAID YOU WERE HERE. I HAD TO COME SEE YOU!
WHY'D MY STUPID OLD MAN HAFTA GO AND DO THAT...

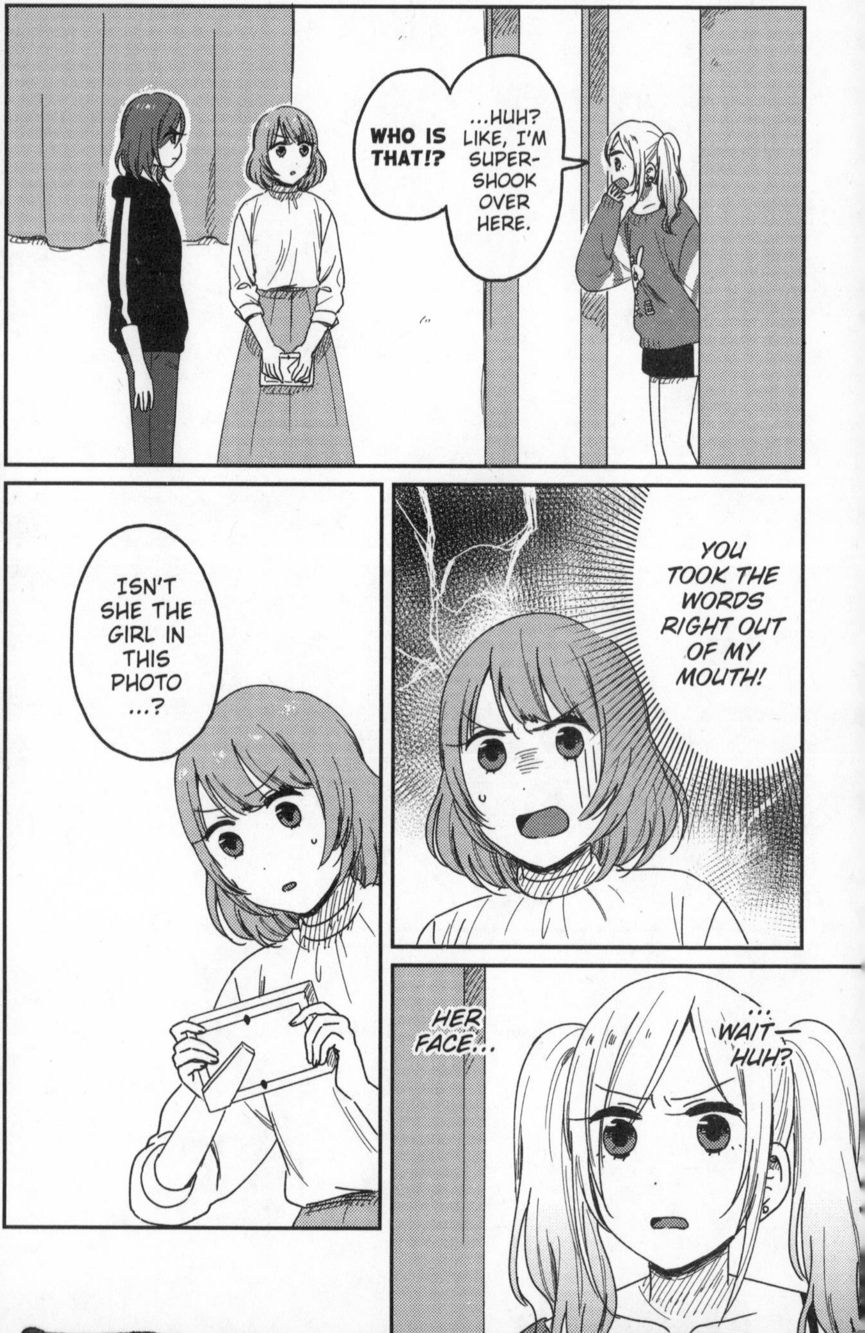
...HUH? LIKE, I'M SUPER-SHOOK OVER HERE.
WHO IS THAT!?
YOU TOOK THE WORDS RIGHT OUT OF MY MOUTH!
...WAIT—HUH?
HER FACE...
ISN'T SHE THE GIRL IN THIS PHOTO ...?

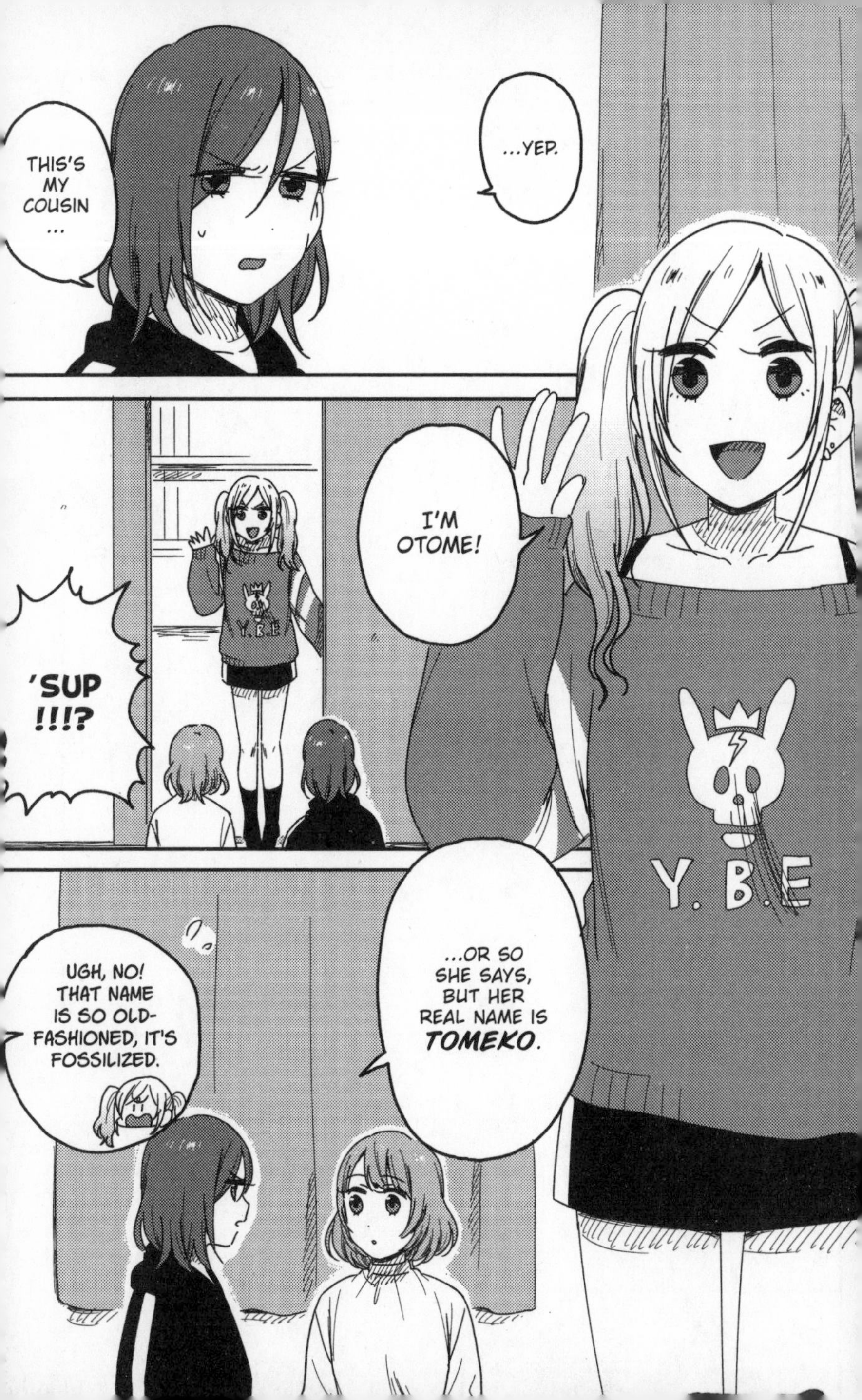
...YEP.
THIS'S MY COUSIN...
I'M OTOME!
'SUP !!!?
...OR SO SHE SAYS, BUT HER REAL NAME IS *TOMEKO*.
UGH, NO! THAT NAME IS SO OLD-FASHIONED, IT'S FOSSILIZED.

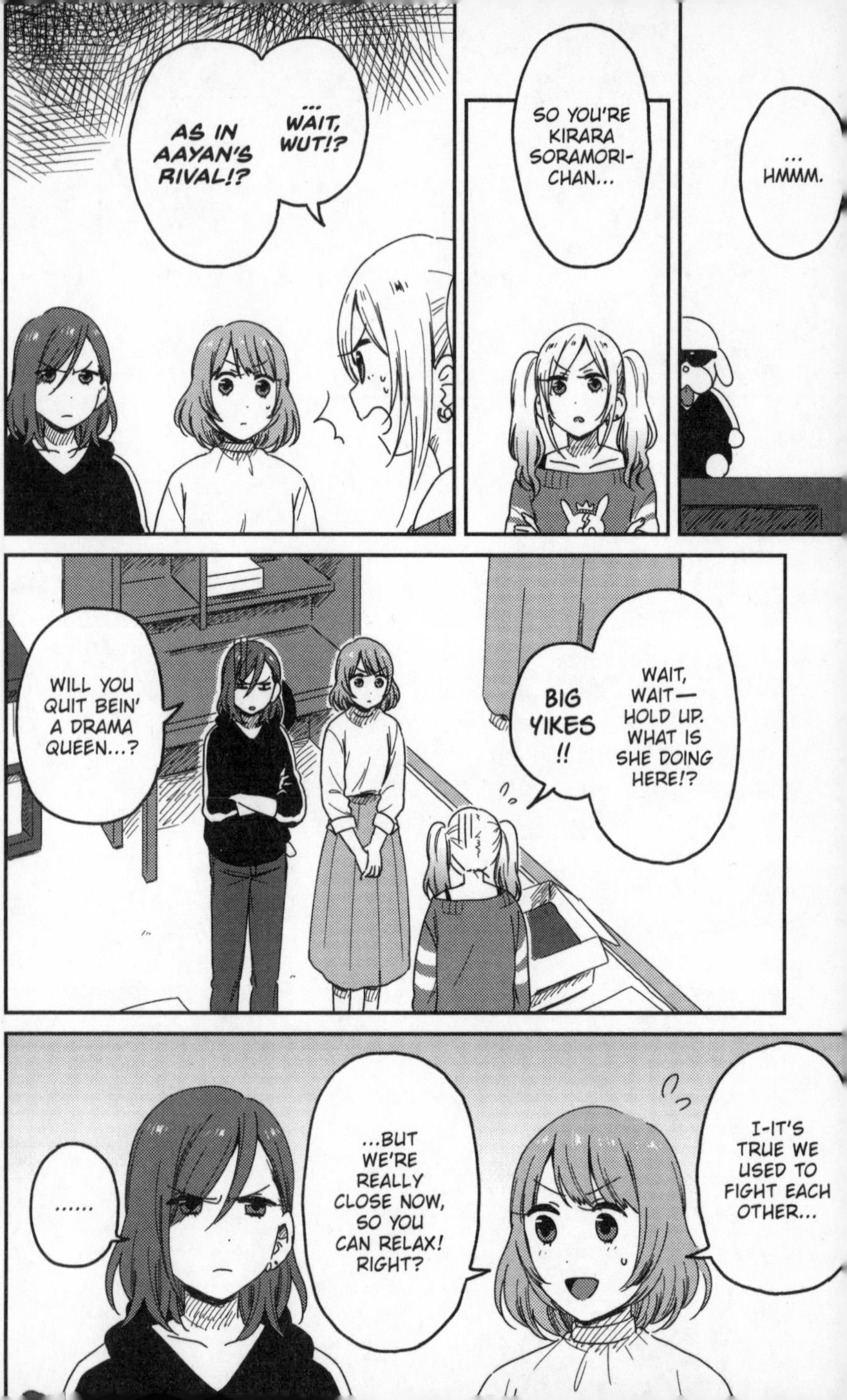
... HMMM.
SO YOU'RE KIRARA SORAMORI-CHAN...
... WAIT, WUT!?
AS IN AAYAN'S RIVAL!?
WAIT, WAIT— HOLD UP. WHAT IS SHE DOING HERE!?
BIG YIKES !!
WILL YOU QUIT BEIN' A DRAMA QUEEN...?
I-IT'S TRUE WE USED TO FIGHT EACH OTHER...
...BUT WE'RE REALLY CLOSE NOW, SO YOU CAN RELAX! RIGHT?
......

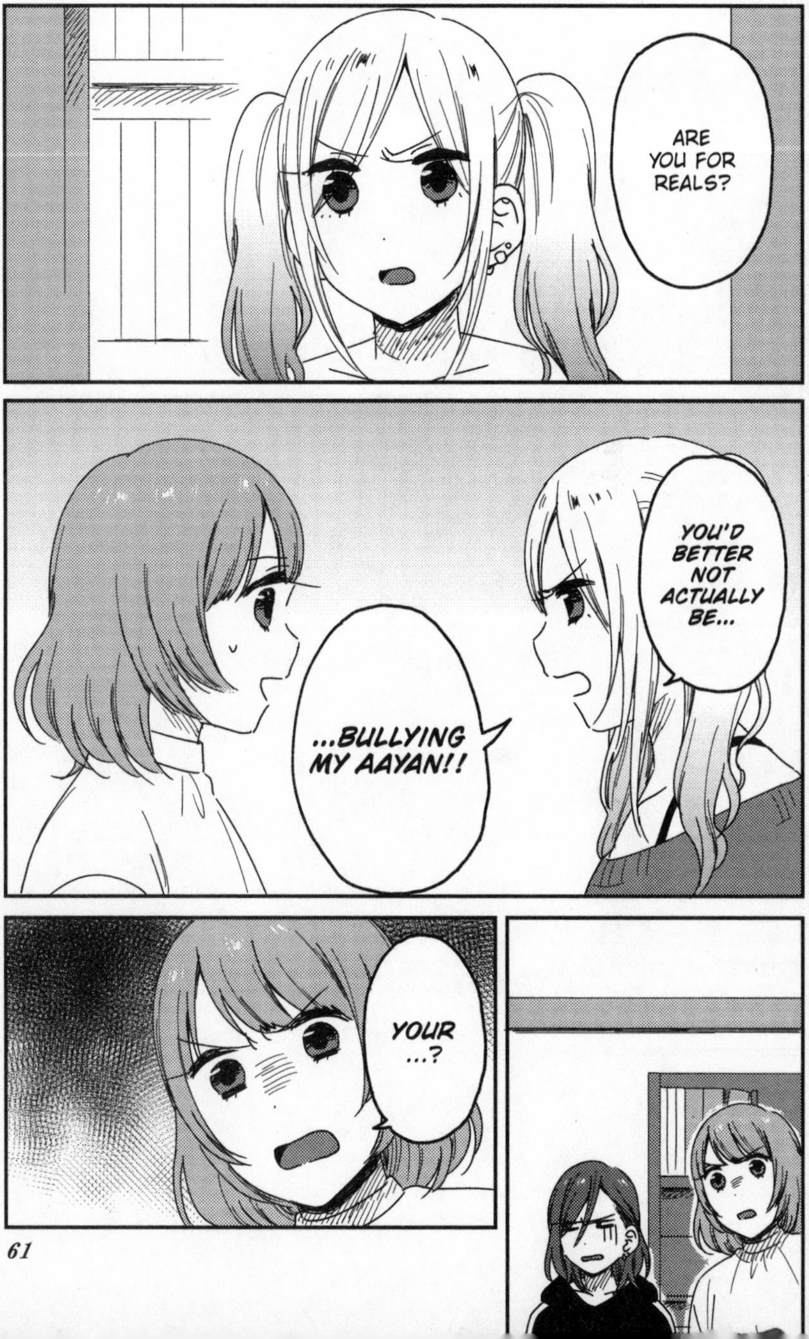
ARE YOU FOR REALS?
YOU'D BETTER NOT ACTUALLY BE...
...BULLYING MY AAYAN!!
YOUR ...?

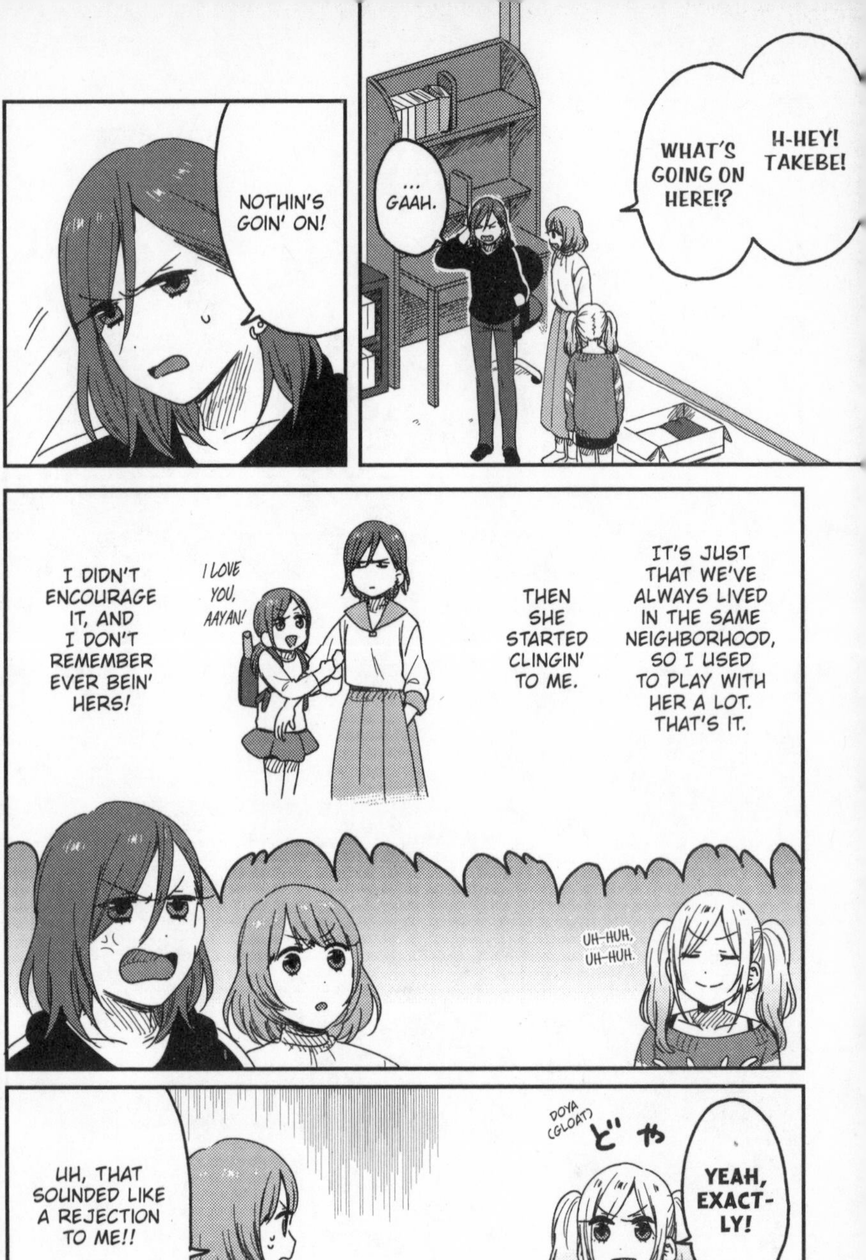
H-HEY! TAKEBE!
WHAT'S GOING ON HERE!?
... GAAH.
NOTHIN'S GOIN' ON!
IT'S JUST THAT WE'VE ALWAYS LIVED IN THE SAME NEIGHBORHOOD, SO I USED TO PLAY WITH HER A LOT. THAT'S IT.
THEN SHE STARTED CLINGIN' TO ME.
I LOVE YOU, AAYAN!
I DIDN'T ENCOURAGE IT, AND I DON'T REMEMBER EVER BEIN' HERS!
UH-HUH, UH-HUH.
DOYA (GLOAT)
どや
YEAH, EXACT-LY!
UH, THAT SOUNDED LIKE A REJECTION TO ME!!

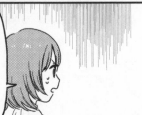

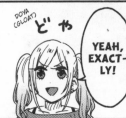

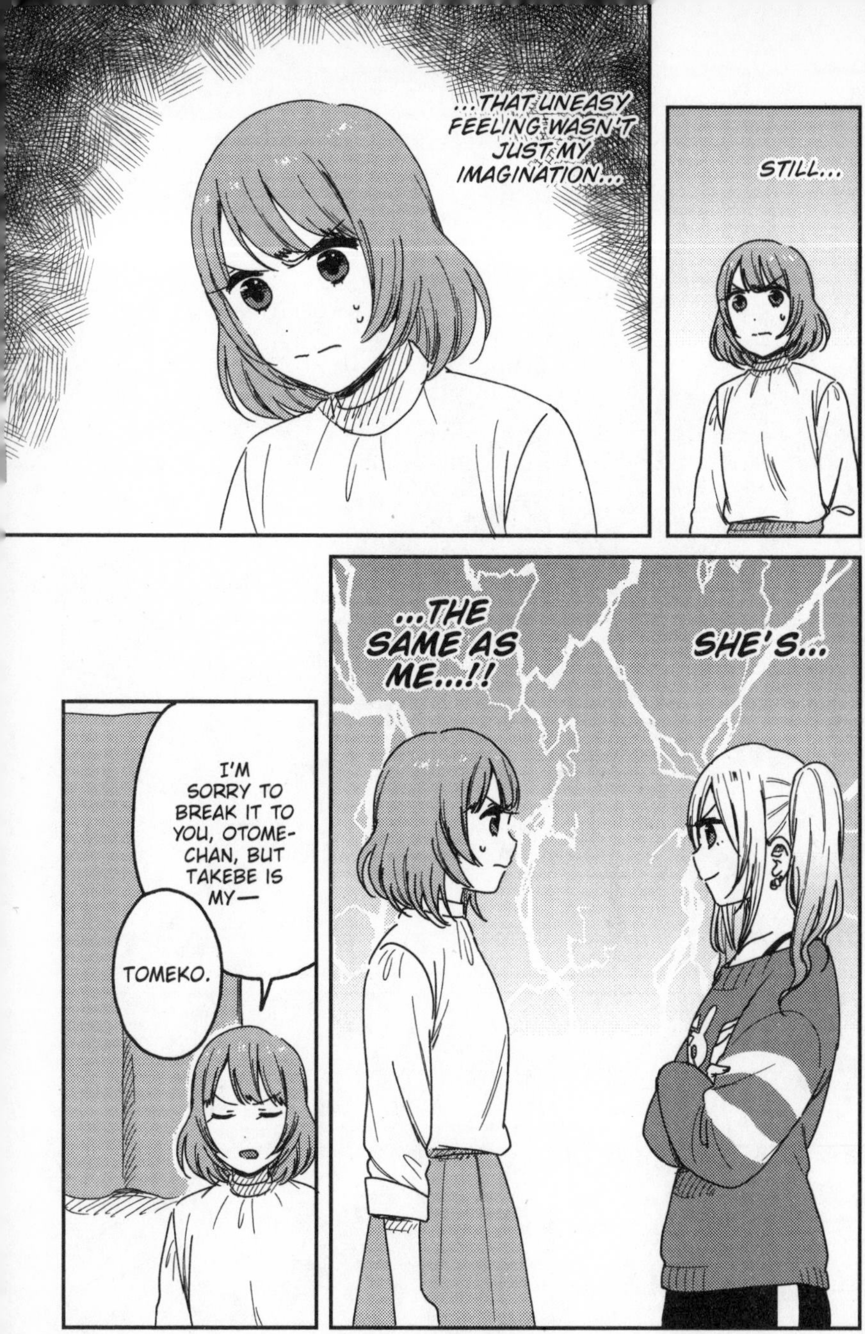
STILL...
...THAT UNEASY FEELING WASN'T JUST MY IMAGINATION...
SHE'S...
...THE SAME AS ME...!!
I'M SORRY TO BREAK IT TO YOU, OTOME-CHAN, BUT TAKEBE IS MY—
TOMEKO.

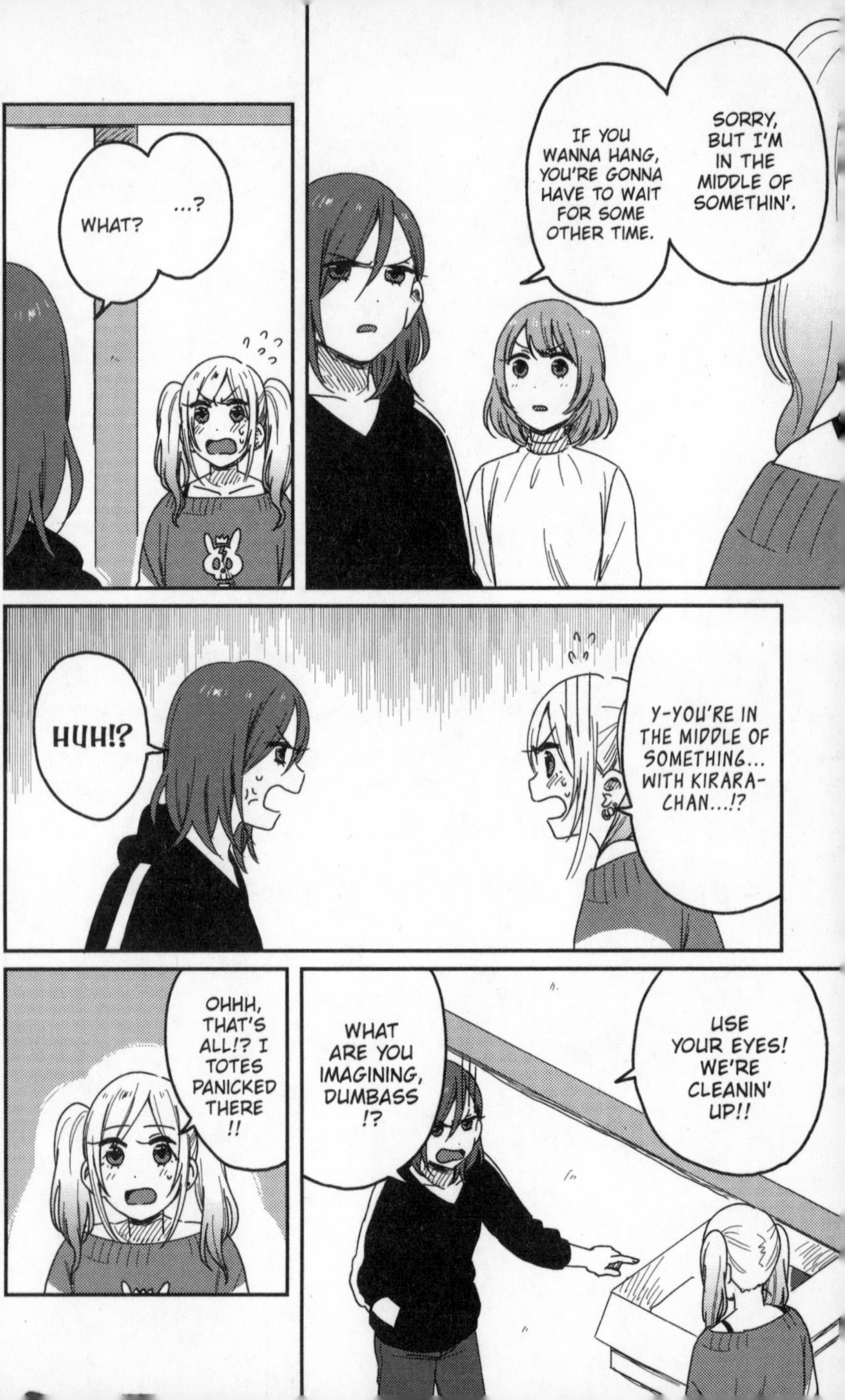
SORRY, BUT I'M IN THE MIDDLE OF SOMETHIN'.
IF YOU WANNA HANG, YOU'RE GONNA HAVE TO WAIT FOR SOME OTHER TIME.
...?
WHAT?
Y-YOU'RE IN THE MIDDLE OF SOMETHING... WITH KIRARA-CHAN...!?
HUH!?
USE YOUR EYES! WE'RE CLEANIN' UP!!
WHAT ARE YOU IMAGINING, DUMBASS!?
OHHH, THAT'S ALL!? I TOTES PANICKED THERE!!

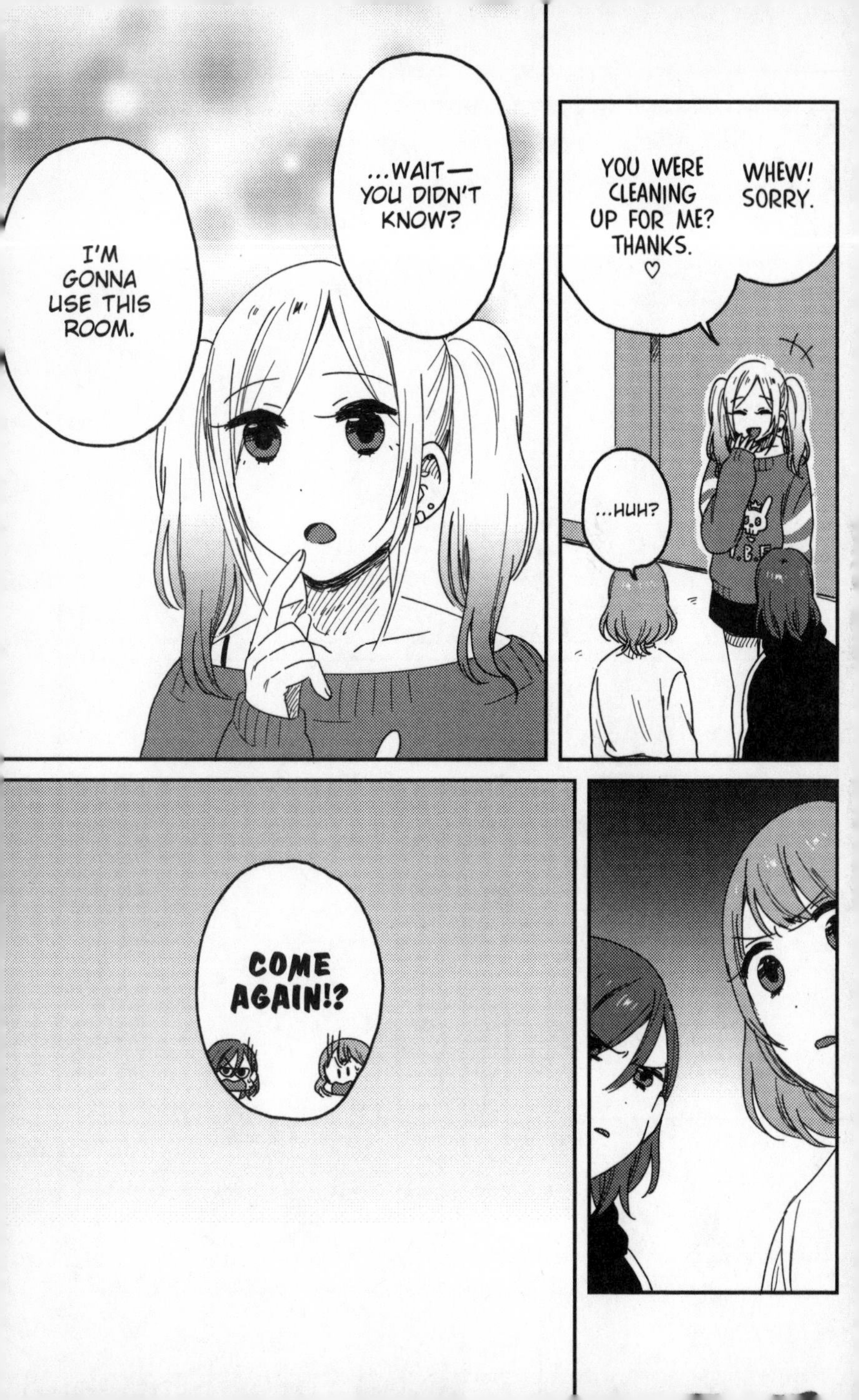
WHEW! SORRY.
YOU WERE CLEANING UP FOR ME? THANKS. ♡
...HUH?
...WAIT— YOU DIDN'T KNOW?
I'M GONNA USE THIS ROOM.
COME AGAIN!?

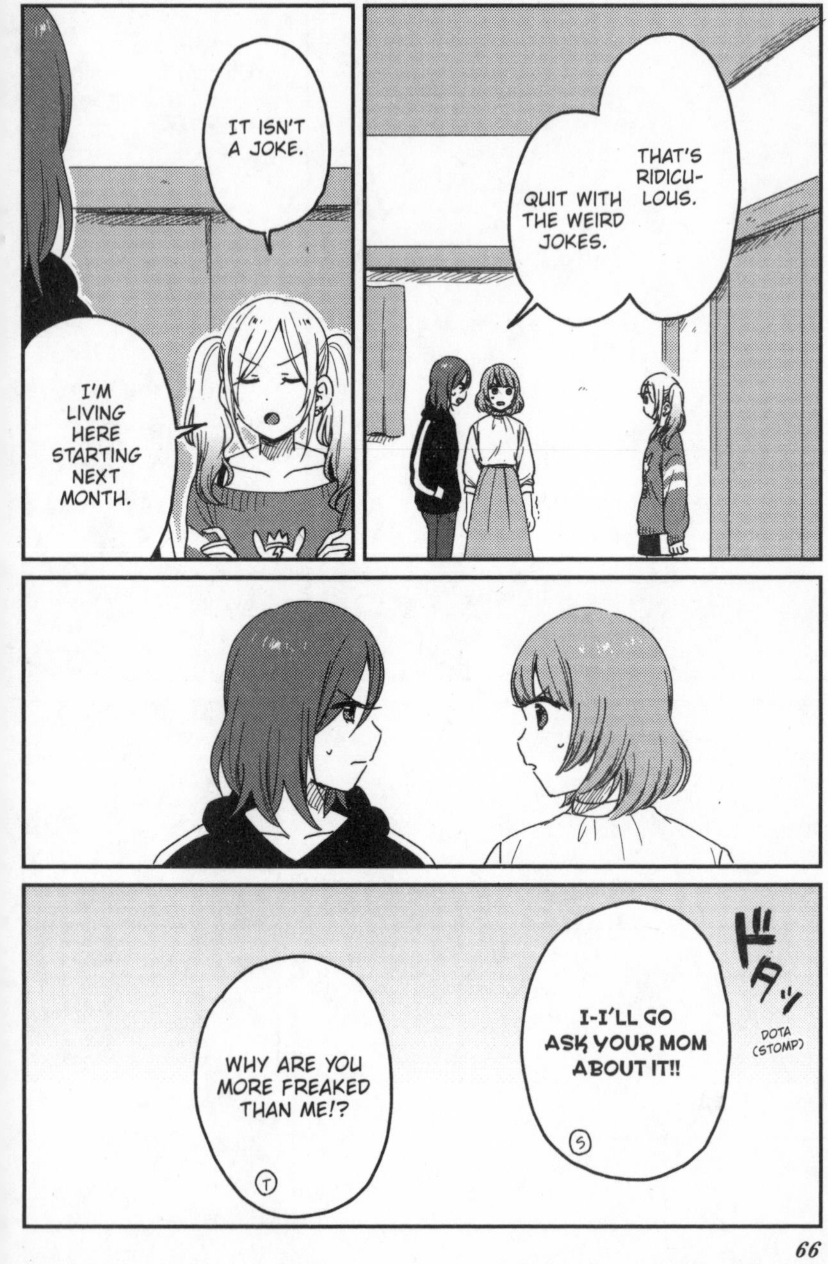
THAT'S RIDICULOUS.
QUIT WITH THE WEIRD JOKES.
IT ISN'T A JOKE.
I'M LIVING HERE STARTING NEXT MONTH.
ドタッ
DOTA (STOMP)
I-I'LL GO ASK YOUR MOM ABOUT IT!!
WHY ARE YOU MORE FREAKED THAN ME!?

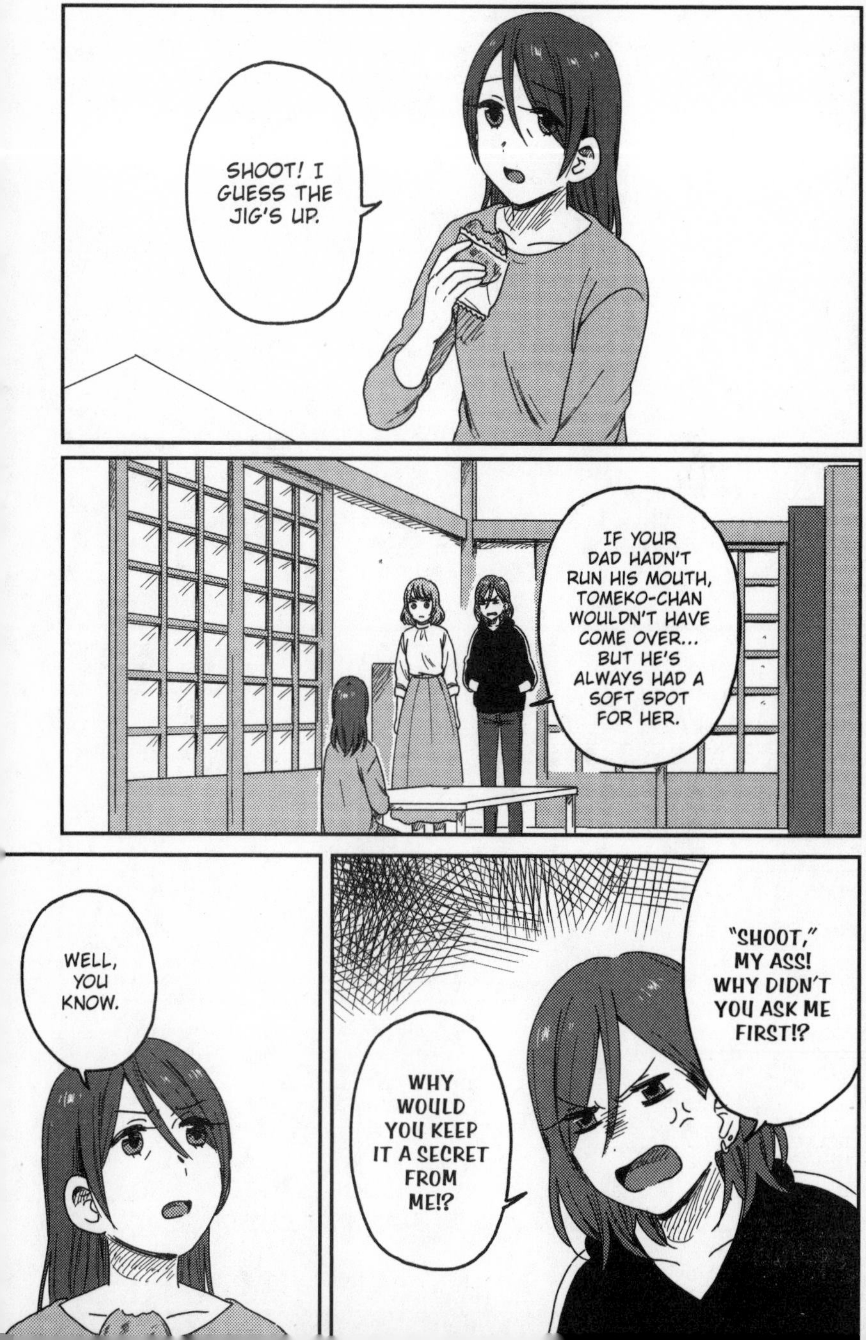
SHOOT! I GUESS THE JIG'S UP.
IF YOUR DAD HADN'T RUN HIS MOUTH, TOMEKO-CHAN WOULDN'T HAVE COME OVER... BUT HE'S ALWAYS HAD A SOFT SPOT FOR HER.
"SHOOT," MY ASS! WHY DIDN'T YOU ASK ME FIRST!?
WHY WOULD YOU KEEP IT A SECRET FROM ME!?
WELL, YOU KNOW.

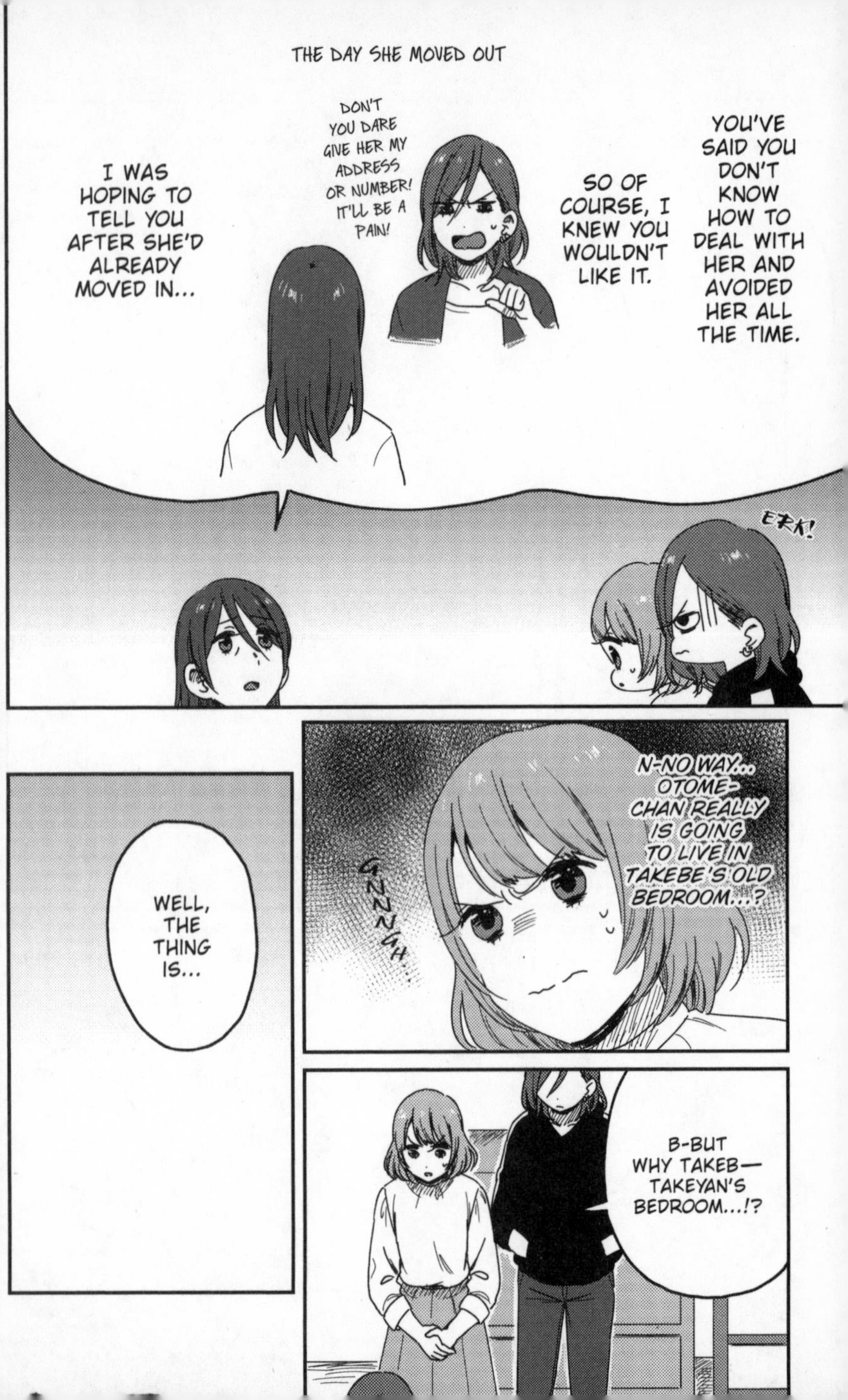
THE DAY SHE MOVED OUT
YOU'VE SAID YOU DON'T KNOW HOW TO DEAL WITH HER AND AVOIDED HER ALL THE TIME.
SO OF COURSE, I KNEW YOU WOULDN'T LIKE IT.
DON'T YOU DARE GIVE HER MY ADDRESS OR NUMBER! IT'LL BE A PAIN!
I WAS HOPING TO TELL YOU AFTER SHE'D ALREADY MOVED IN...
ERK!
N-NO WAY... OTOME-CHAN REALLY IS GOING TO LIVE IN TAKEBE'S OLD BEDROOM...?
GNNNGH...
B-BUT WHY TAKEB— TAKEYAN'S BEDROOM...!?
WELL, THE THING IS...

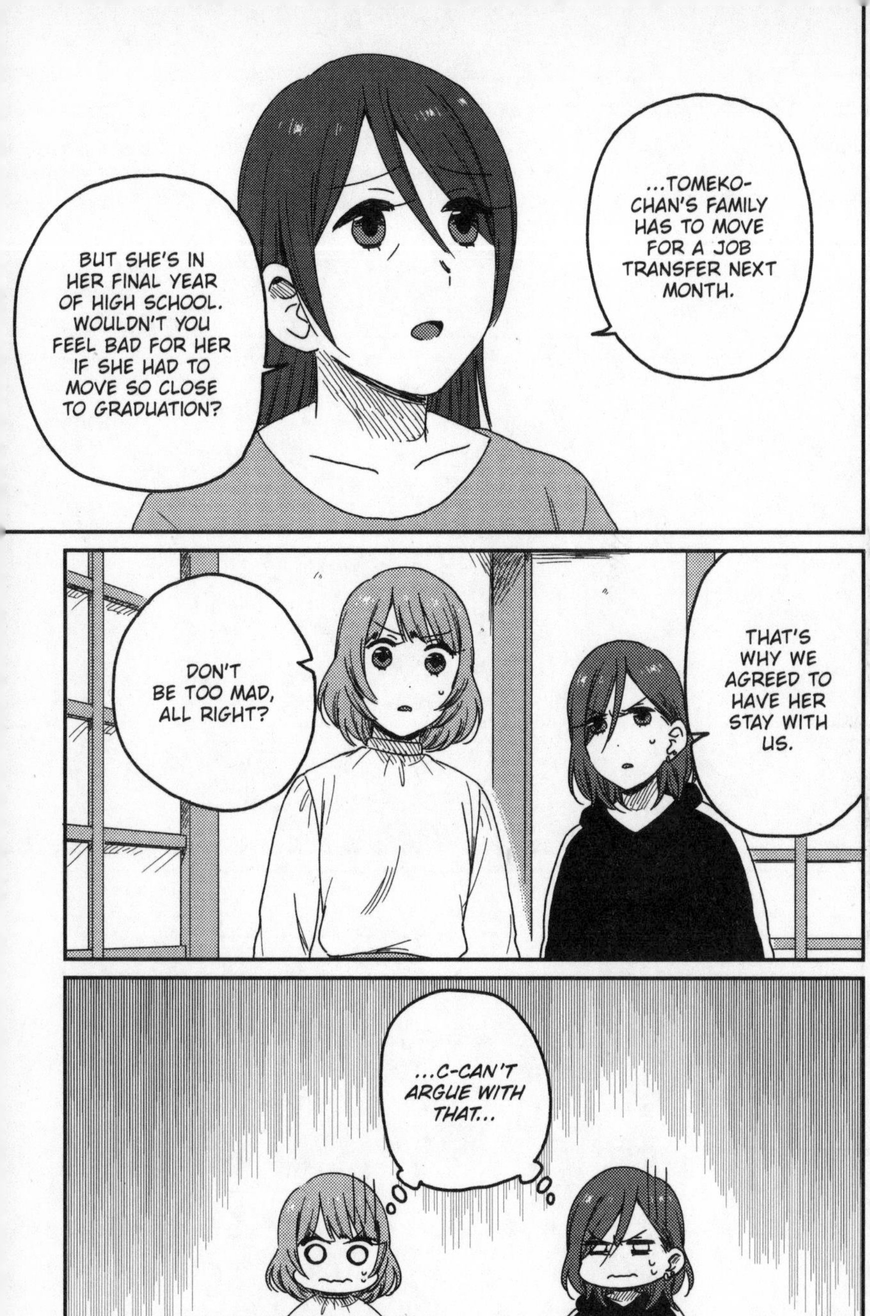
...TOMEKO-CHAN'S FAMILY HAS TO MOVE FOR A JOB TRANSFER NEXT MONTH.
BUT SHE'S IN HER FINAL YEAR OF HIGH SCHOOL. WOULDN'T YOU FEEL BAD FOR HER IF SHE HAD TO MOVE SO CLOSE TO GRADUATION?
THAT'S WHY WE AGREED TO HAVE HER STAY WITH US.
DON'T BE TOO MAD, ALL RIGHT?
...C-CAN'T ARGUE WITH THAT...

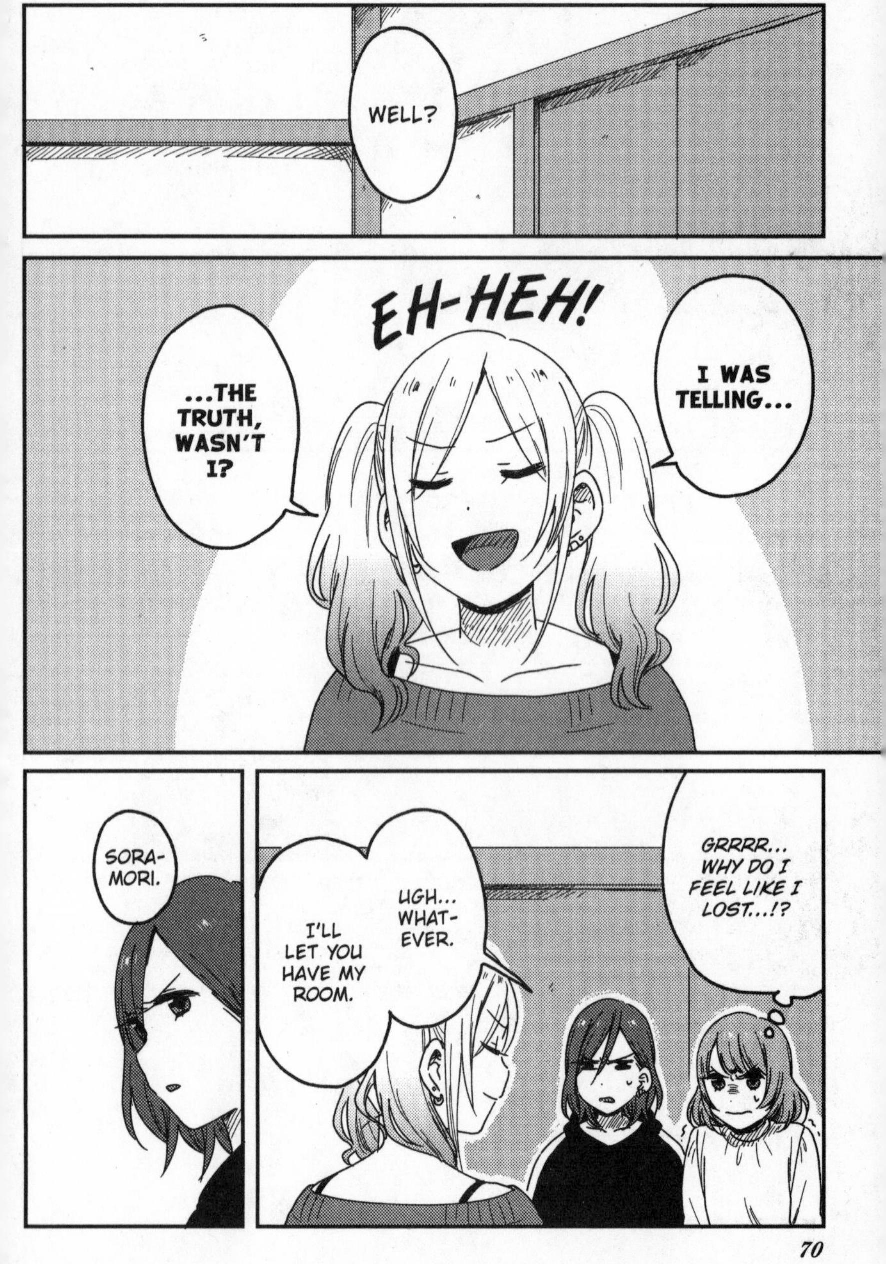
WELL?
EH-HEH!
I WAS TELLING...
...THE TRUTH, WASN'T I?
GRRRR... WHY DO I FEEL LIKE I LOST...!?
UGH... WHAT-EVER.
I'LL LET YOU HAVE MY ROOM.
SORA-MORI.

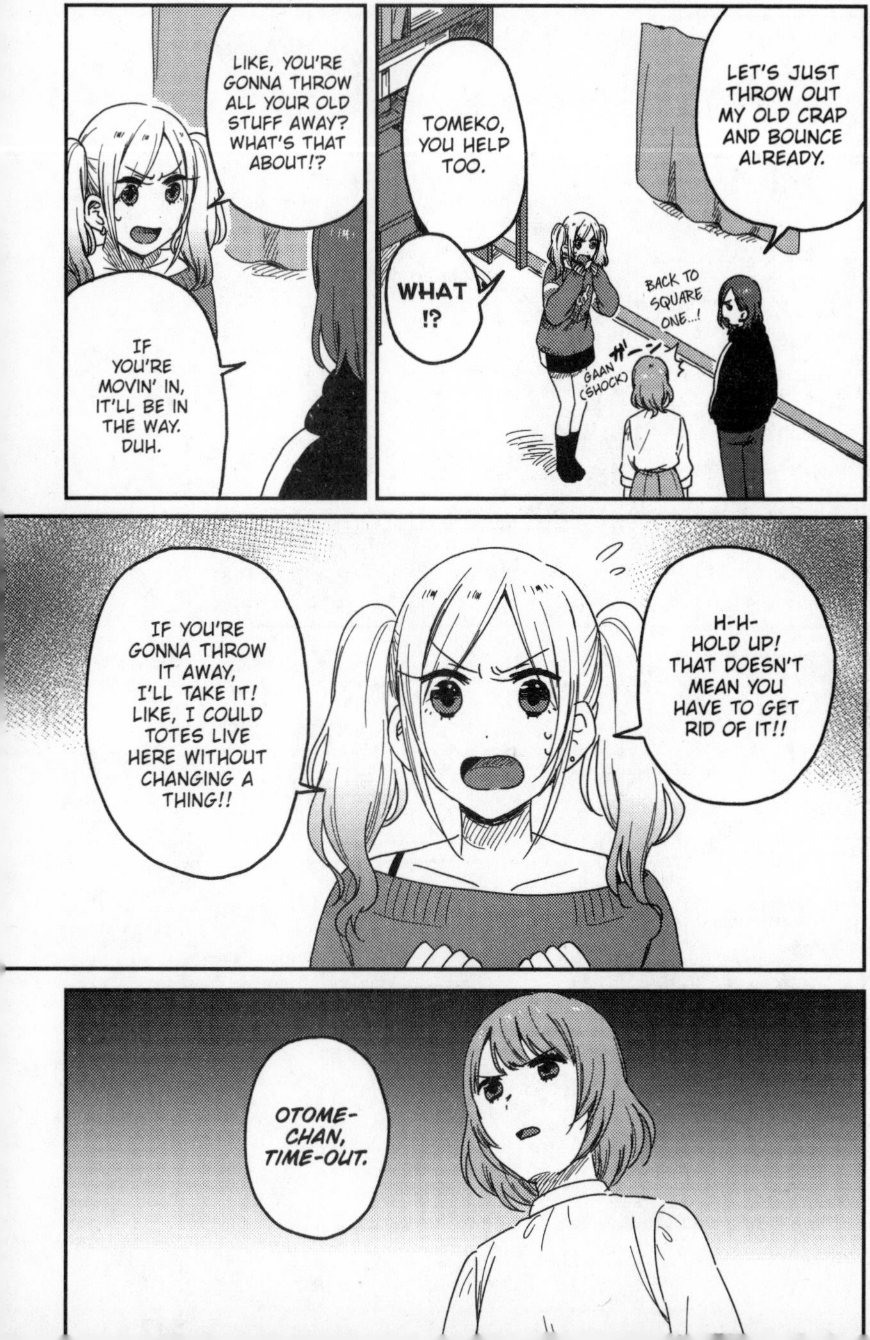
LET'S JUST THROW OUT MY OLD CRAP AND BOUNCE ALREADY.
TOMEKO, YOU HELP TOO.
WHAT !?
BACK TO SQUARE ONE...!
ガーン
GAAN (SHOCK)
LIKE, YOU'RE GONNA THROW ALL YOUR OLD STUFF AWAY? WHAT'S THAT ABOUT!?
IF YOU'RE MOVIN' IN, IT'LL BE IN THE WAY. DUH.
H-H-HOLD UP! THAT DOESN'T MEAN YOU HAVE TO GET RID OF IT!!
IF YOU'RE GONNA THROW IT AWAY, I'LL TAKE IT! LIKE, I COULD TOTES LIVE HERE WITHOUT CHANGING A THING!!
OTOME-CHAN, TIME-OUT.

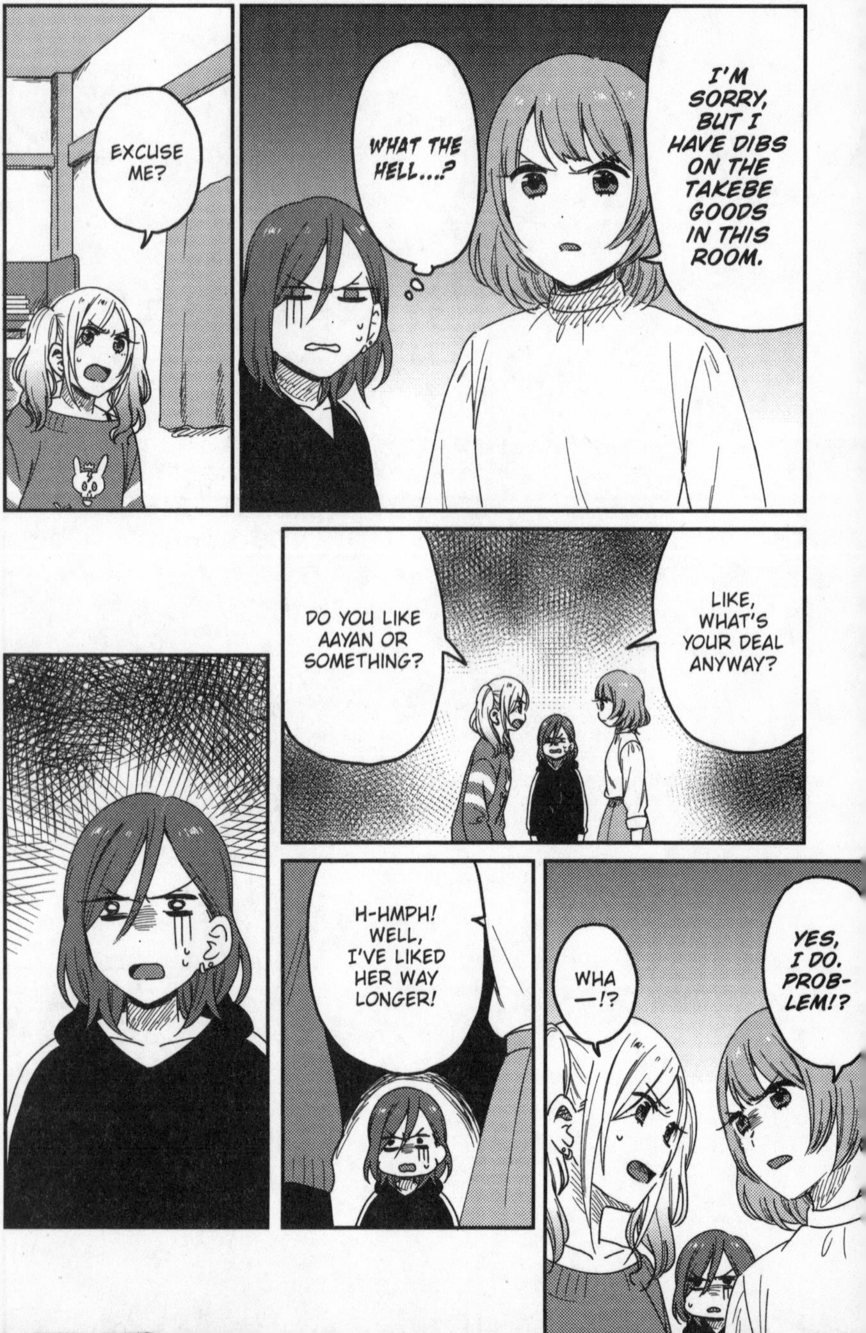
I'M SORRY, BUT I HAVE DIBS ON THE TAKEBE GOODS IN THIS ROOM.
WHAT THE HELL...?
EXCUSE ME?
LIKE, WHAT'S YOUR DEAL ANYWAY?
DO YOU LIKE AAYAN OR SOMETHING?
YES, I DO. PROB-LEM!?
WHA—!?
H-HMPH! WELL, I'VE LIKED HER WAY LONGER!

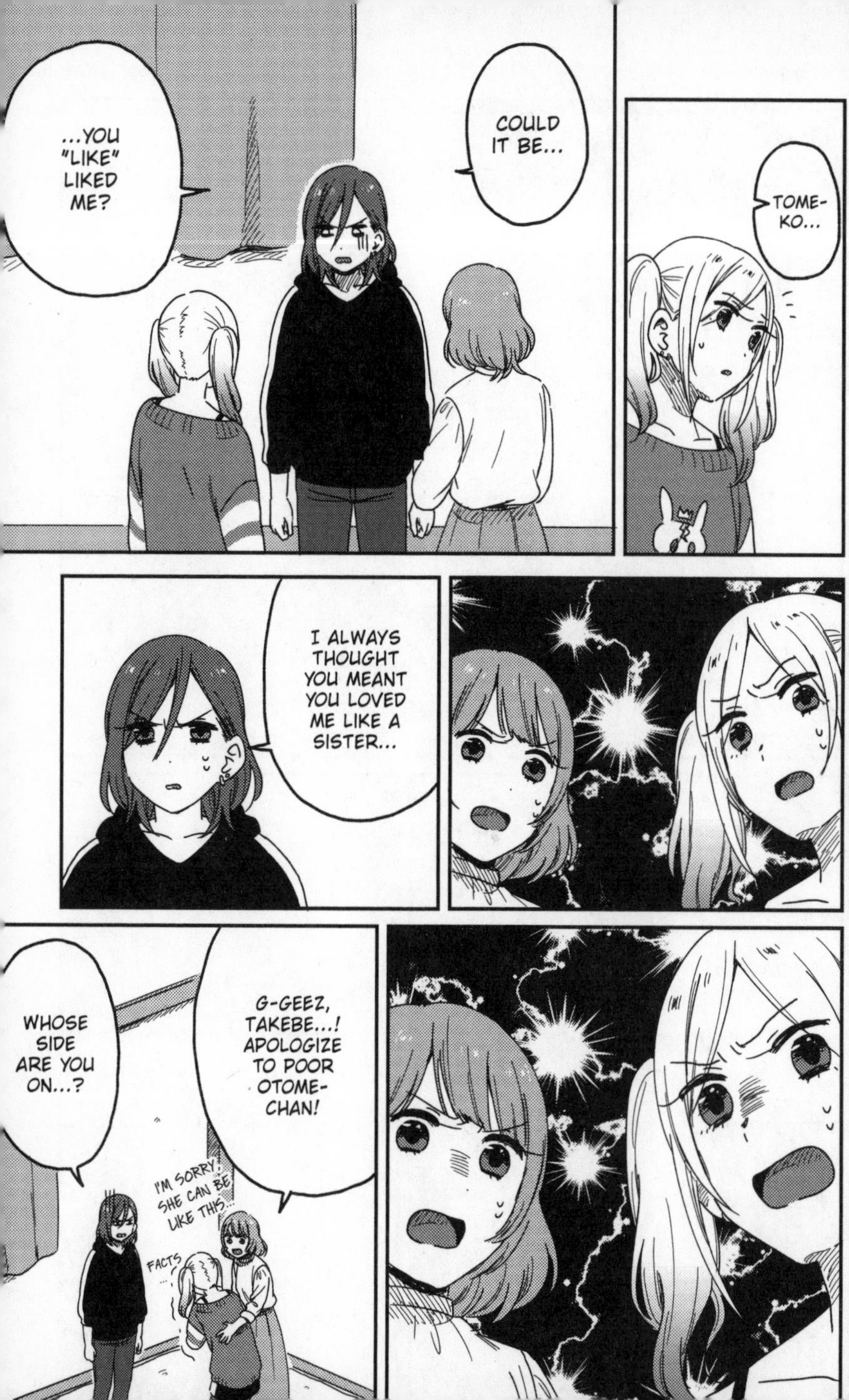
TOME-KO...
COULD IT BE...
...YOU "LIKE" LIKED ME?
I ALWAYS THOUGHT YOU MEANT YOU LOVED ME LIKE A SISTER...
G-GEEZ, TAKEBE...! APOLOGIZE TO POOR OTOME-CHAN!
WHOSE SIDE ARE YOU ON...?
I'M SORRY. SHE CAN BE LIKE THIS...
FACTS ...

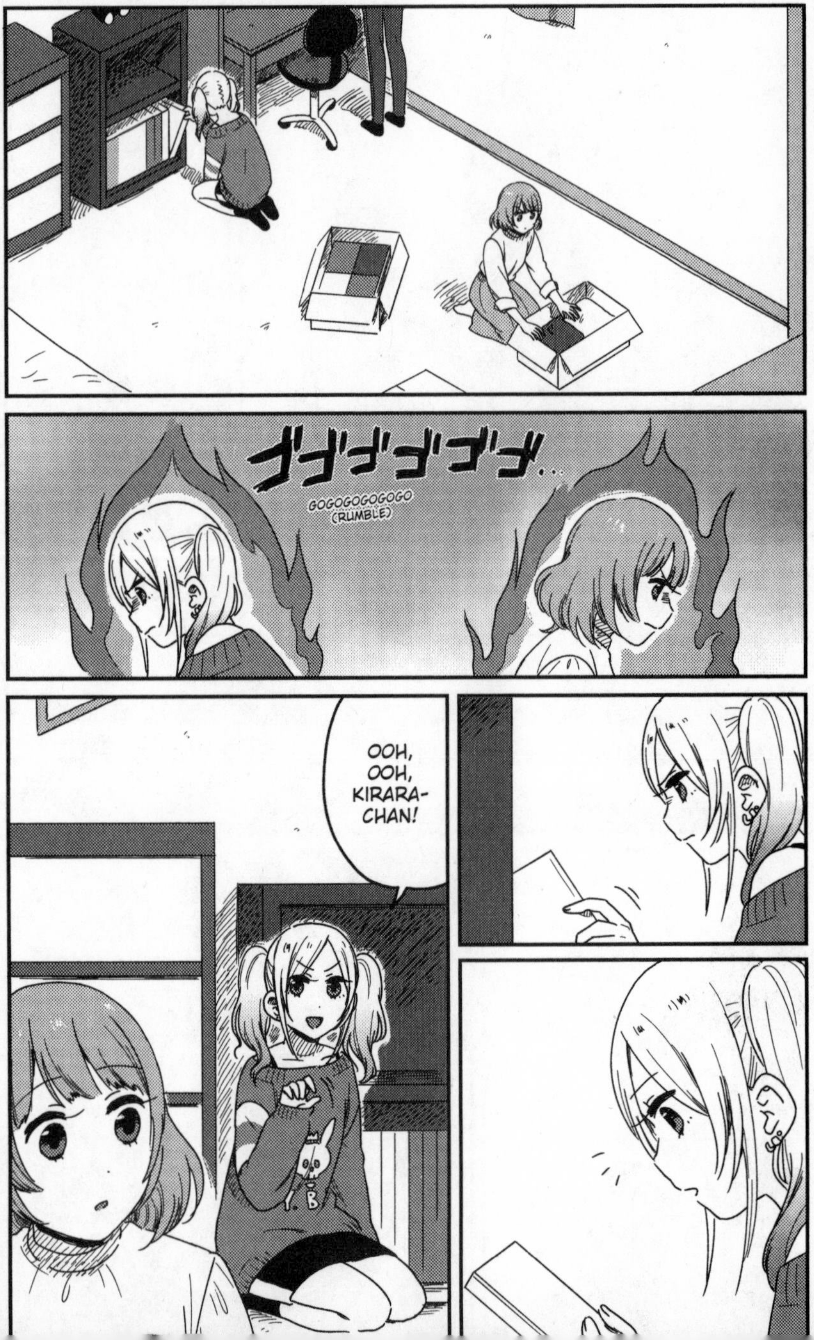
ゴゴゴゴゴゴ…
GOGOGOGOGOGO
(RUMBLE)
OOH, OOH, KIRARA-CHAN!

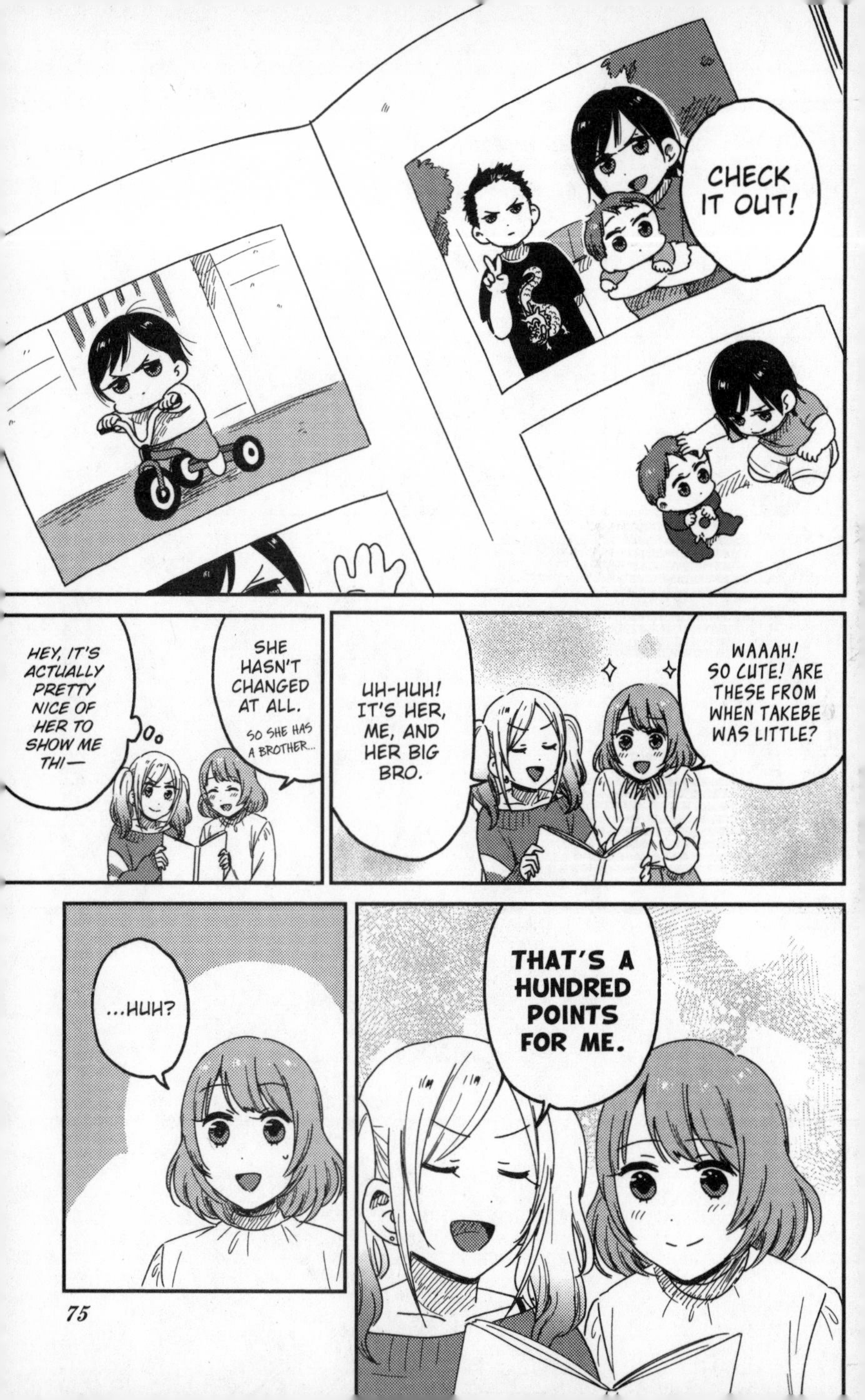
CHECK IT OUT!
WAAAH! SO CUTE! ARE THESE FROM WHEN TAKEBE WAS LITTLE?
UH-HUH! IT'S HER, ME, AND HER BIG BRO.
SHE HASN'T CHANGED AT ALL.
SO SHE HAS A BROTHER...
HEY, IT'S ACTUALLY PRETTY NICE OF HER TO SHOW ME THI—
THAT'S A HUNDRED POINTS FOR ME.
...HUH?

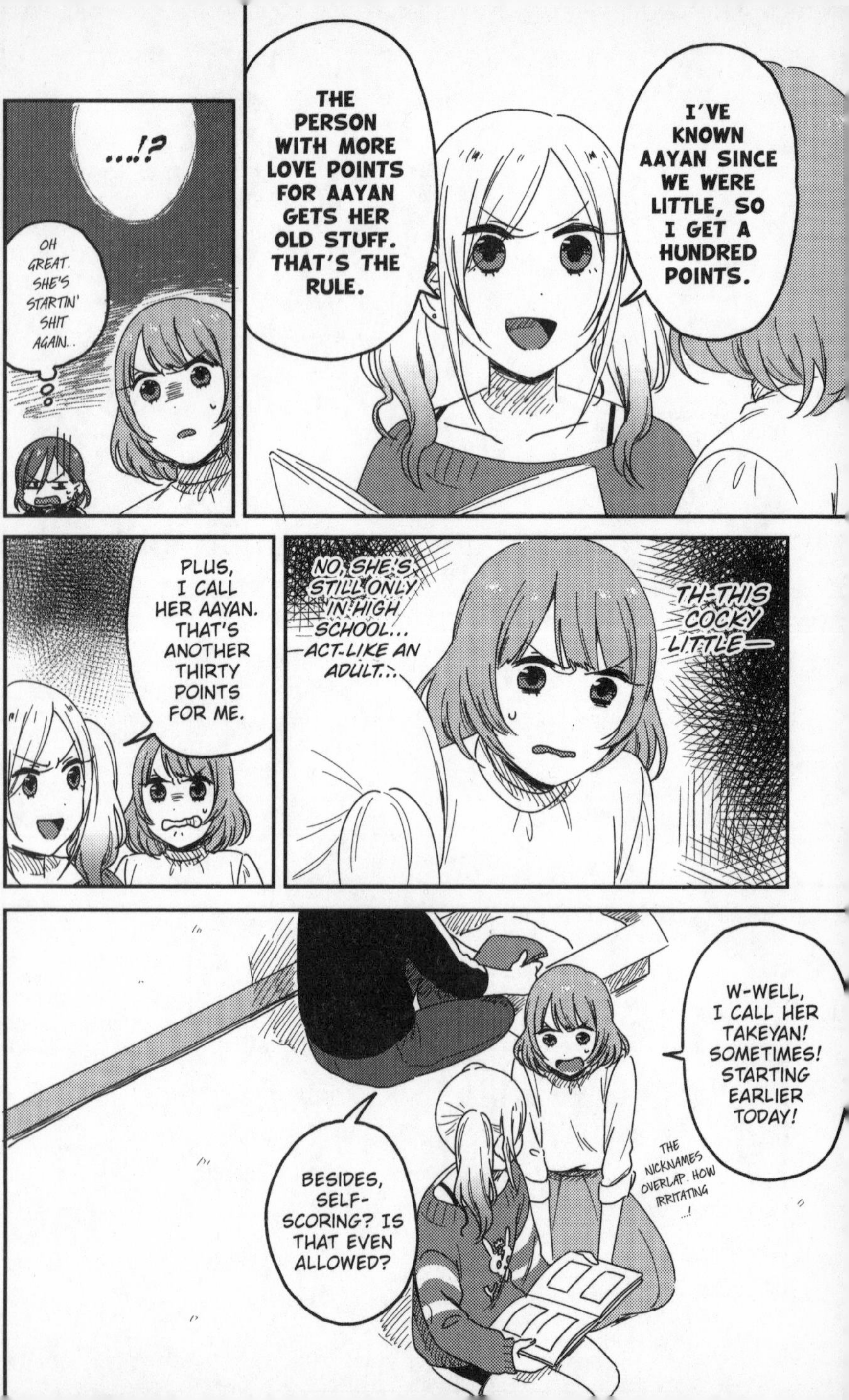
I'VE KNOWN AAYAN SINCE WE WERE LITTLE, SO I GET A HUNDRED POINTS.
THE PERSON WITH MORE LOVE POINTS FOR AAYAN GETS HER OLD STUFF. THAT'S THE RULE.
...!?
OH GREAT. SHE'S STARTIN' SHIT AGAIN...
TH-THIS COCKY LITTLE—
NO, SHE'S STILL ONLY IN HIGH SCHOOL... ACT LIKE AN ADULT...
PLUS, I CALL HER AAYAN. THAT'S ANOTHER THIRTY POINTS FOR ME.
W-WELL, I CALL HER TAKEYAN! SOMETIMES! STARTING EARLIER TODAY!
THE NICKNAMES OVERLAP. HOW IRRITATING ...!
BESIDES, SELF-SCORING? IS THAT EVEN ALLOWED?

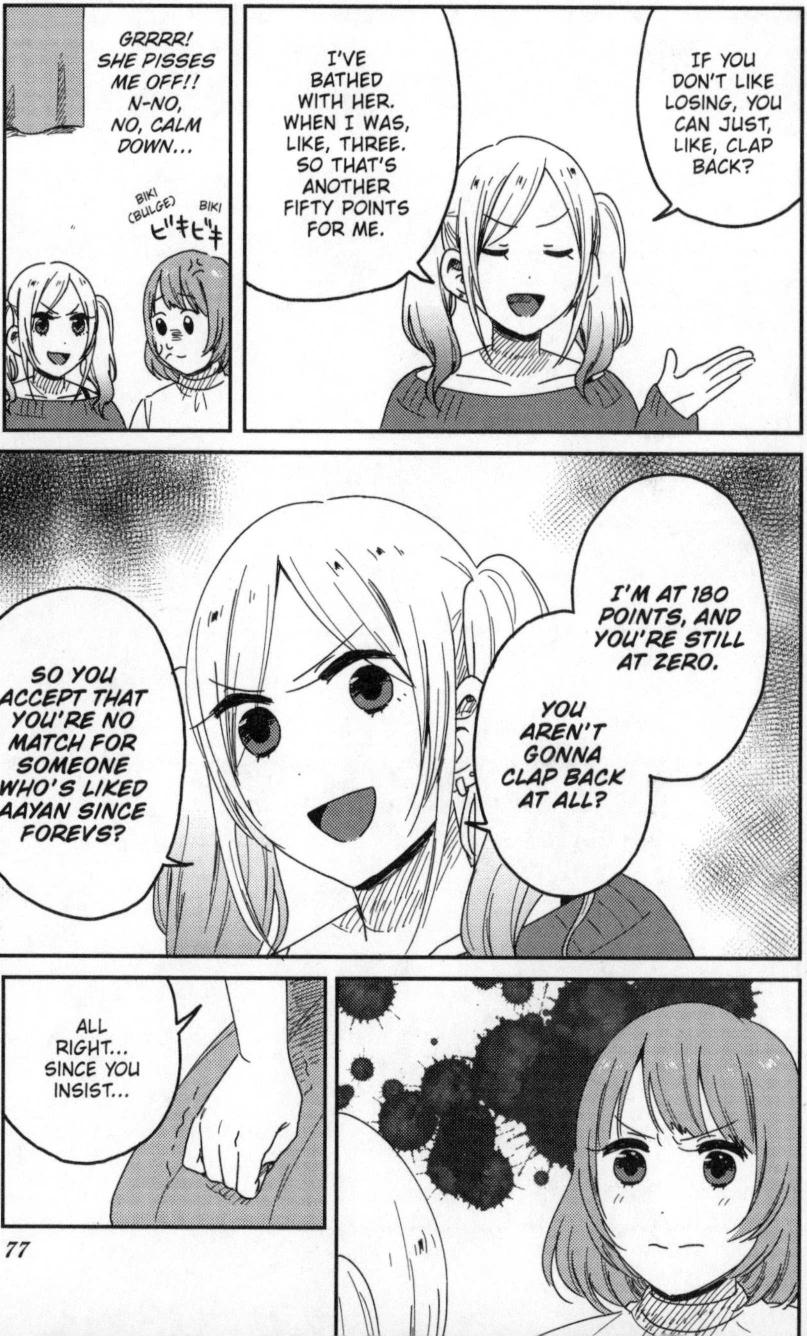
IF YOU DON'T LIKE LOSING, YOU CAN JUST, LIKE, CLAP BACK?
I'VE BATHED WITH HER. WHEN I WAS, LIKE, THREE. SO THAT'S ANOTHER FIFTY POINTS FOR ME.
GRRRR! SHE PISSES ME OFF!! N-NO, NO, CALM DOWN...
BIKI (BULGE) BIKI
ビキビキ
I'M AT 180 POINTS, AND YOU'RE STILL AT ZERO.
YOU AREN'T GONNA CLAP BACK AT ALL?
SO YOU ACCEPT THAT YOU'RE NO MATCH FOR SOMEONE WHO'S LIKED AAYAN SINCE FOREVS?
ALL RIGHT... SINCE YOU INSIST...

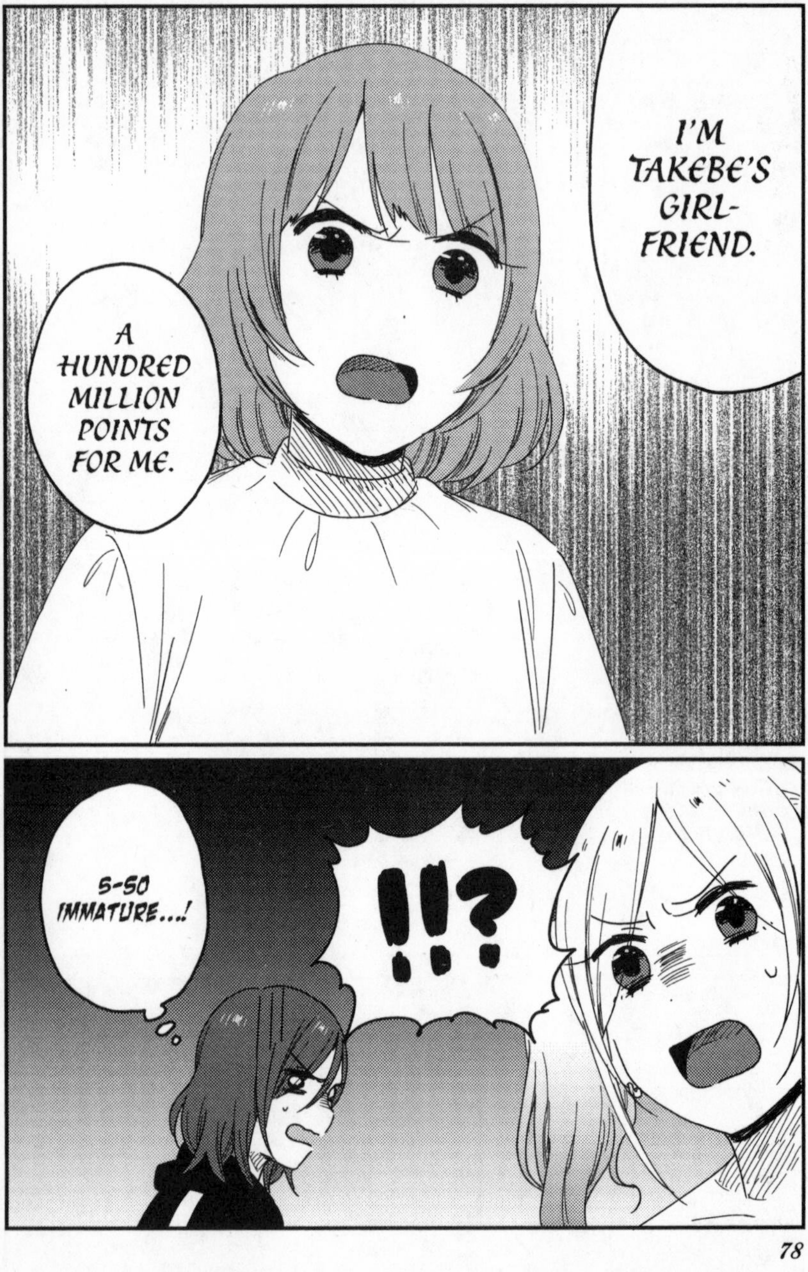
I'M TAKEBE'S GIRL-FRIEND.
A HUNDRED MILLION POINTS FOR ME.
!!?
S-SO IMMATURE...!

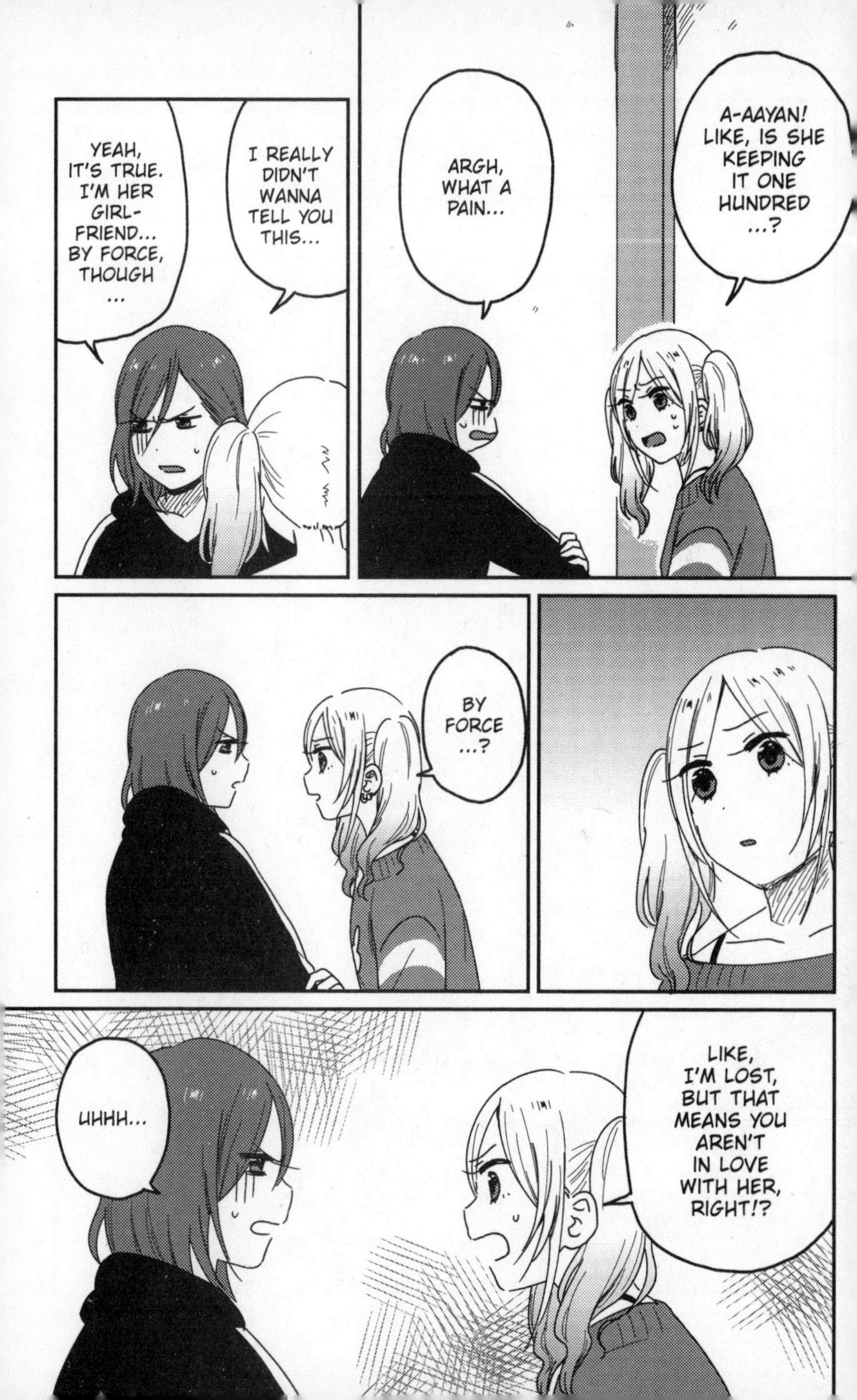
A-AAYAN! LIKE, IS SHE KEEPING IT ONE HUNDRED ...?
ARGH, WHAT A PAIN...
I REALLY DIDN'T WANNA TELL YOU THIS...
YEAH, IT'S TRUE. I'M HER GIRL-FRIEND... BY FORCE, THOUGH ...
BY FORCE ...?
LIKE, I'M LOST, BUT THAT MEANS YOU AREN'T IN LOVE WITH HER, RIGHT!?
UHHH...

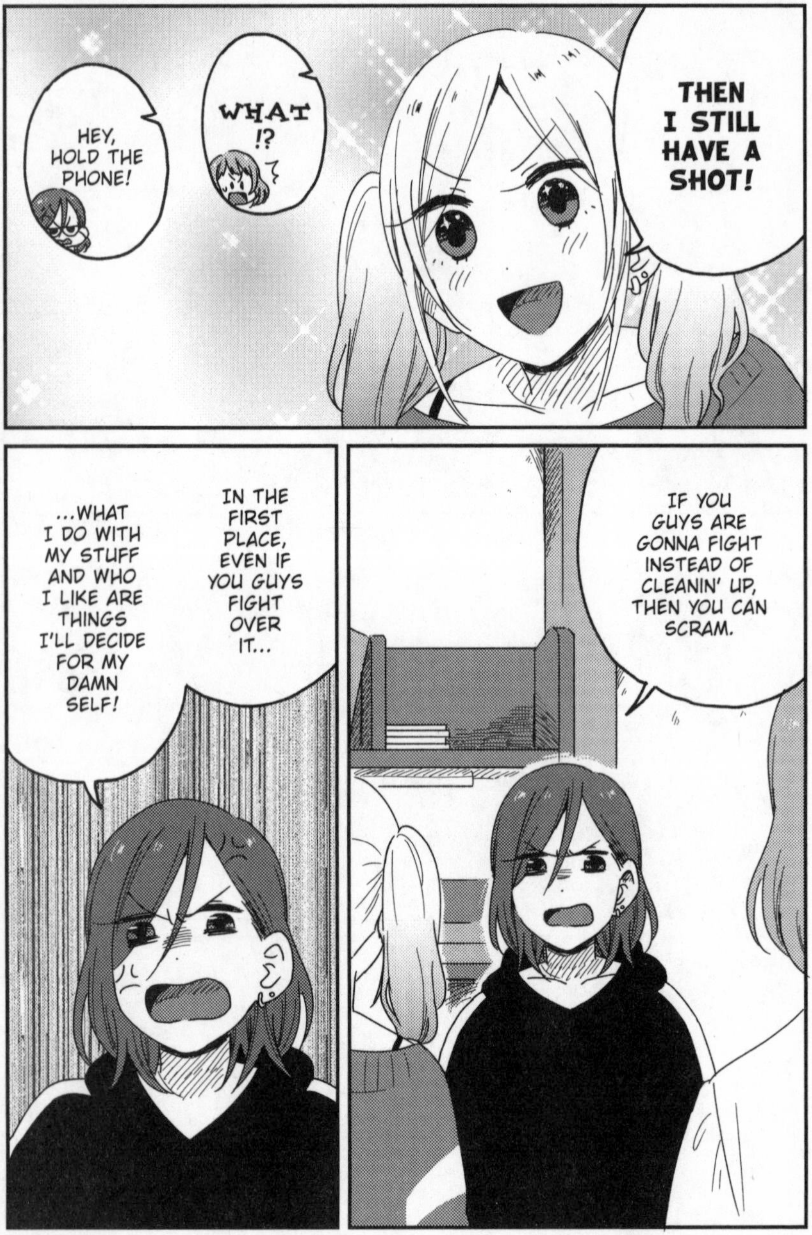
THEN I STILL HAVE A SHOT!
WHAT !?
HEY, HOLD THE PHONE!
IF YOU GUYS ARE GONNA FIGHT INSTEAD OF CLEANIN' UP, THEN YOU CAN SCRAM.
IN THE FIRST PLACE, EVEN IF YOU GUYS FIGHT OVER IT...
...WHAT I DO WITH MY STUFF AND WHO I LIKE ARE THINGS I'LL DECIDE FOR MY DAMN SELF!

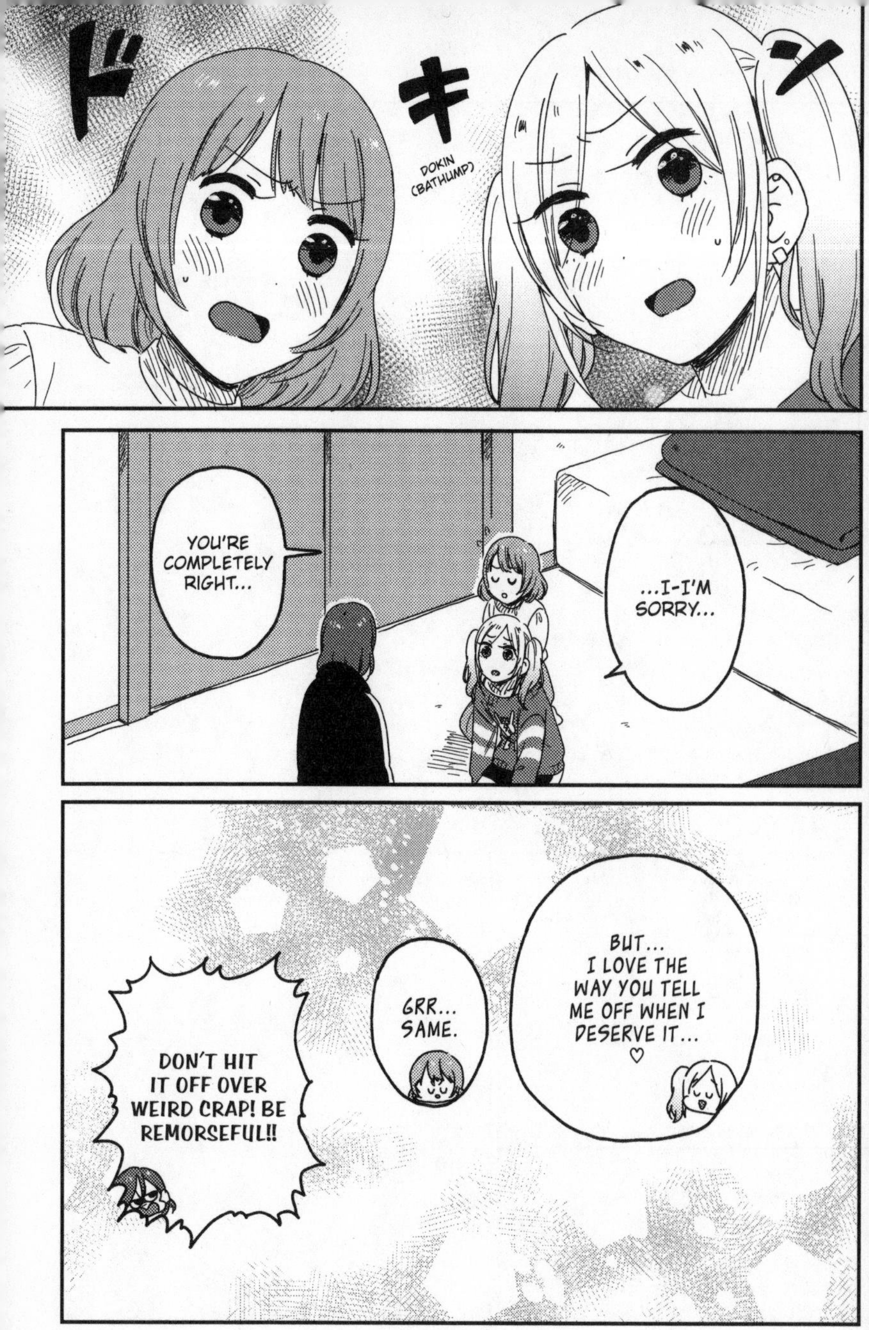
ドキン
DOKIN (BATHUMP)
...I-I'M SORRY...
YOU'RE COMPLETELY RIGHT...
BUT... I LOVE THE WAY YOU TELL ME OFF WHEN I DESERVE IT... ♡
GRR... SAME.
DON'T HIT IT OFF OVER WEIRD CRAP! BE REMORSEFUL!!

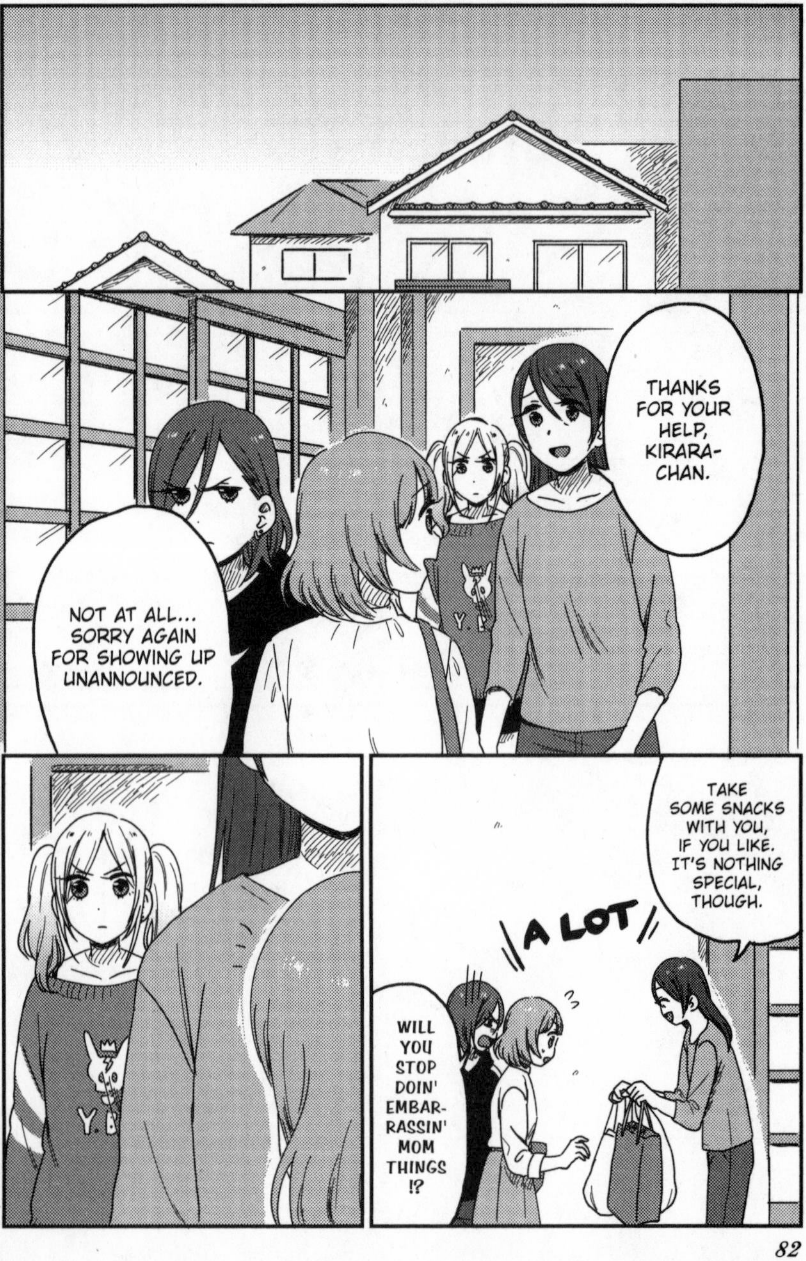

THANKS FOR YOUR HELP, KIRARA-CHAN.
NOT AT ALL... SORRY AGAIN FOR SHOWING UP UNANNOUNCED.
TAKE SOME SNACKS WITH YOU, IF YOU LIKE. IT'S NOTHING SPECIAL, THOUGH.
A LOT
WILL YOU STOP DOIN' EMBARRASSIN' MOM THINGS!?

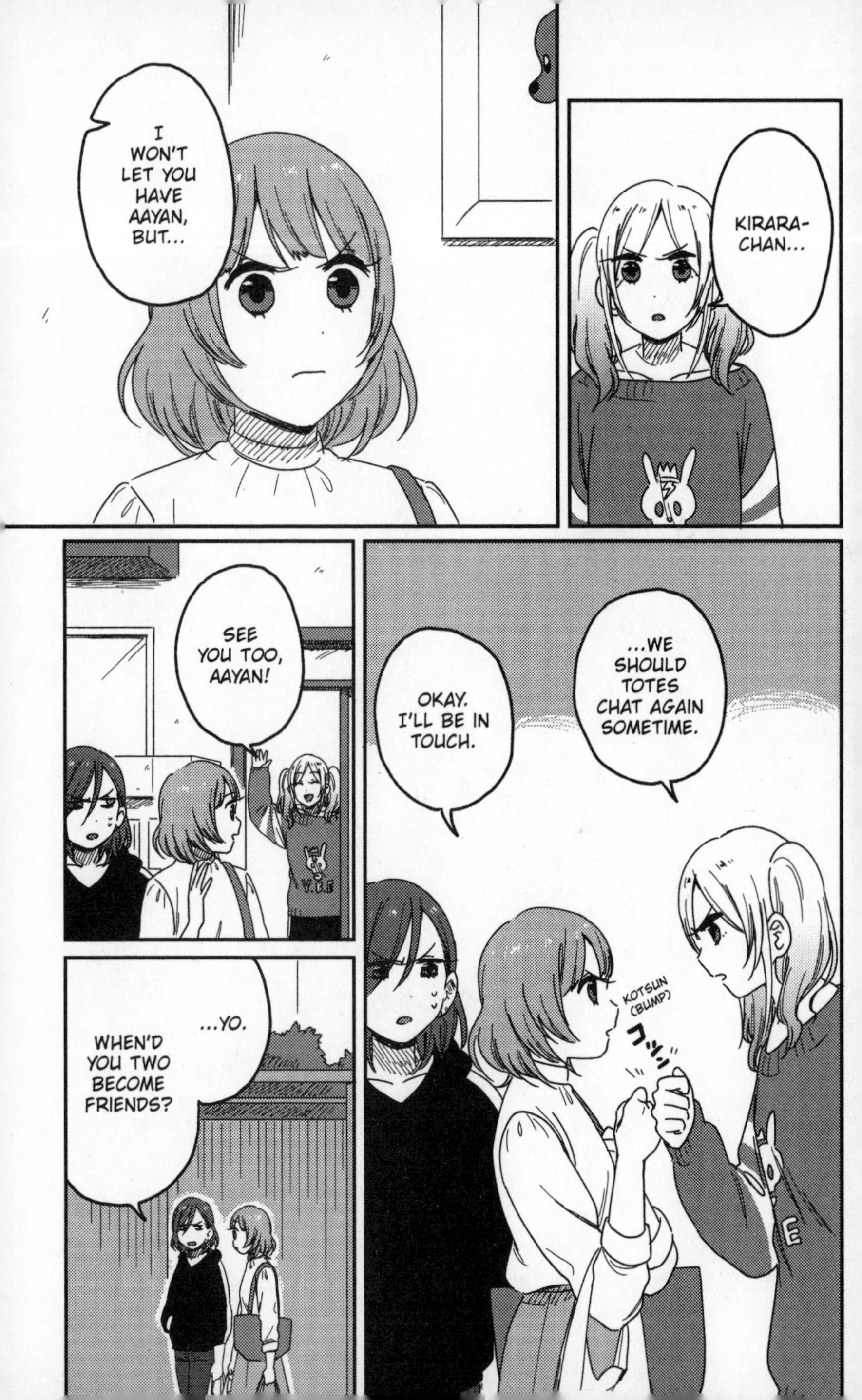
KIRARA-CHAN...
I WON'T LET YOU HAVE AAYAN, BUT...
...WE SHOULD TOTES CHAT AGAIN SOMETIME.
OKAY. I'LL BE IN TOUCH.
KOTSUN (BUMP)
SEE YOU TOO, AAYAN!
...YO.
WHEN'D YOU TWO BECOME FRIENDS?

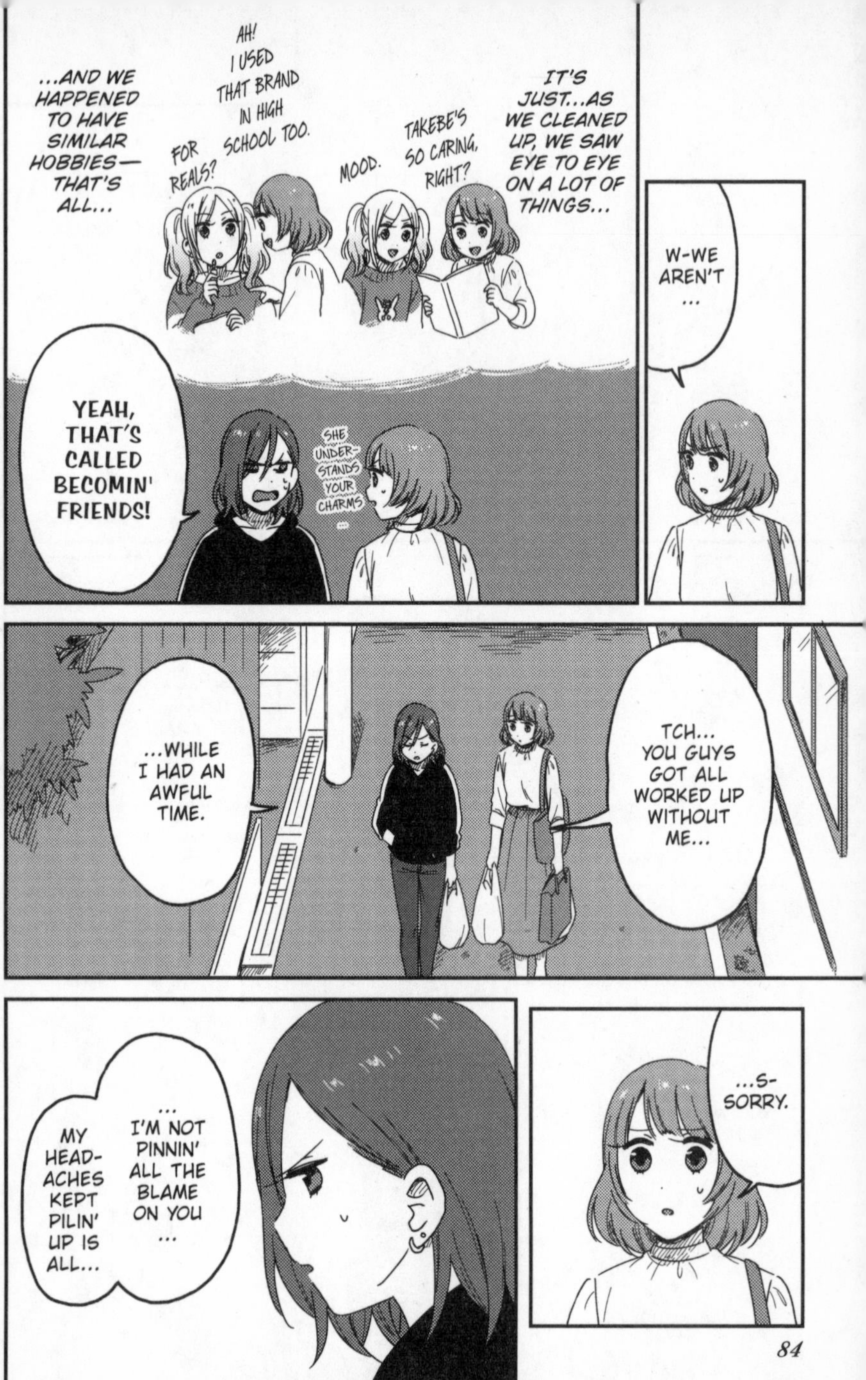
W-WE AREN'T ...
IT'S JUST...AS WE CLEANED UP, WE SAW EYE TO EYE ON A LOT OF THINGS...
TAKEBE'S SO CARING, RIGHT?
MOOD.
AH! I USED THAT BRAND IN HIGH SCHOOL TOO.
FOR REALS?
...AND WE HAPPENED TO HAVE SIMILAR HOBBIES—THAT'S ALL...
SHE UNDERSTANDS YOUR CHARMS ...
YEAH, THAT'S CALLED BECOMIN' FRIENDS!
TCH... YOU GUYS GOT ALL WORKED UP WITHOUT ME...
...WHILE I HAD AN AWFUL TIME.
...S-SORRY.
... I'M NOT PINNIN' ALL THE BLAME ON YOU ...
MY HEAD-ACHES KEPT PILIN' UP IS ALL...

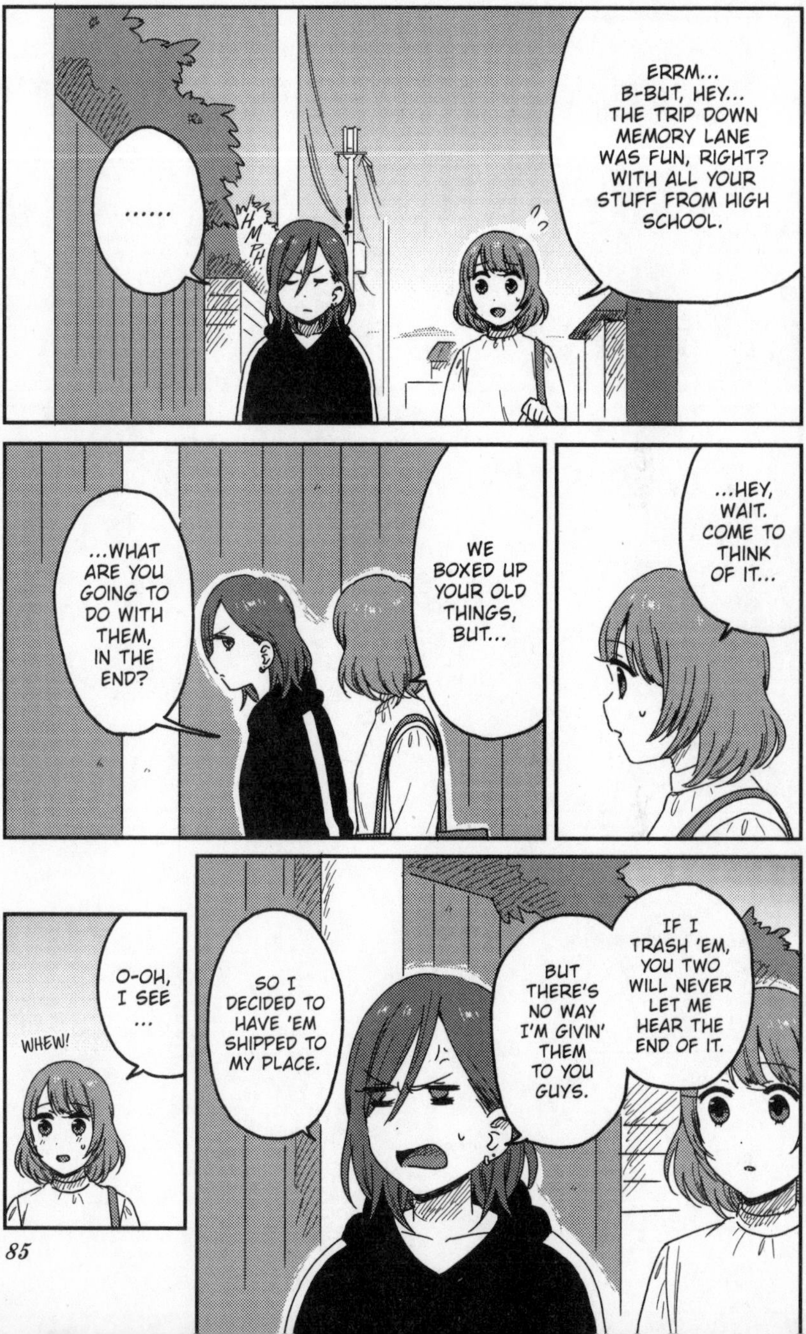
ERRM... B-BUT, HEY... THE TRIP DOWN MEMORY LANE WAS FUN, RIGHT? WITH ALL YOUR STUFF FROM HIGH SCHOOL.
HMPH
......
...HEY, WAIT. COME TO THINK OF IT...
WE BOXED UP YOUR OLD THINGS, BUT...
...WHAT ARE YOU GOING TO DO WITH THEM, IN THE END?
IF I TRASH 'EM, YOU TWO WILL NEVER LET ME HEAR THE END OF IT.
BUT THERE'S NO WAY I'M GIVIN' THEM TO YOU GUYS.
SO I DECIDED TO HAVE 'EM SHIPPED TO MY PLACE.
O-OH, I SEE...
WHEW!

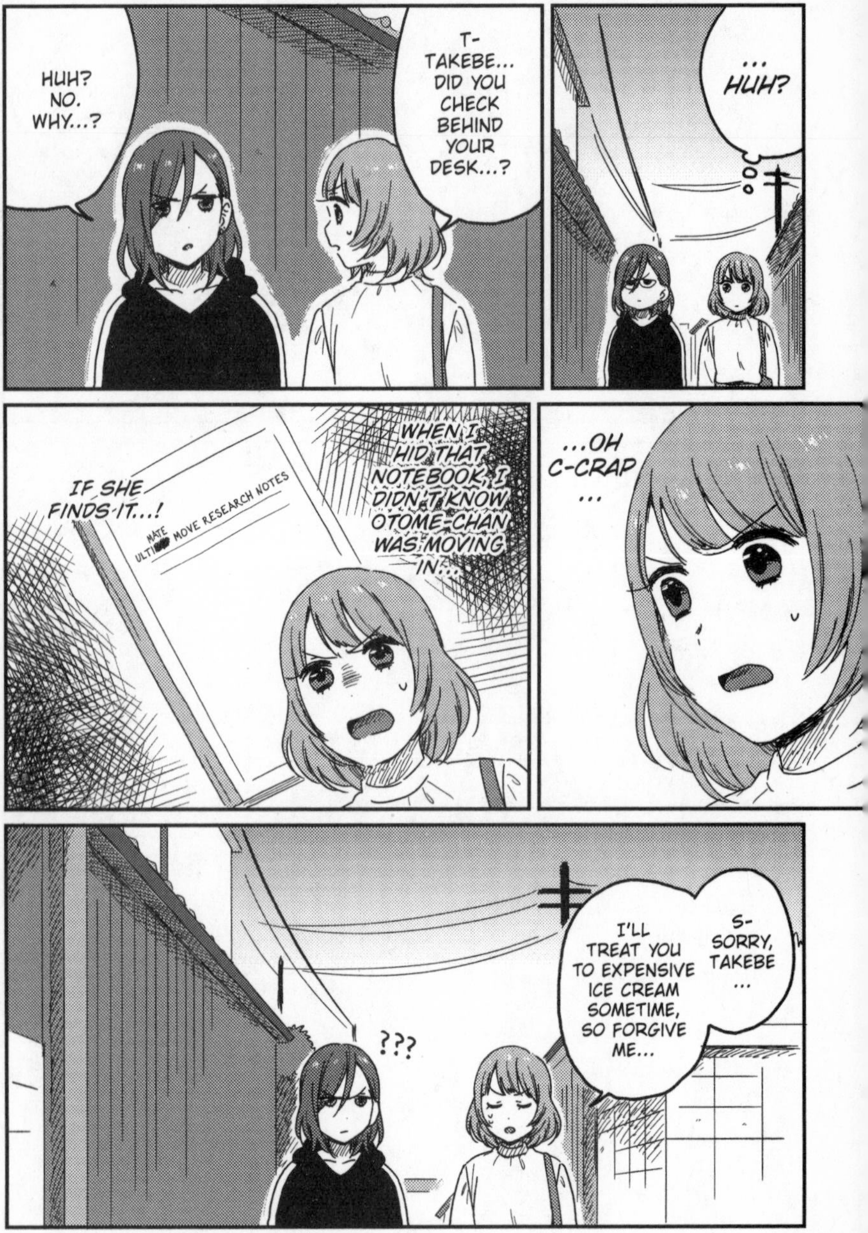

... HUH?
T- TAKEBE... DID YOU CHECK BEHIND YOUR DESK...?
HUH? NO. WHY...?
...OH C-CRAP ...
WHEN I HID THAT NOTEBOOK, I DIDN'T KNOW OTOME-CHAN WAS MOVING IN...
IF SHE FINDS IT...!
ULTIMATE MOVE RESEARCH NOTES
S- SORRY, TAKEBE ...
I'LL TREAT YOU TO EXPENSIVE ICE CREAM SOMETIME, SO FORGIVE ME...
???

CHAPTER 9

Catch These Hands!

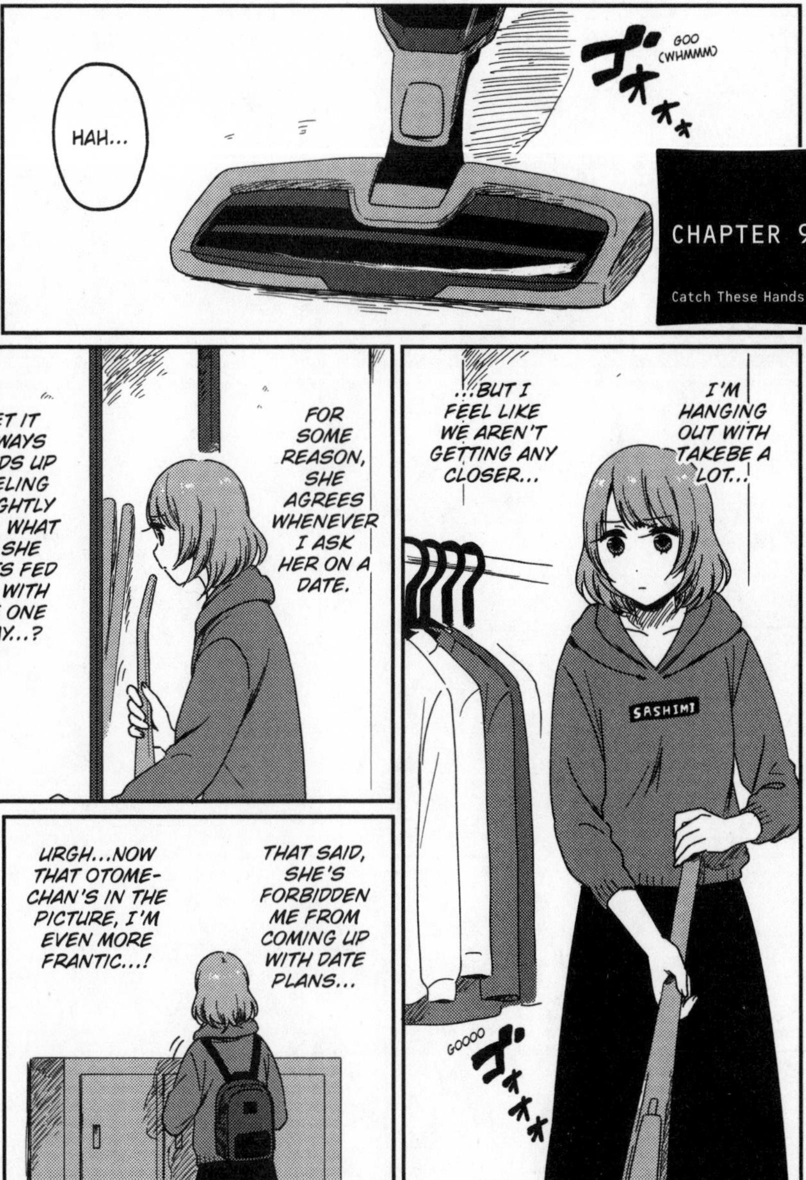

HAH...
GOO (WHMMM)
I'M HANGING OUT WITH TAKEBE A LOT...
...BUT I FEEL LIKE WE AREN'T GETTING ANY CLOSER...
SASHIMI
GOOOO
FOR SOME REASON, SHE AGREES WHENEVER I ASK HER ON A DATE.
YET IT ALWAYS WINDS UP FEELING SLIGHTLY OFF. WHAT IF SHE GETS FED UP WITH ME ONE DAY...?
THAT SAID, SHE'S FORBIDDEN ME FROM COMING UP WITH DATE PLANS...
URGH...NOW THAT OTOME-CHAN'S IN THE PICTURE, I'M EVEN MORE FRANTIC...!

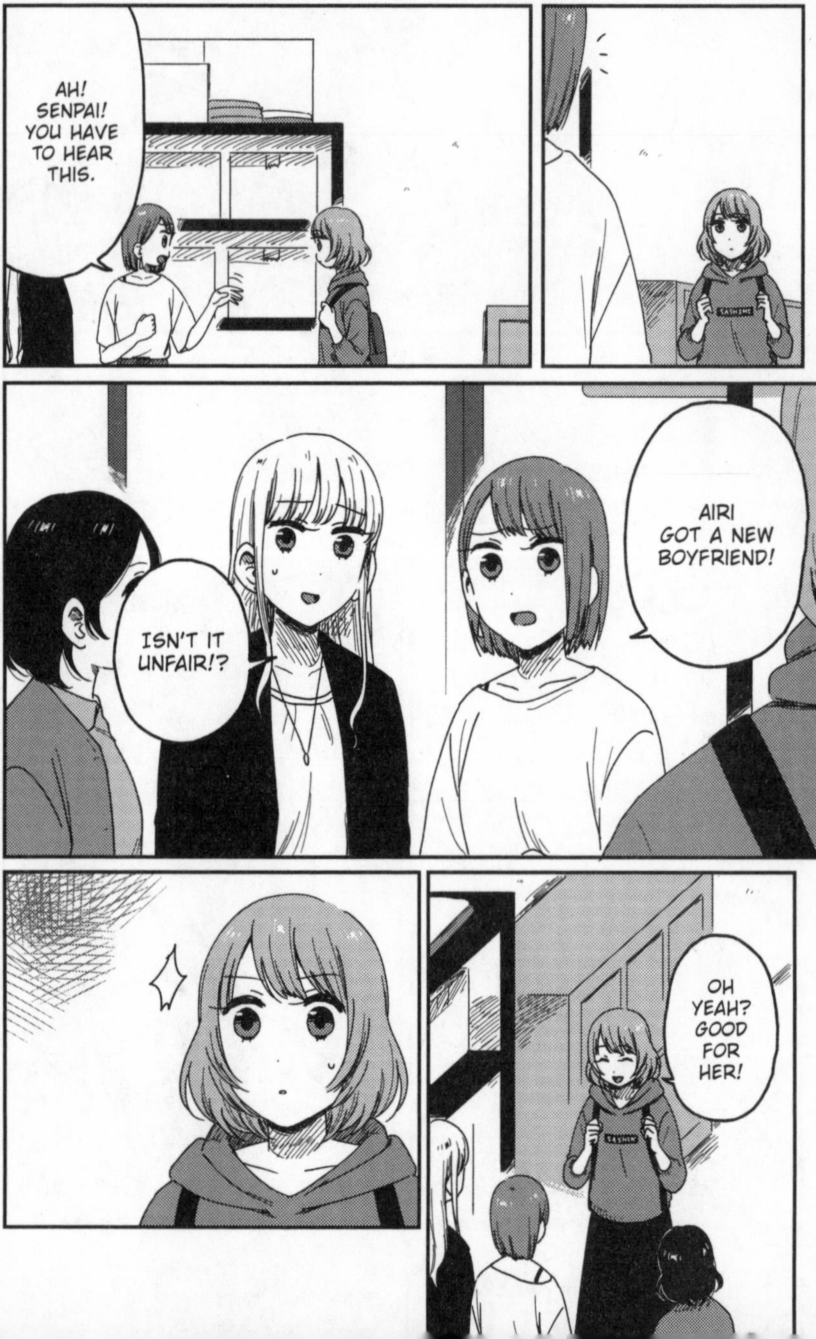
AH! SENPAI! YOU HAVE TO HEAR THIS.
AIRI GOT A NEW BOYFRIEND!
ISN'T IT UNFAIR!?
OH YEAH? GOOD FOR HER!

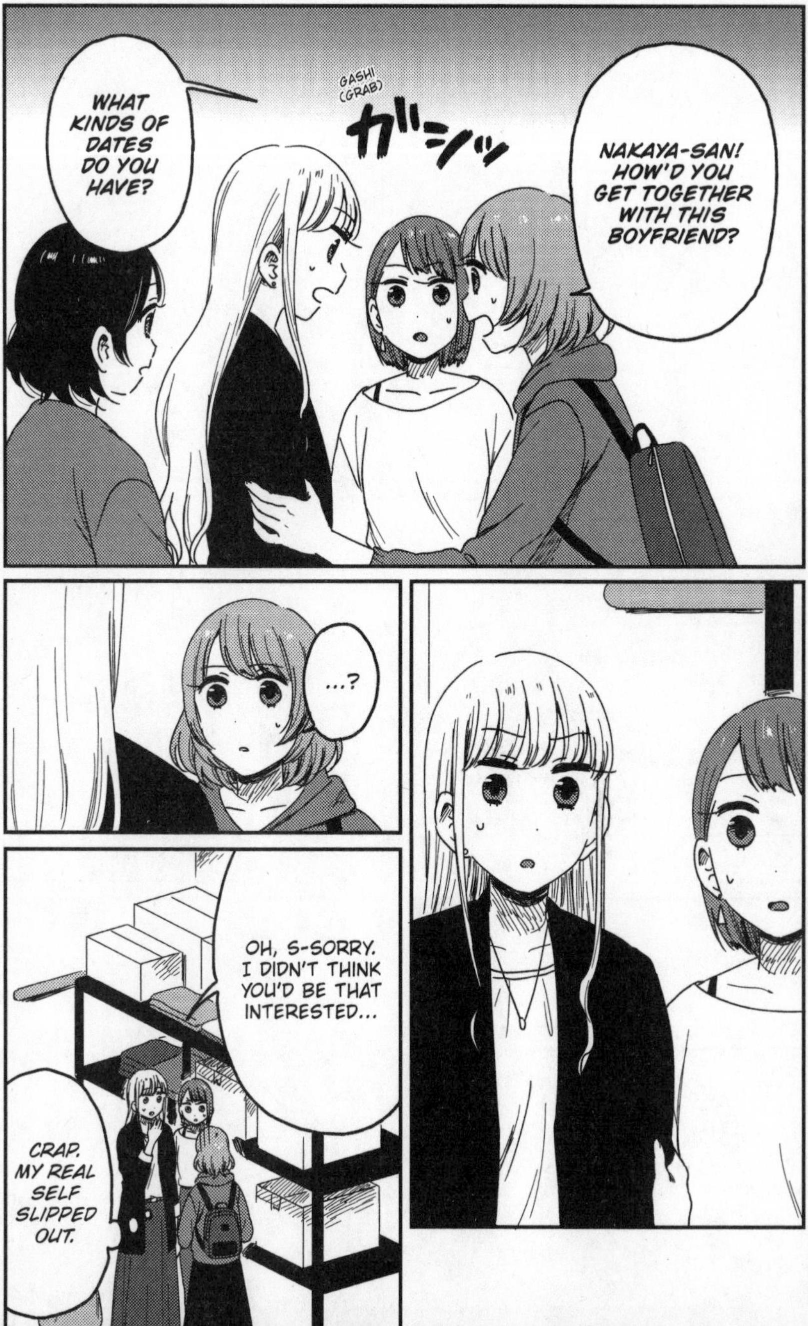

NAKAYA-SAN! HOW'D YOU GET TOGETHER WITH THIS BOYFRIEND?
ガシッ
GASHI (GRAB)
WHAT KINDS OF DATES DO YOU HAVE?
...?
OH, S-SORRY. I DIDN'T THINK YOU'D BE THAT INTERESTED...
CRAP. MY REAL SELF SLIPPED OUT.

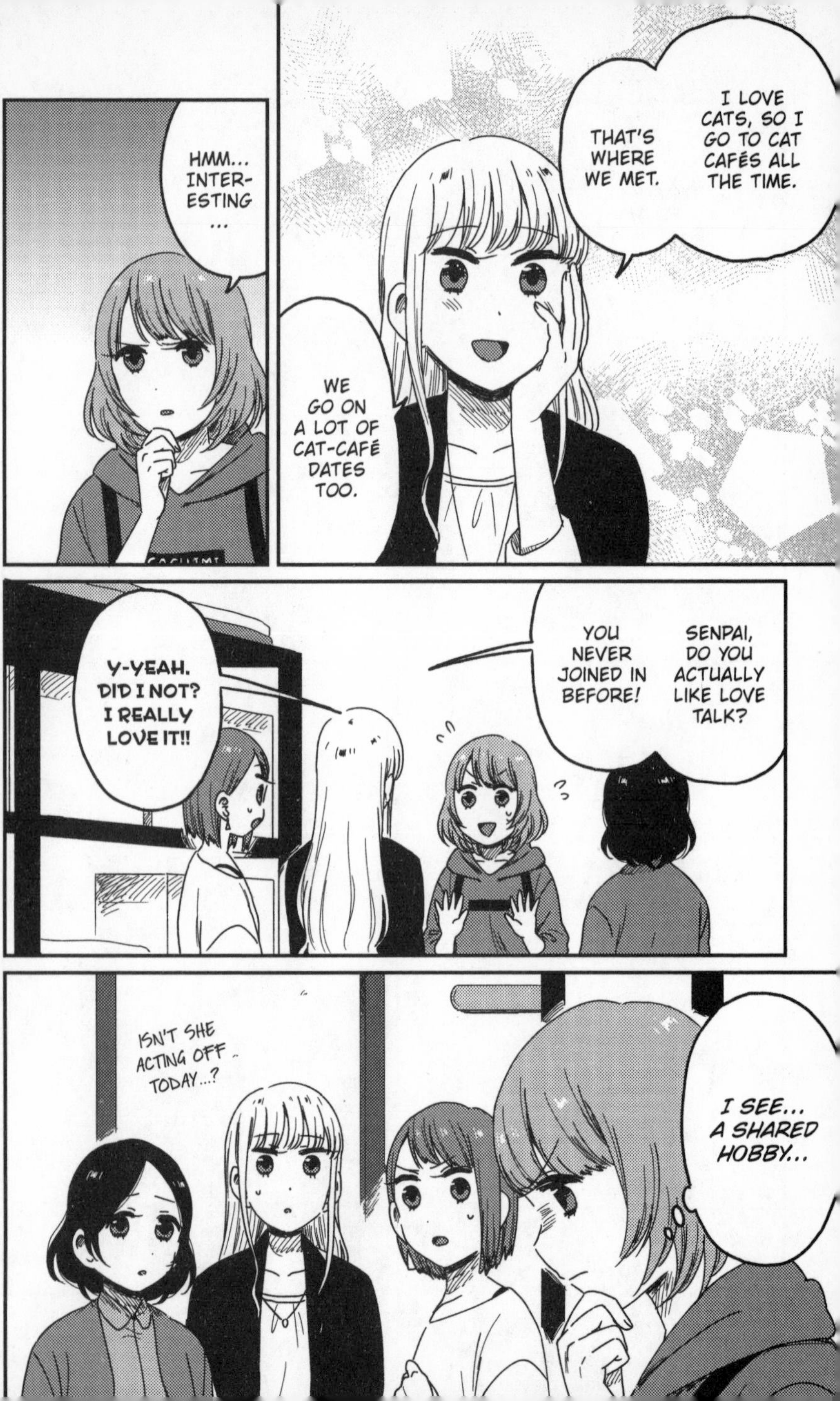
I LOVE CATS, SO I GO TO CAT CAFÉS ALL THE TIME.
THAT'S WHERE WE MET.
WE GO ON A LOT OF CAT-CAFÉ DATES TOO.
HMM... INTER-ESTING...
SENPAI, DO YOU ACTUALLY LIKE LOVE TALK?
YOU NEVER JOINED IN BEFORE!
Y-YEAH. DID I NOT? I REALLY LOVE IT!!
I SEE... A SHARED HOBBY...
ISN'T SHE ACTING OFF TODAY...?

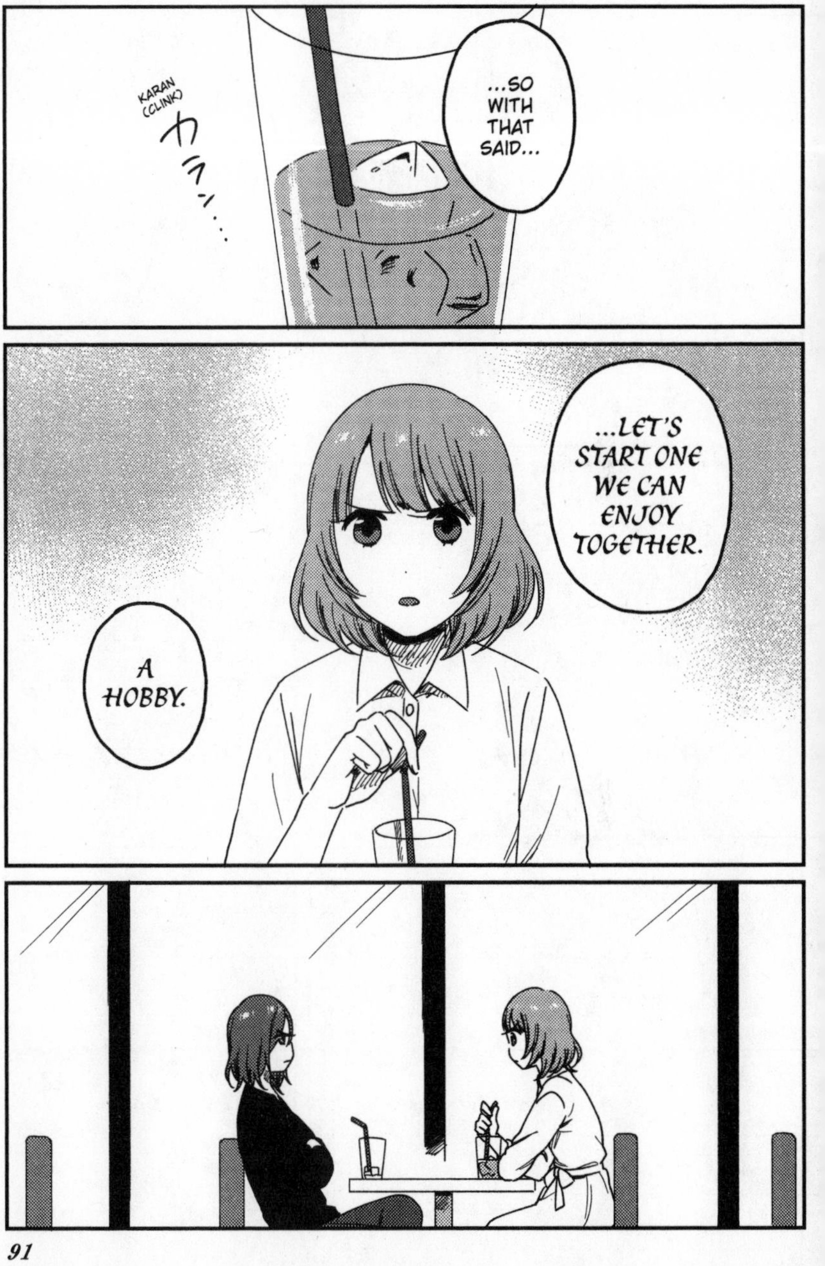
...SO WITH THAT SAID...
KARAN (CLINK)
カラン…
...LET'S START ONE WE CAN ENJOY TOGETHER.
A HOBBY.

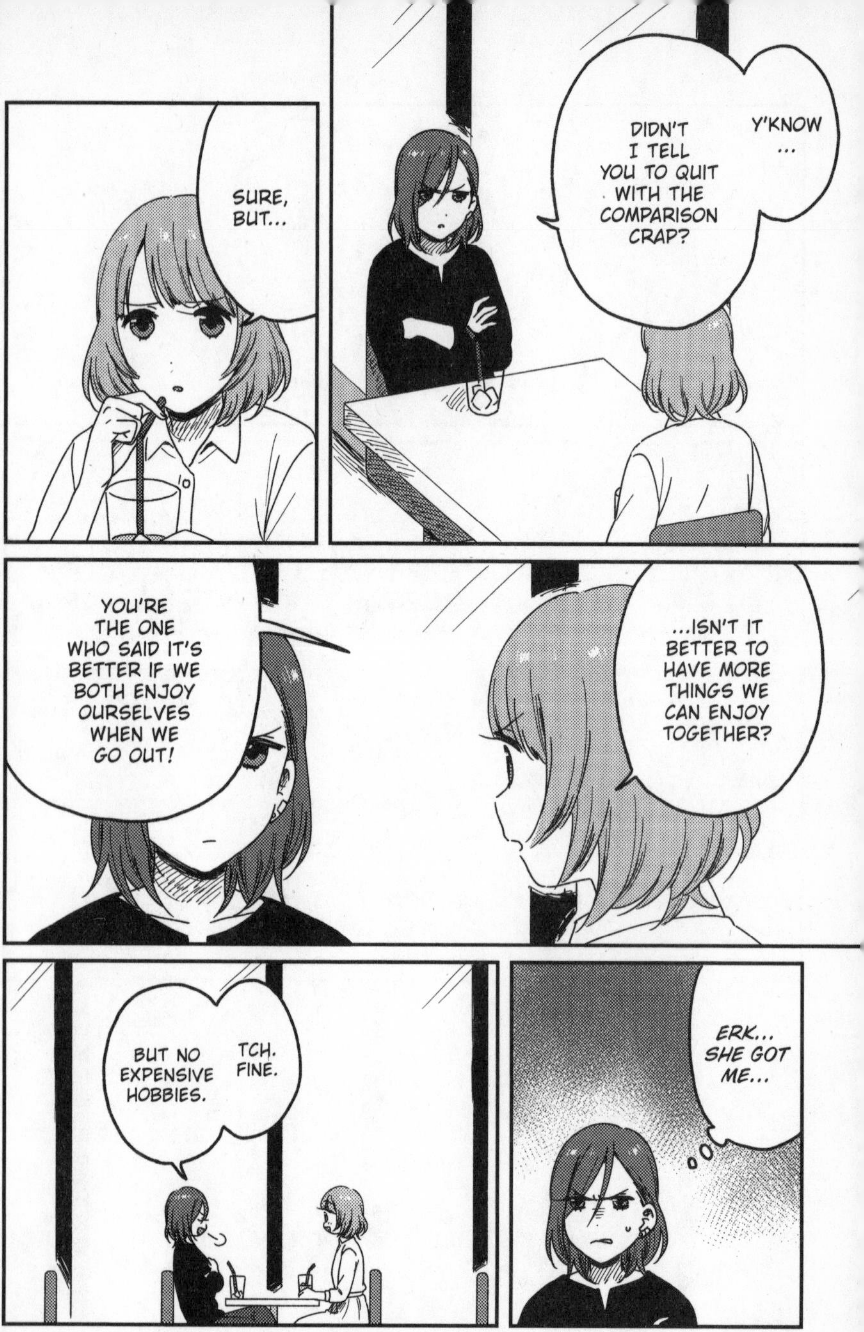
Y'KNOW...
DIDN'T I TELL YOU TO QUIT WITH THE COMPARISON CRAP?
SURE, BUT...
...ISN'T IT BETTER TO HAVE MORE THINGS WE CAN ENJOY TOGETHER?
YOU'RE THE ONE WHO SAID IT'S BETTER IF WE BOTH ENJOY OURSELVES WHEN WE GO OUT!
ERK... SHE GOT ME...
TCH. FINE.
BUT NO EXPENSIVE HOBBIES.

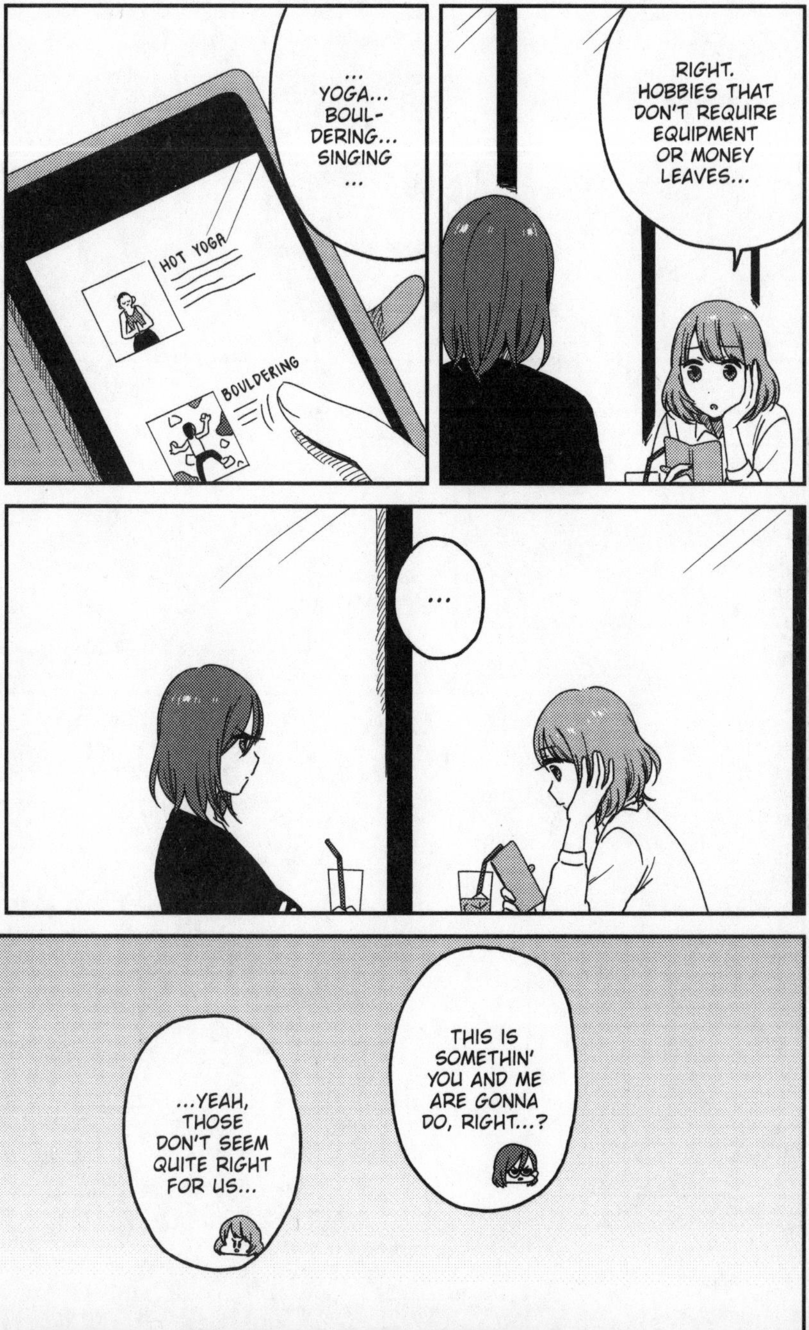
RIGHT. HOBBIES THAT DON'T REQUIRE EQUIPMENT OR MONEY LEAVES...
... YOGA... BOUL-DERING... SINGING ...
HOT YOGA
BOULDERING
...
THIS IS SOMETHIN' YOU AND ME ARE GONNA DO, RIGHT...?
...YEAH, THOSE DON'T SEEM QUITE RIGHT FOR US...

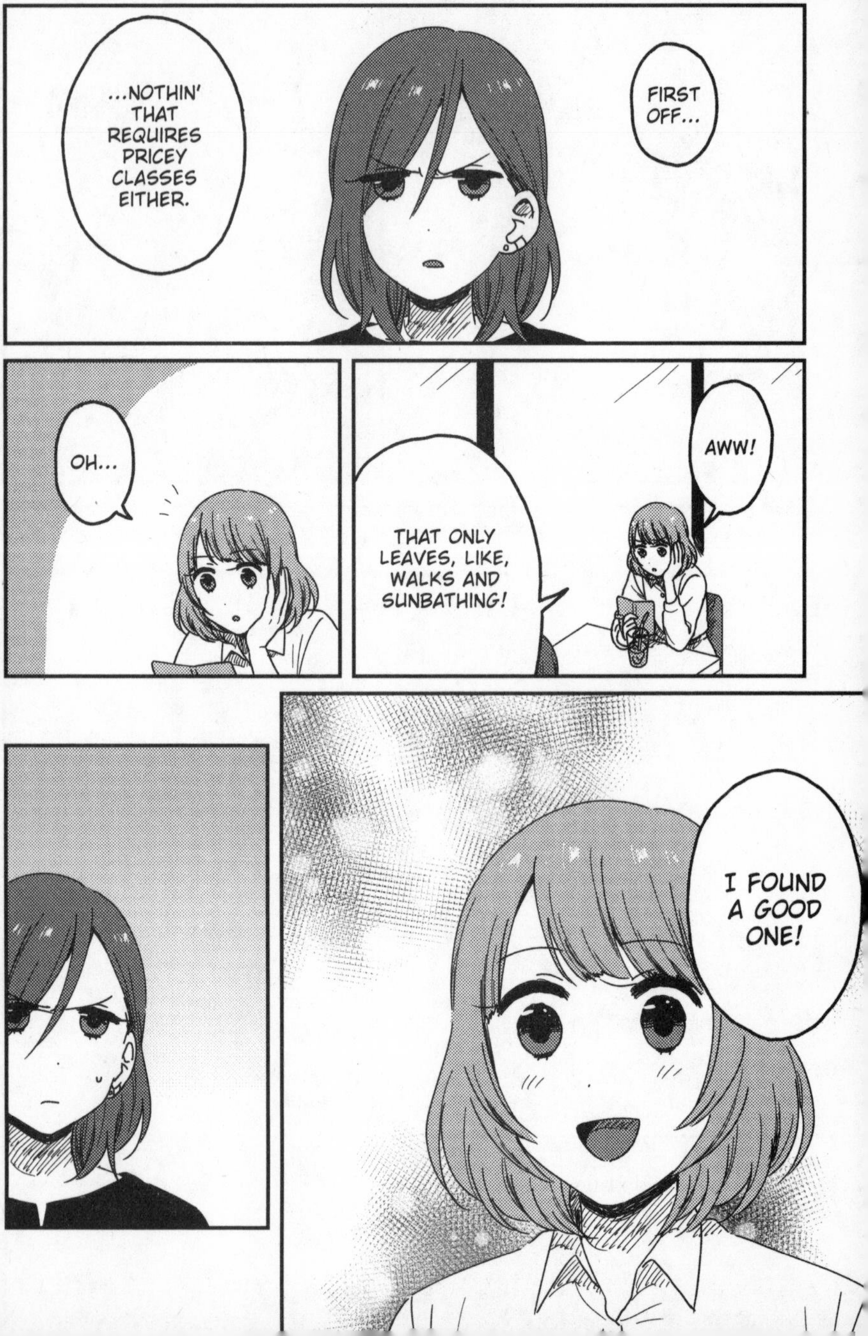
FIRST OFF...
...NOTHIN' THAT REQUIRES PRICEY CLASSES EITHER.
AWW!
THAT ONLY LEAVES, LIKE, WALKS AND SUNBATHING!
OH...
I FOUND A GOOD ONE!

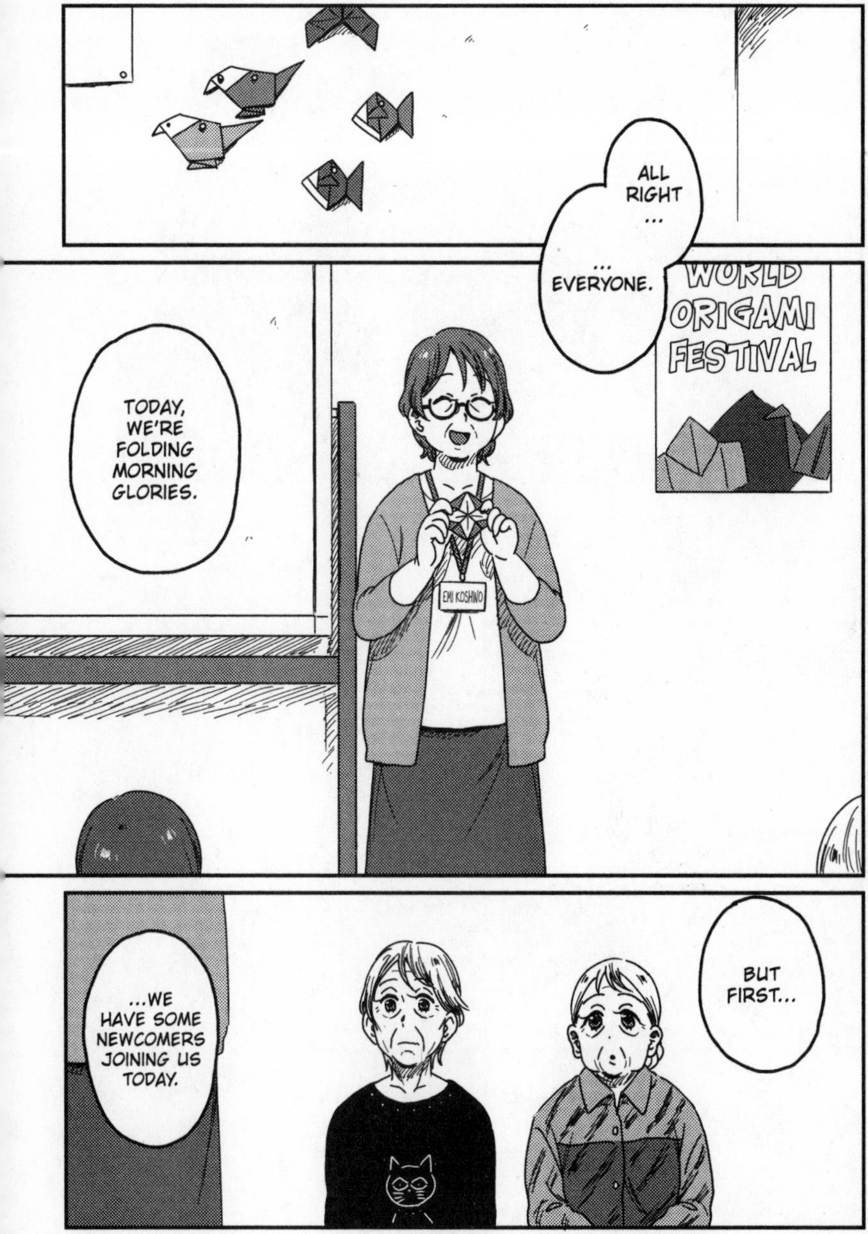
ALL RIGHT...
...EVERYONE.
WORLD ORIGAMI FESTIVAL
TODAY, WE'RE FOLDING MORNING GLORIES.
EMI KOSHINO
BUT FIRST...
...WE HAVE SOME NEWCOMERS JOINING US TODAY.

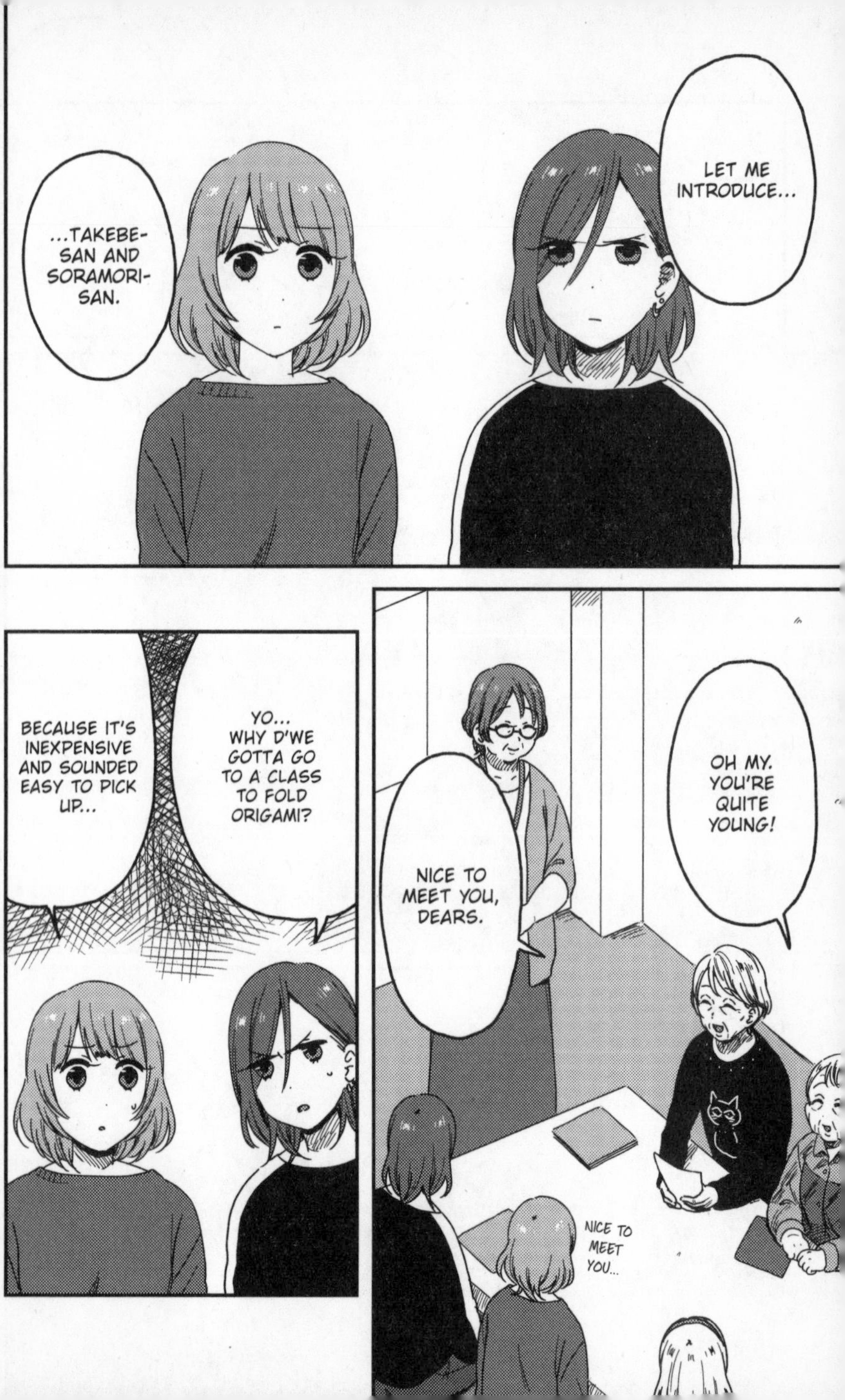
LET ME INTRODUCE...
...TAKEBE-SAN AND SORAMORI-SAN.
OH MY. YOU'RE QUITE YOUNG!
NICE TO MEET YOU, DEARS.
NICE TO MEET YOU...
YO... WHY D'WE GOTTA GO TO A CLASS TO FOLD ORIGAMI?
BECAUSE IT'S INEXPENSIVE AND SOUNDED EASY TO PICK UP...

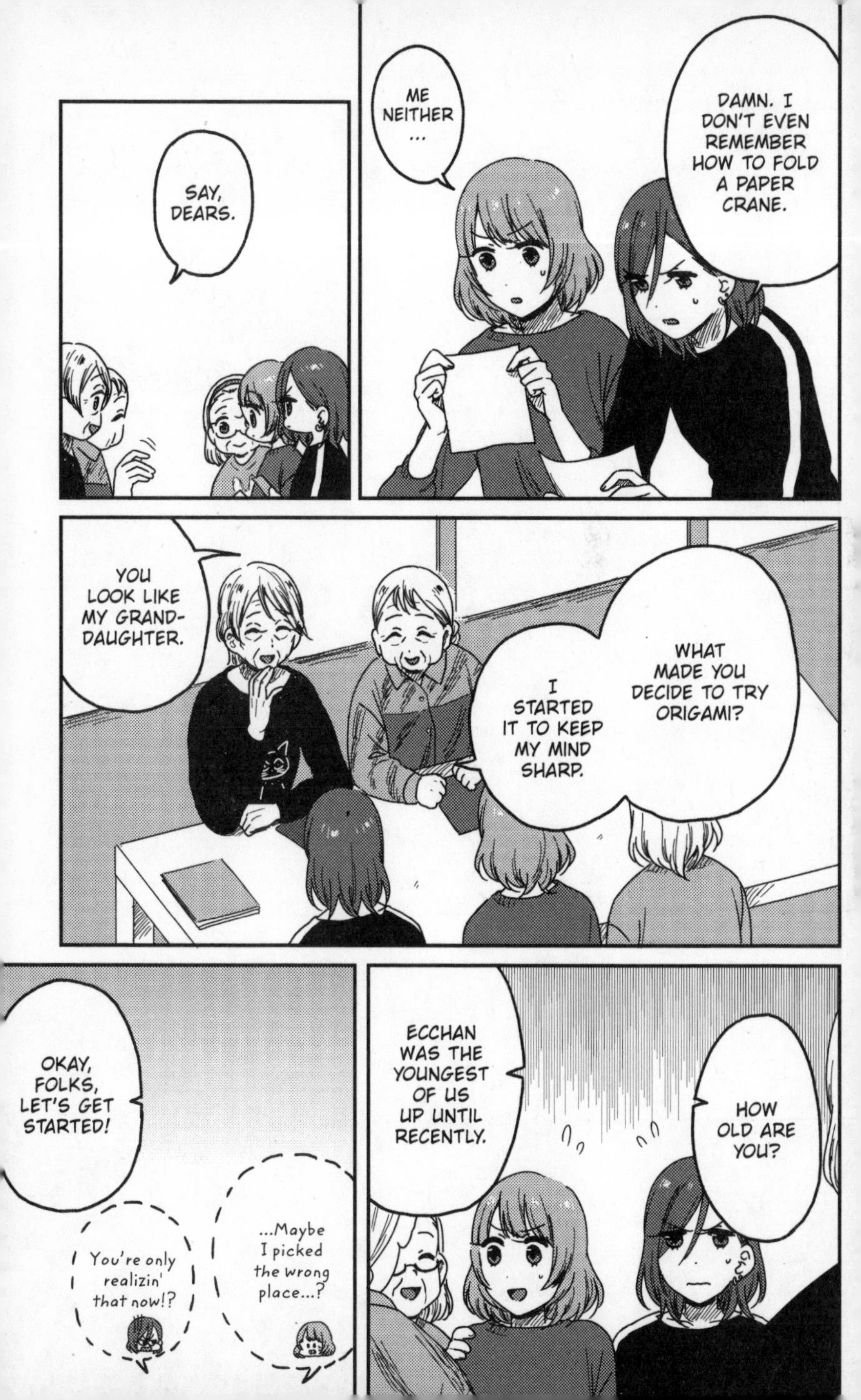
DAMN. I DON'T EVEN REMEMBER HOW TO FOLD A PAPER CRANE.
ME NEITHER ...
SAY, DEARS.
WHAT MADE YOU DECIDE TO TRY ORIGAMI?
I STARTED IT TO KEEP MY MIND SHARP.
YOU LOOK LIKE MY GRAND-DAUGHTER.
HOW OLD ARE YOU?
ECCHAN WAS THE YOUNGEST OF US UP UNTIL RECENTLY.
OKAY, FOLKS, LET'S GET STARTED!
...Maybe I picked the wrong place...?
You're only realizin' that now!?

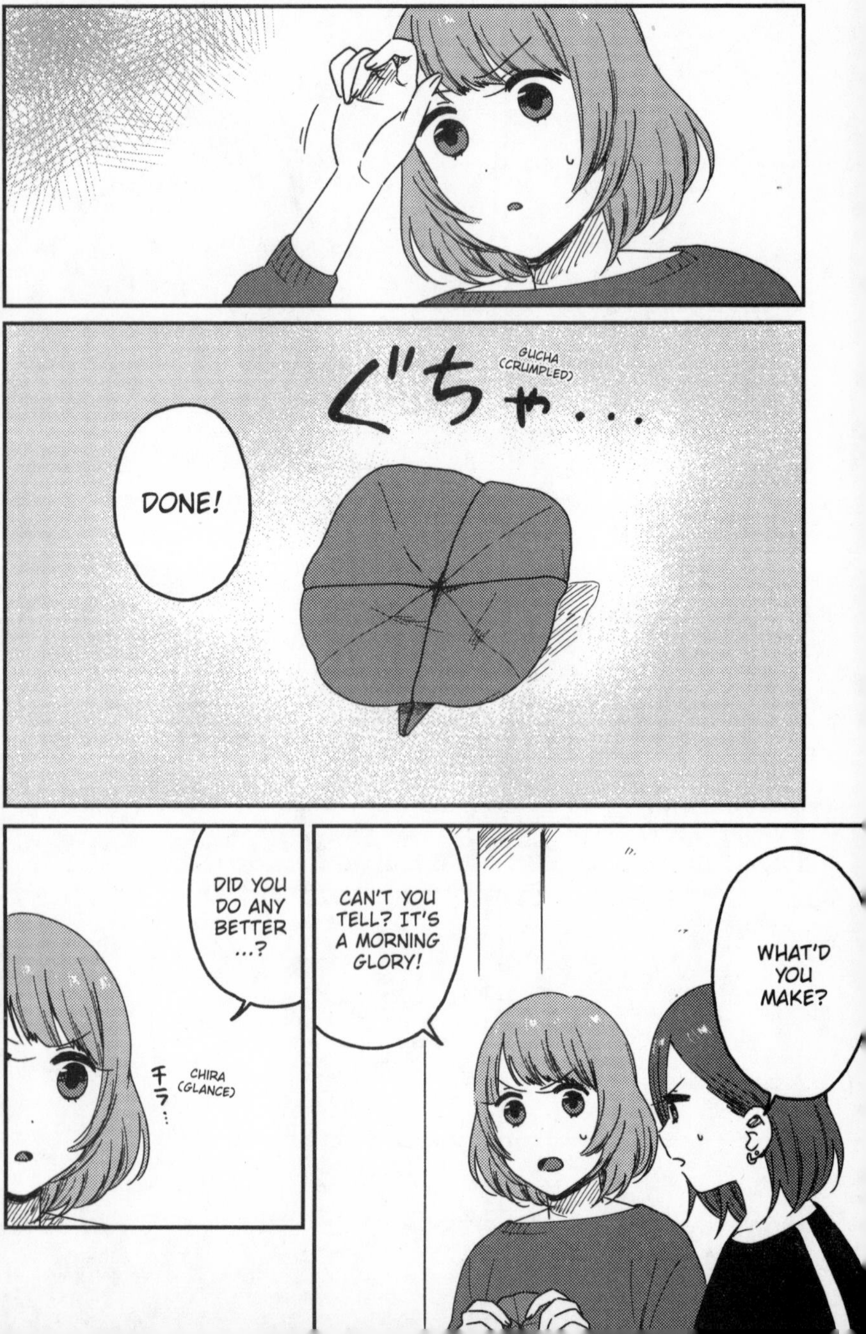
ぐちゃ...
GUCHA (CRUMPLED)
DONE!
WHAT'D YOU MAKE?
CAN'T YOU TELL? IT'S A MORNING GLORY!
DID YOU DO ANY BETTER ...?
チラ...
CHIRA (GLANCE)

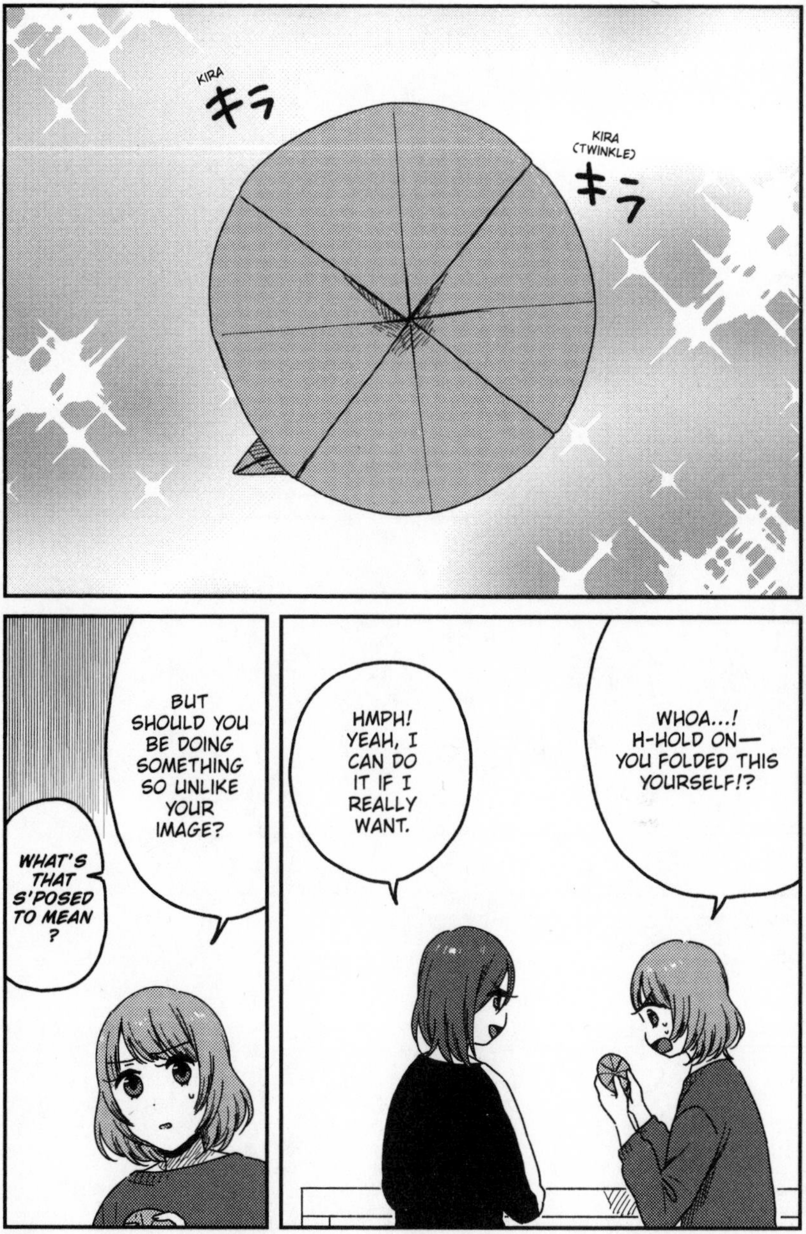
KIRA
キラ
KIRA (TWINKLE)
キラ
WHOA...! H-HOLD ON— YOU FOLDED THIS YOURSELF!?
HMPH! YEAH, I CAN DO IT IF I REALLY WANT.
BUT SHOULD YOU BE DOING SOMETHING SO UNLIKE YOUR IMAGE?
WHAT'S THAT S'POSED TO MEAN?

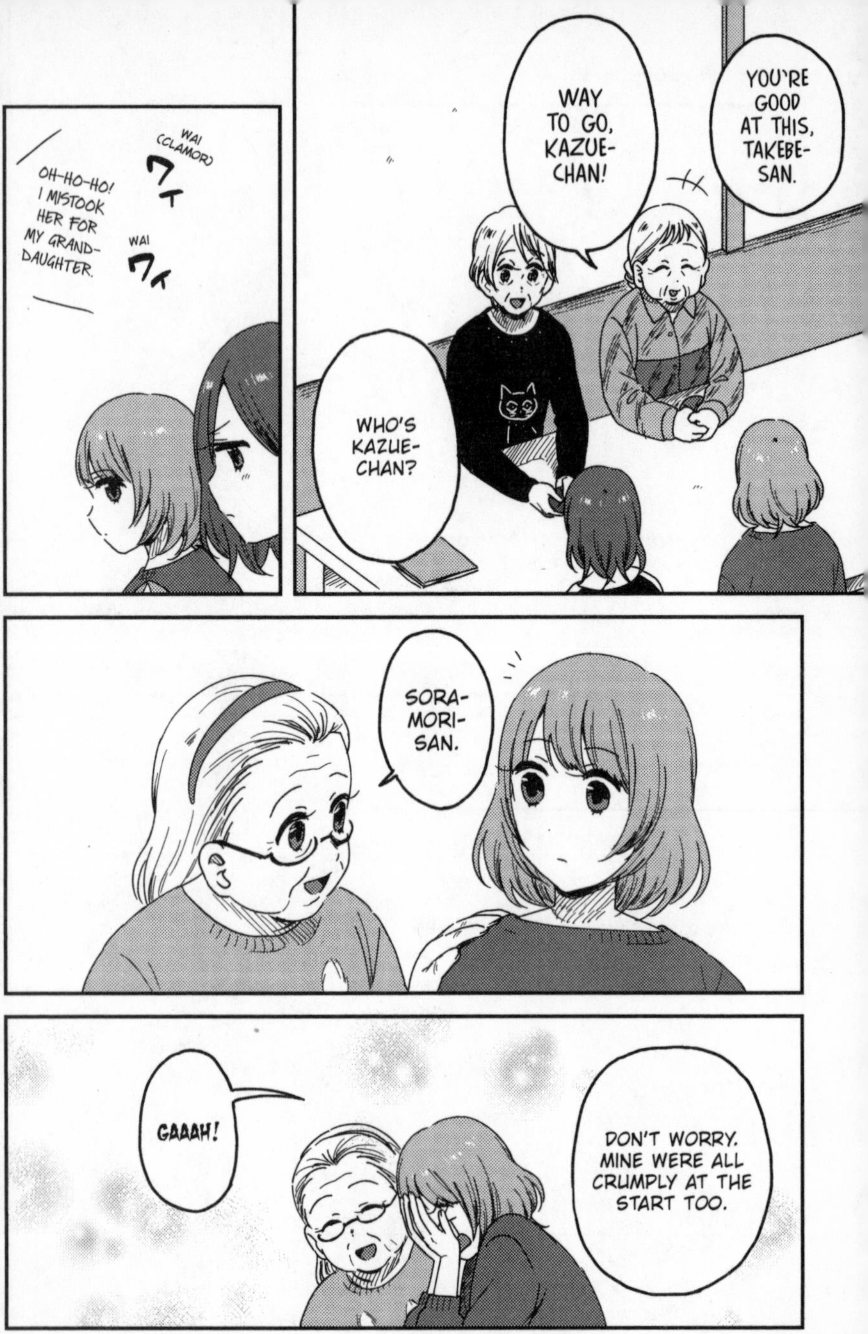
YOU'RE GOOD AT THIS, TAKEBE-SAN.
WAY TO GO, KAZUE-CHAN!
WHO'S KAZUE-CHAN?
WAI (CLAMOR)
ワイ
OH-HO-HO! I MISTOOK HER FOR MY GRAND-DAUGHTER.
WAI
ワイ
SORA-MORI-SAN.
DON'T WORRY. MINE WERE ALL CRUMPLY AT THE START TOO.
GAAAH!

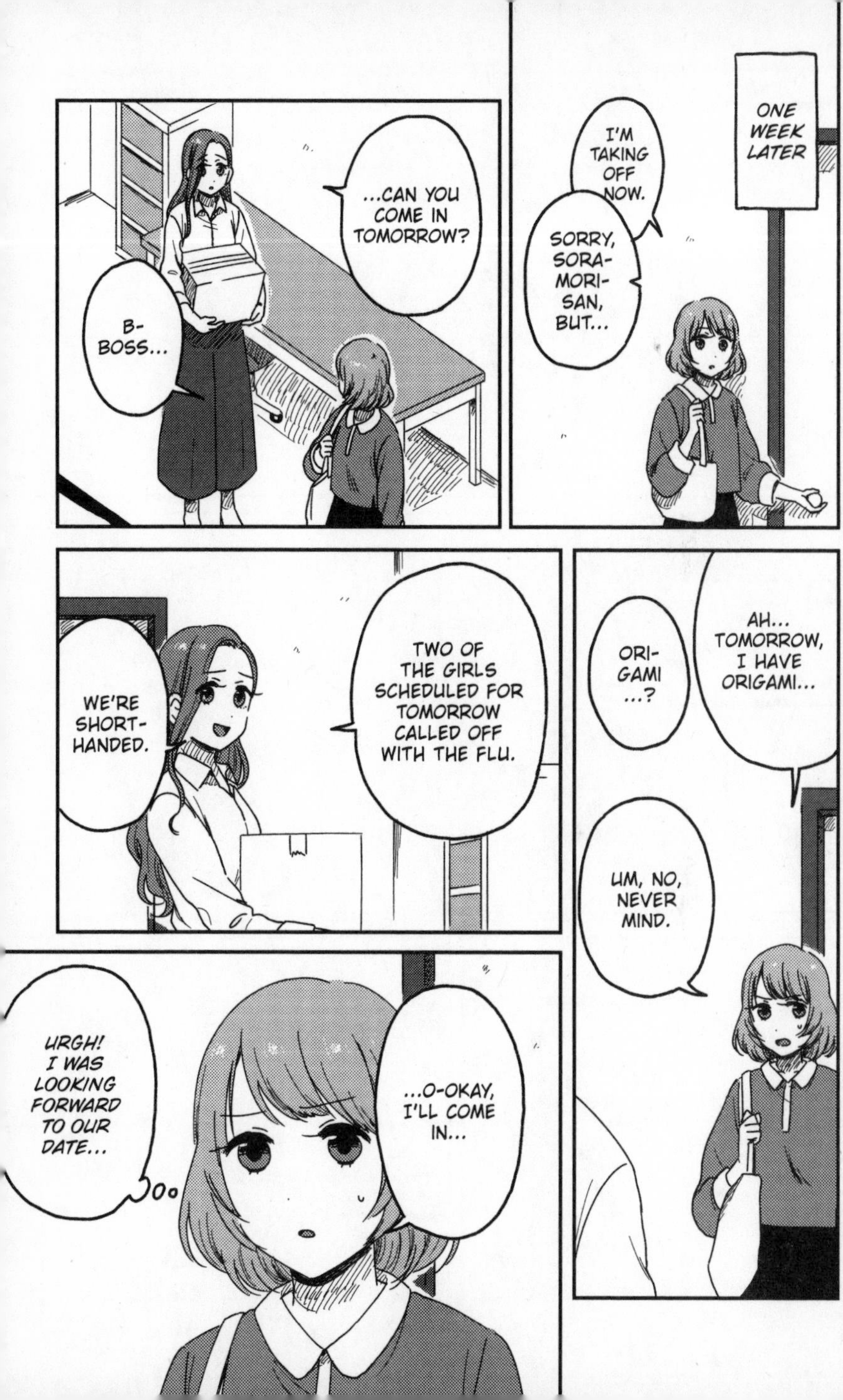
ONE WEEK LATER
I'M TAKING OFF NOW.
SORRY, SORA-MORI-SAN, BUT...
...CAN YOU COME IN TOMORROW?
B-BOSS...
AH... TOMORROW, I HAVE ORIGAMI...
ORI-GAMI ...?
UM, NO, NEVER MIND.
TWO OF THE GIRLS SCHEDULED FOR TOMORROW CALLED OFF WITH THE FLU.
WE'RE SHORT-HANDED.
...O-OKAY, I'LL COME IN...
URGH! I WAS LOOKING FORWARD TO OUR DATE...

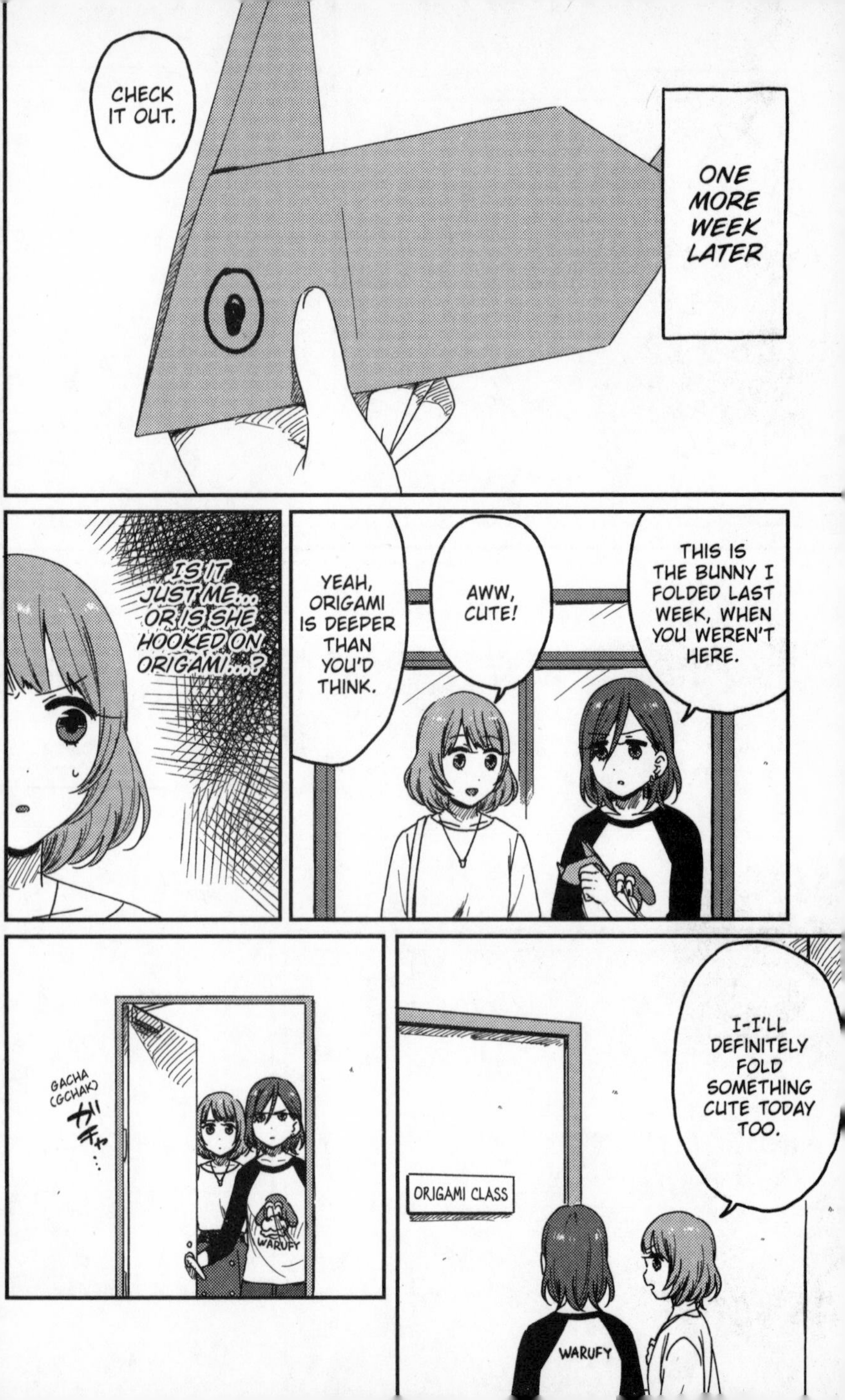
ONE MORE WEEK LATER
CHECK IT OUT.
THIS IS THE BUNNY I FOLDED LAST WEEK, WHEN YOU WEREN'T HERE.
AWW, CUTE!
YEAH, ORIGAMI IS DEEPER THAN YOU'D THINK.
IS IT JUST ME... OR IS SHE HOOKED ON ORIGAMI...?
I-I'LL DEFINITELY FOLD SOMETHING CUTE TODAY TOO.
ORIGAMI CLASS
WARUFY
GACHA (GCHAK)
ガチャ…
WARUFY

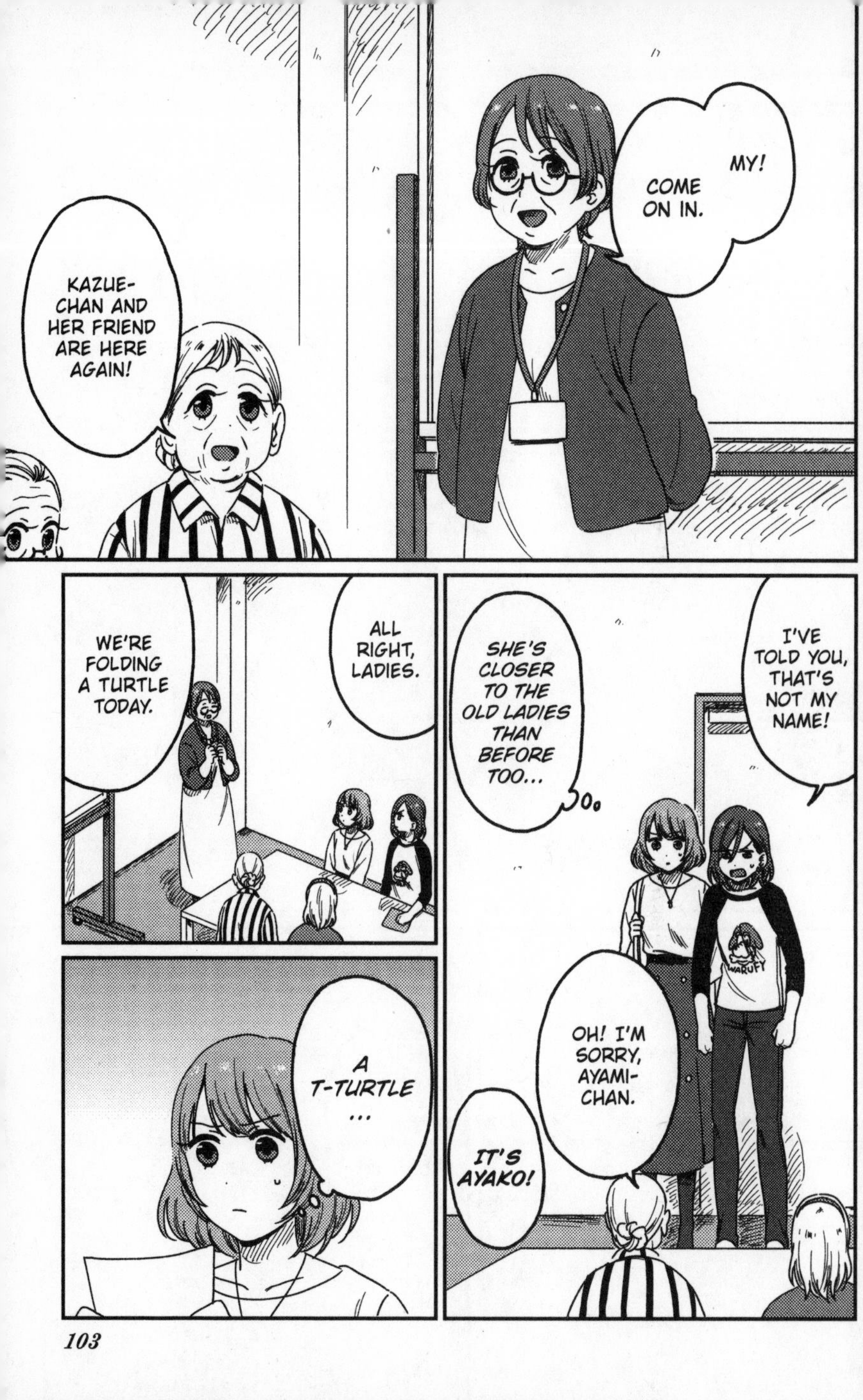
MY!
COME ON IN.
KAZUE-CHAN AND HER FRIEND ARE HERE AGAIN!
I'VE TOLD YOU, THAT'S NOT MY NAME!
SHE'S CLOSER TO THE OLD LADIES THAN BEFORE TOO...
OH! I'M SORRY, AYAMI-CHAN.
IT'S AYAKO!
ALL RIGHT, LADIES.
WE'RE FOLDING A TURTLE TODAY.
A T-TURTLE...
WARUFY

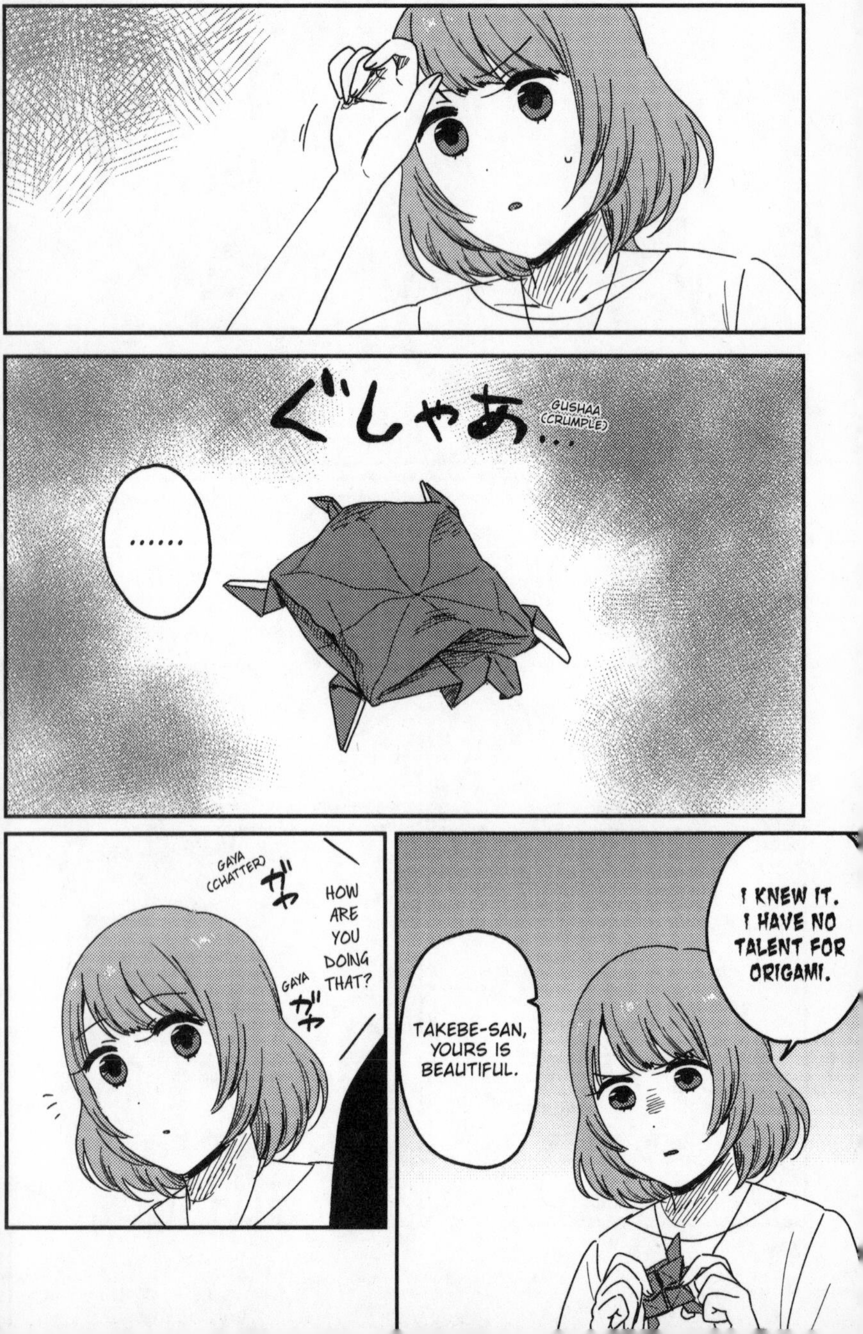
ぐしゃあ…
GUSHAA (CRUMPLE)
......
I KNEW IT. I HAVE NO TALENT FOR ORIGAMI.
TAKEBE-SAN, YOURS IS BEAUTIFUL.
HOW ARE YOU DOING THAT?
GAYA (CHATTER) ガヤ
GAYA ガヤ

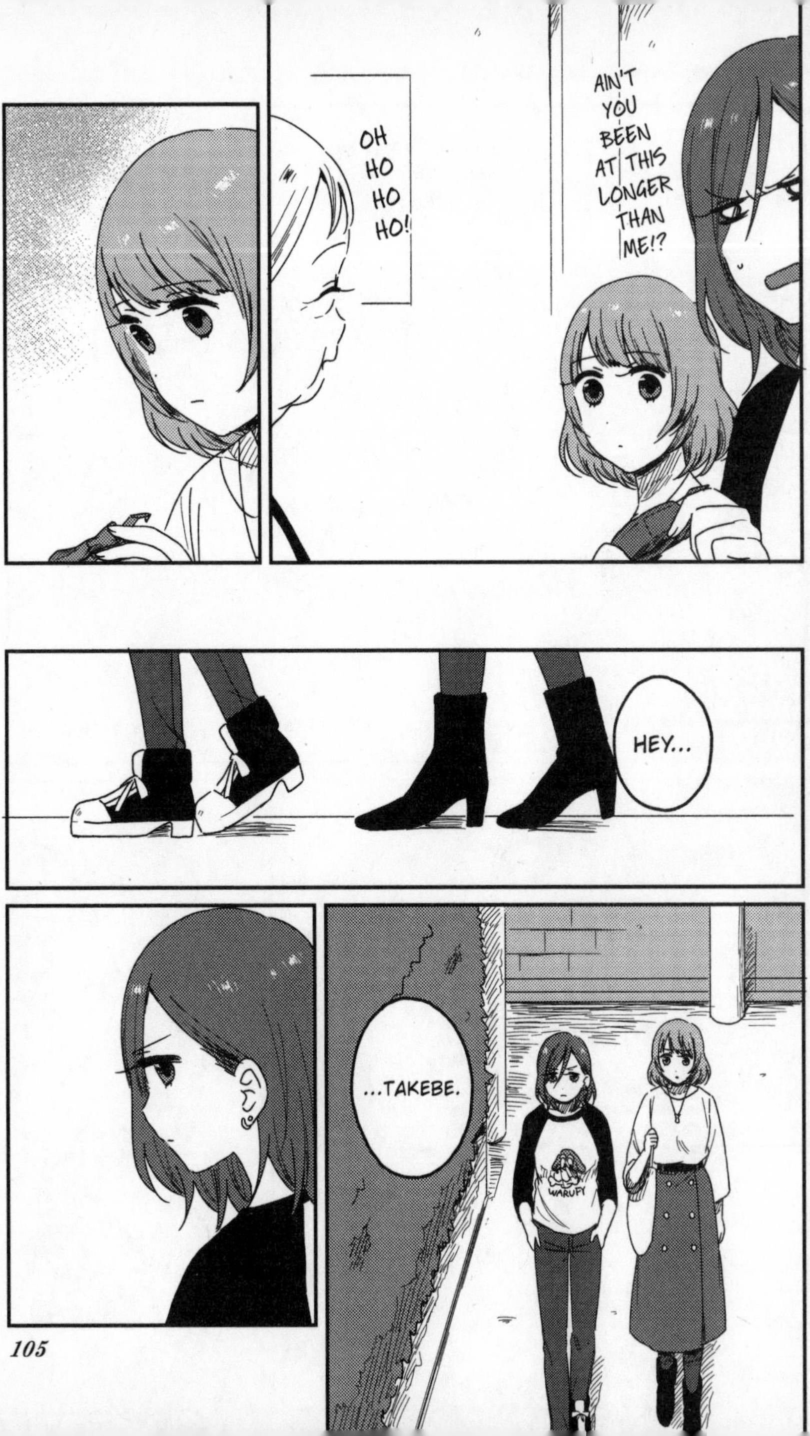
AIN'T YOU BEEN AT THIS LONGER THAN ME!?
OH HO HO HO!
HEY...
...TAKEBE.
WARUFY

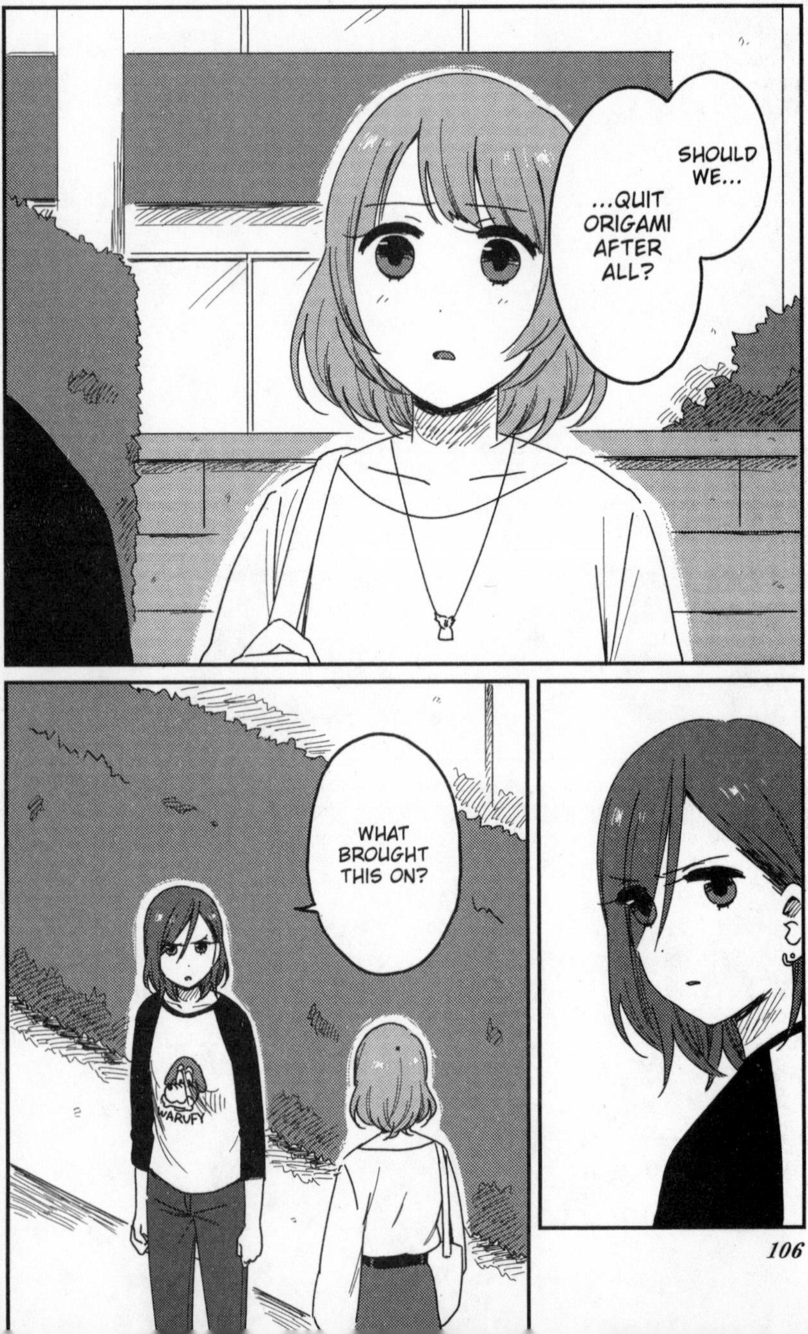
SHOULD WE...
...QUIT ORIGAMI AFTER ALL?
WHAT BROUGHT THIS ON?
WARUFY

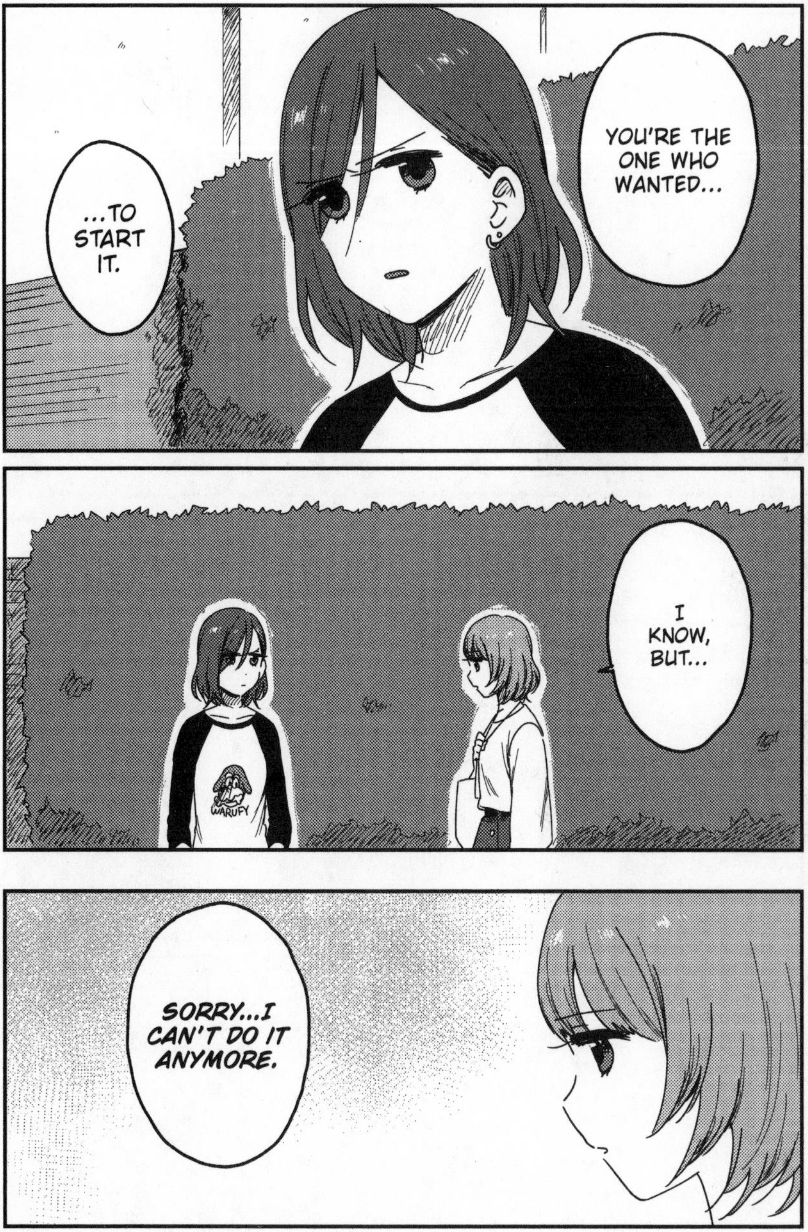
YOU'RE THE ONE WHO WANTED...
...TO START IT.
I KNOW, BUT...
WARUFY
SORRY...I CAN'T DO IT ANYMORE.

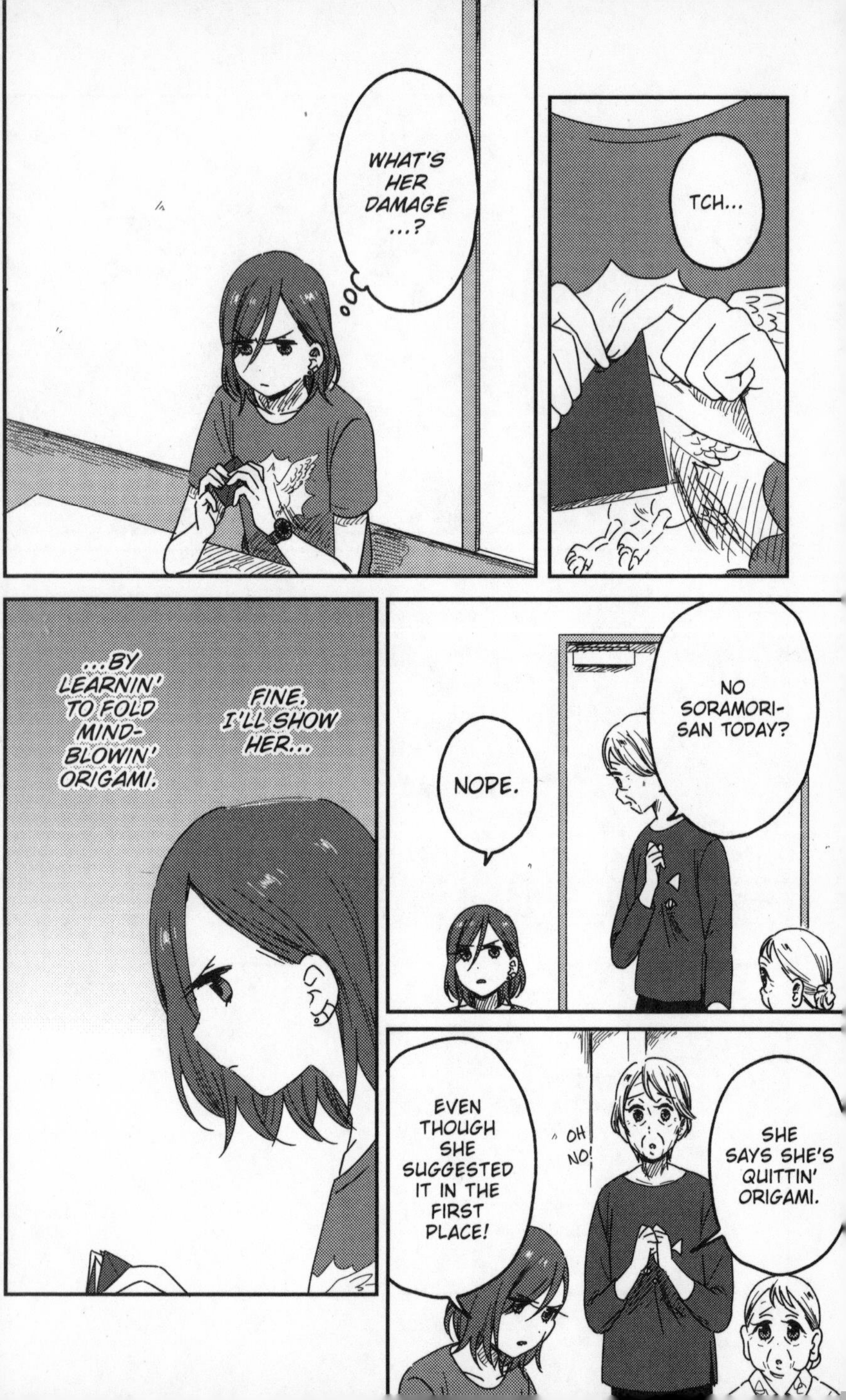
TCH...
WHAT'S HER DAMAGE ...?
NO SORAMORI-SAN TODAY?
NOPE.
SHE SAYS SHE'S QUITTIN' ORIGAMI.
OH NO!
EVEN THOUGH SHE SUGGESTED IT IN THE FIRST PLACE!
FINE. I'LL SHOW HER...
...BY LEARNIN' TO FOLD MIND-BLOWIN' ORIGAMI.

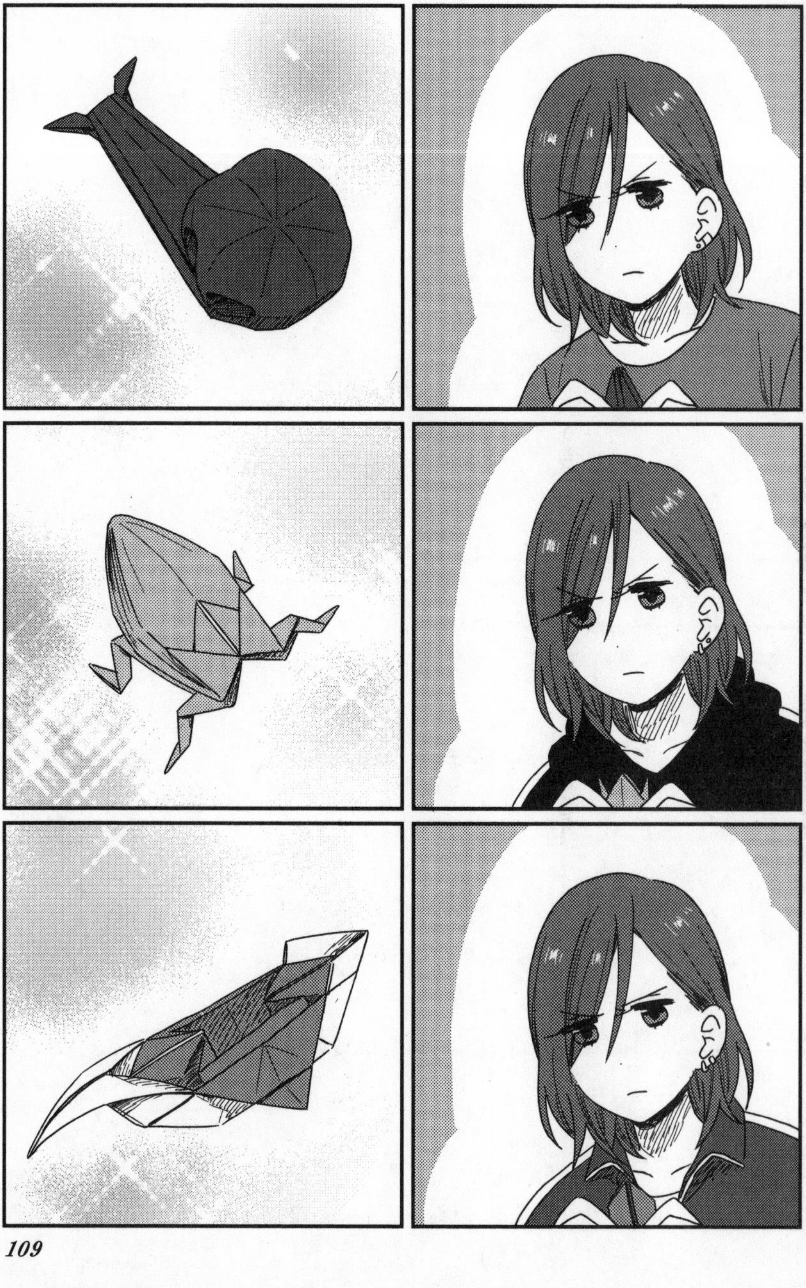

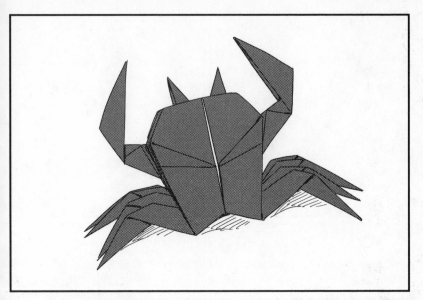

THAT'S QUITE SOMETHING, TAKEBE-SAN.

YOU'RE VERY GOOD AT THIS.

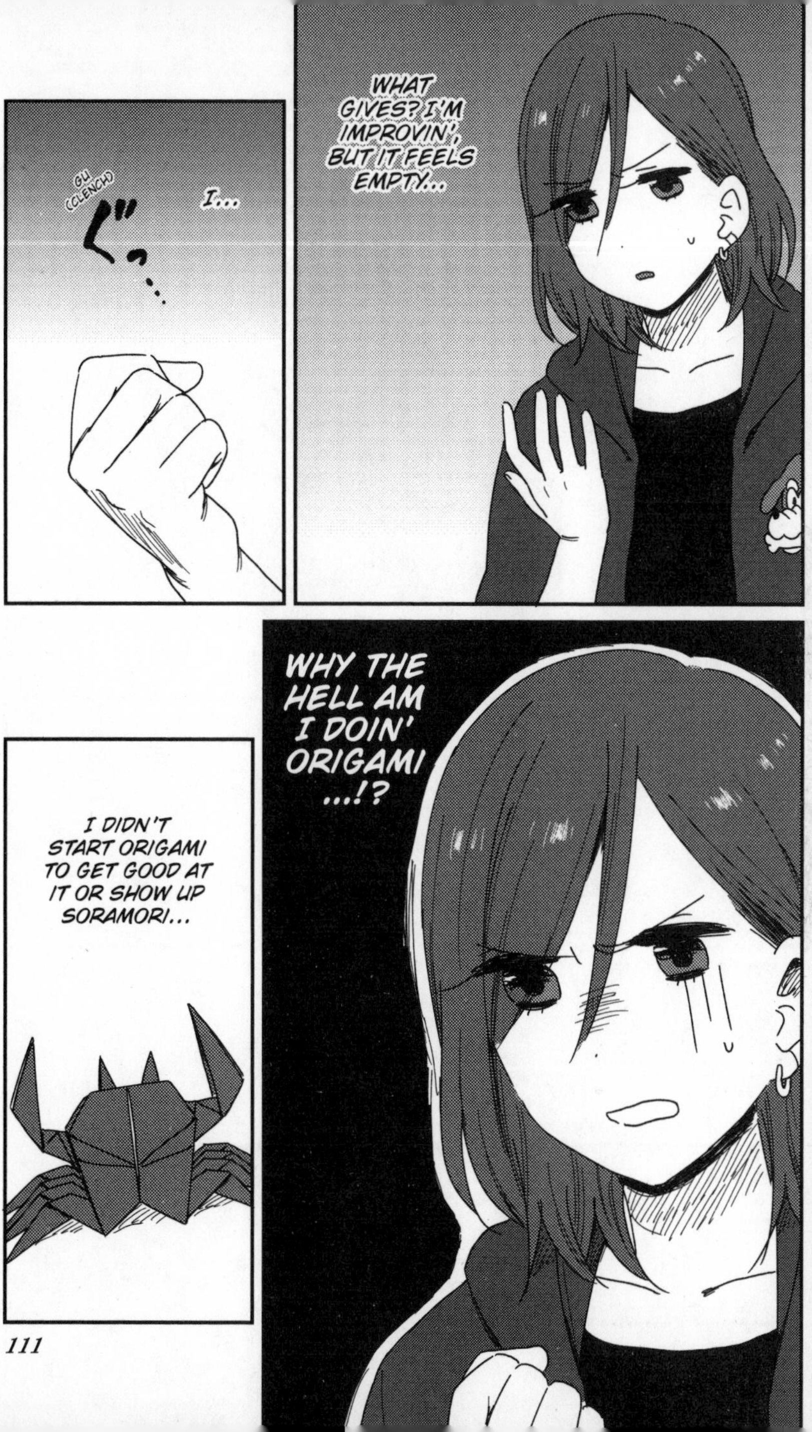
WHAT GIVES? I'M IMPROVIN', BUT IT FEELS EMPTY...
GU (CLENCH)
ぐっ
I...
WHY THE HELL AM I DOIN' ORIGAMI ...!?
I DIDN'T START ORIGAMI TO GET GOOD AT IT OR SHOW UP SORAMORI...

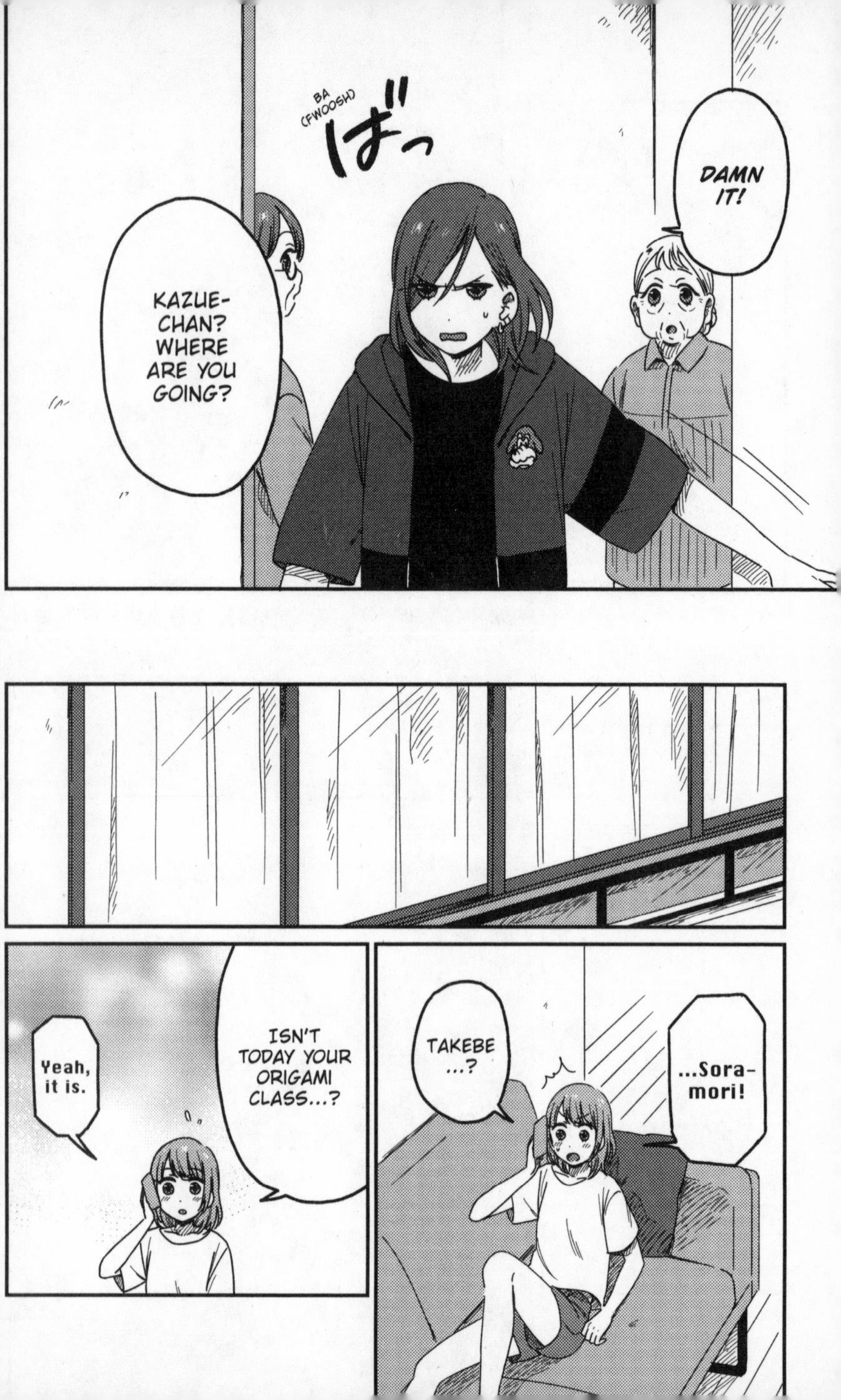
DAMN IT!
ばっ
BA (FWOOSH)
KAZUE-CHAN? WHERE ARE YOU GOING?
...Sora-mori!
TAKEBE ...?
ISN'T TODAY YOUR ORIGAMI CLASS...?
Yeah, it is.

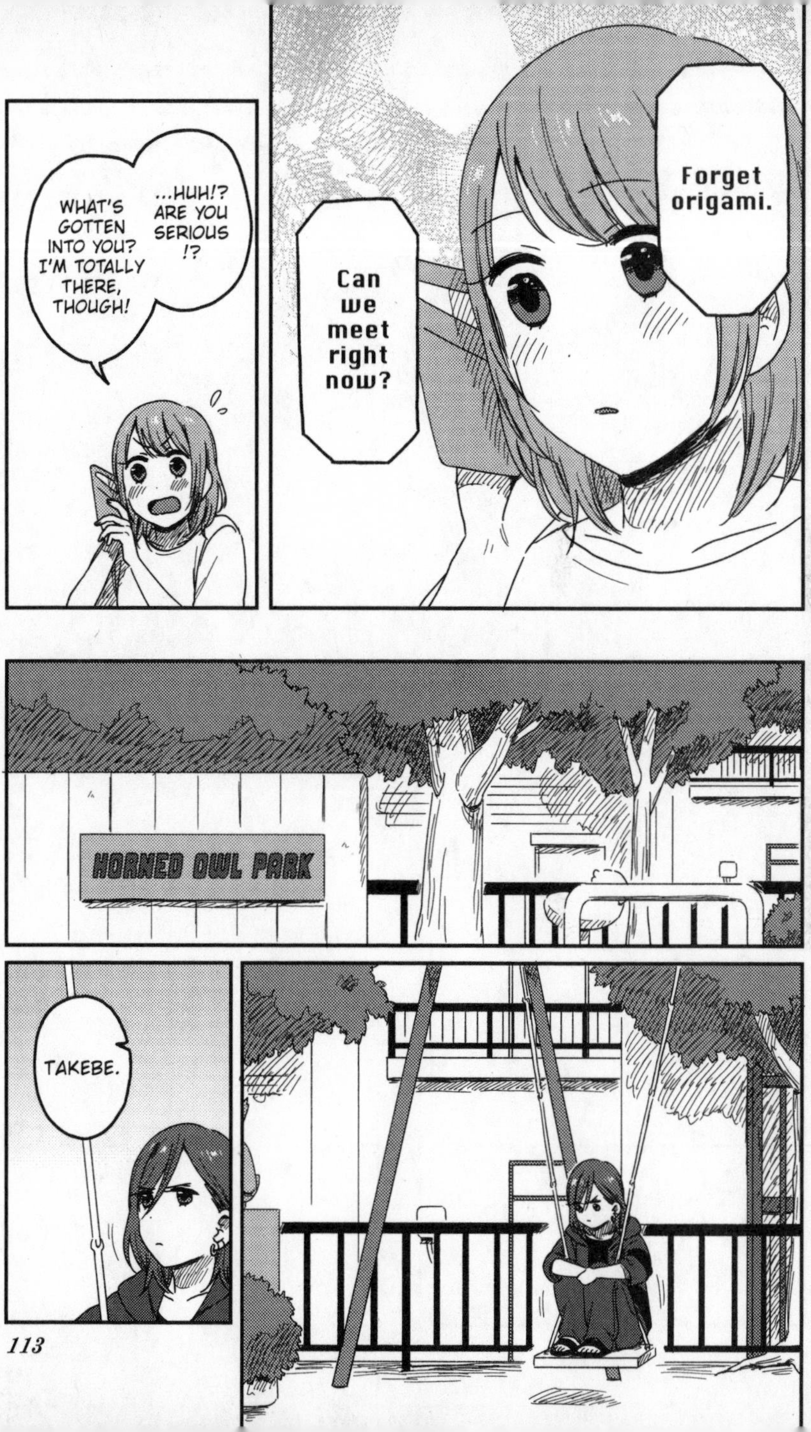
Forget origami.
Can we meet right now?
...HUH!? ARE YOU SERIOUS!?
WHAT'S GOTTEN INTO YOU? I'M TOTALLY THERE, THOUGH!
HORNED OWL PARK
TAKEBE.

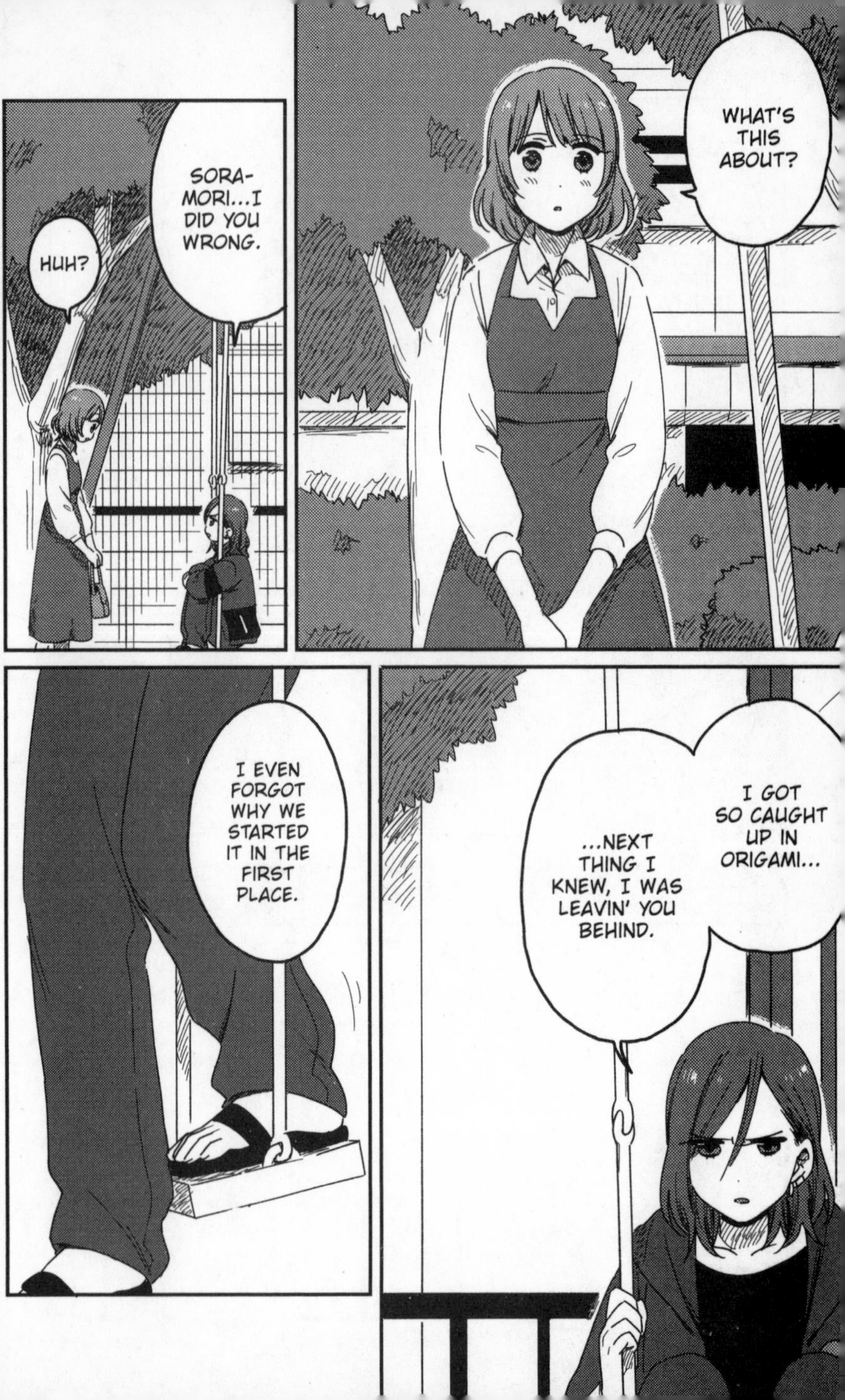
WHAT'S THIS ABOUT?
SORA-MORI...I DID YOU WRONG.
HUH?
I GOT SO CAUGHT UP IN ORIGAMI...
...NEXT THING I KNEW, I WAS LEAVIN' YOU BEHIND.
I EVEN FORGOT WHY WE STARTED IT IN THE FIRST PLACE.

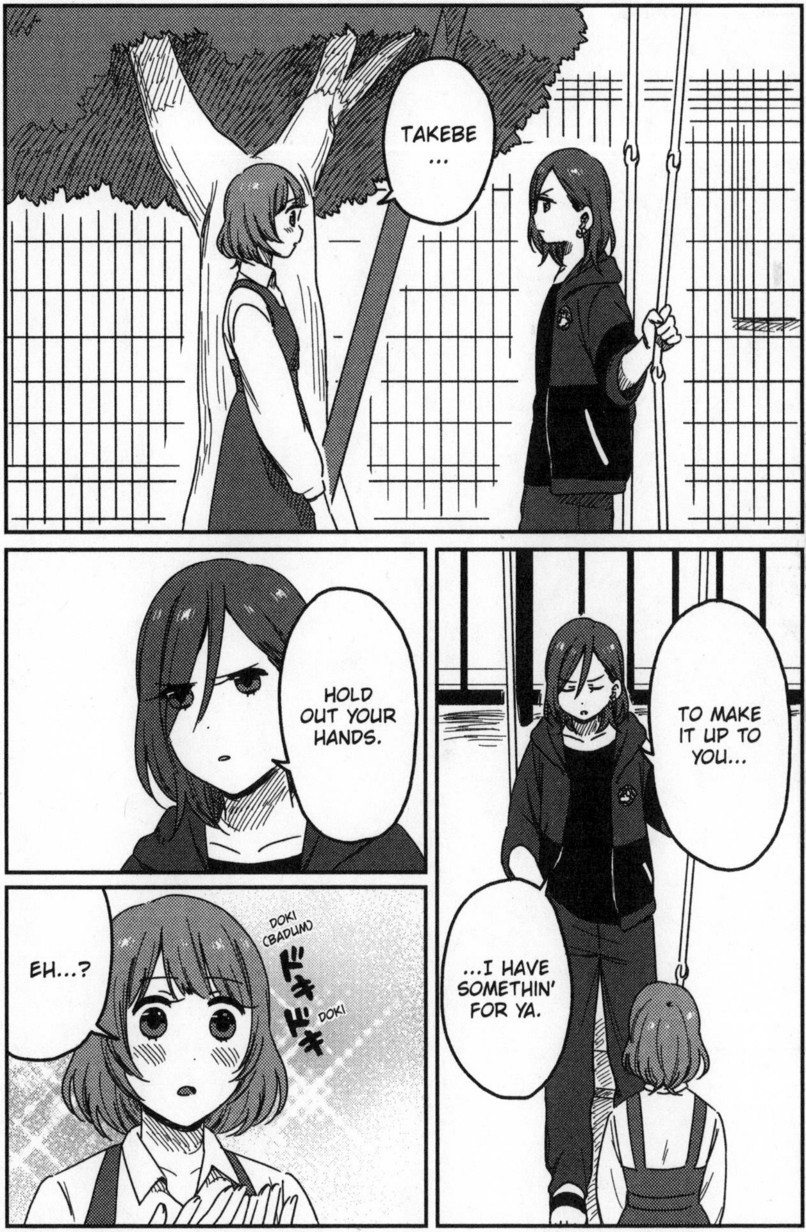
TAKEBE ...
TO MAKE IT UP TO YOU...
...I HAVE SOMETHIN' FOR YA.
HOLD OUT YOUR HANDS.
EH...?
ドキドキ
DOKI (BADUM) DOKI

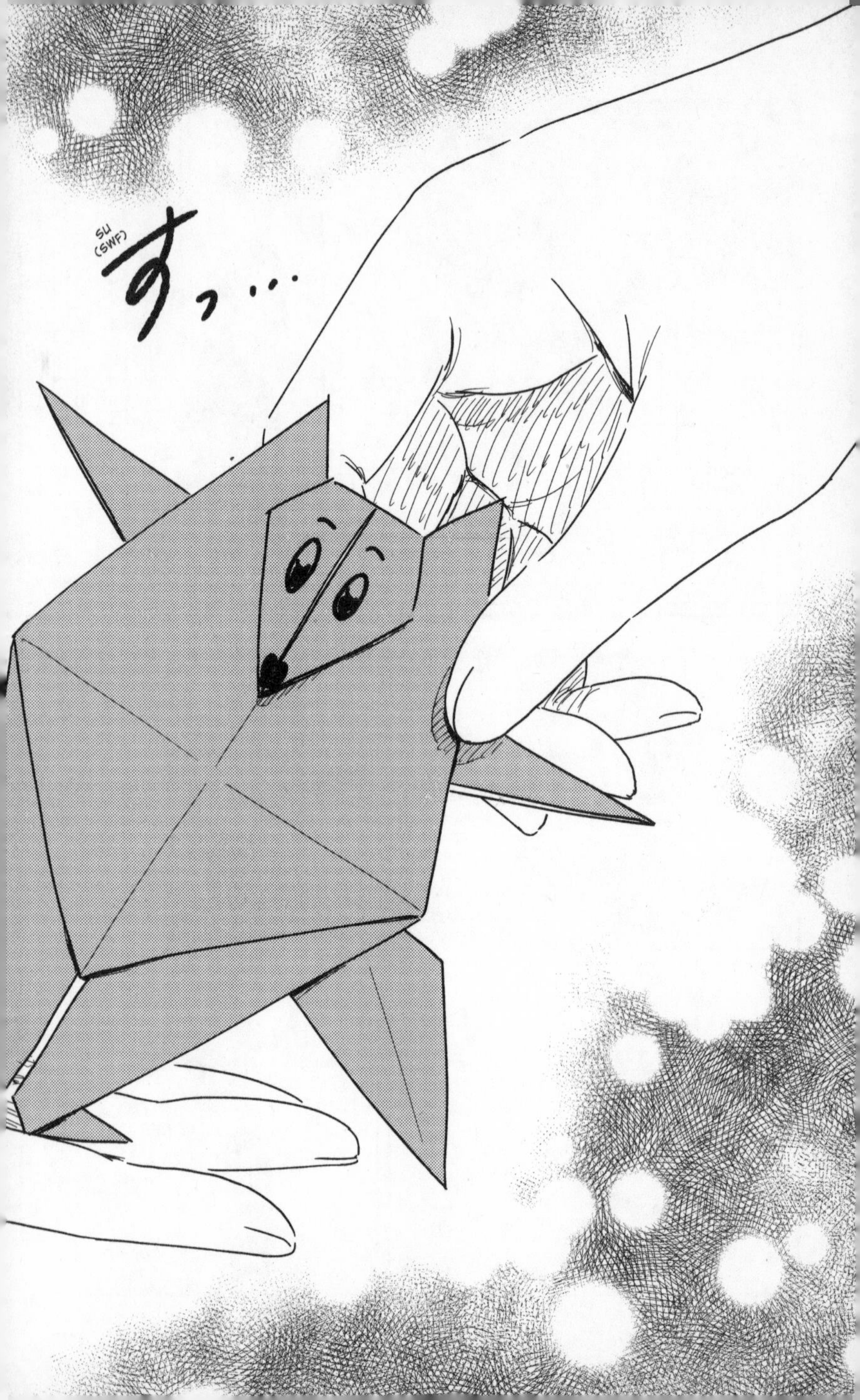
SU
(SWF)
すっ…

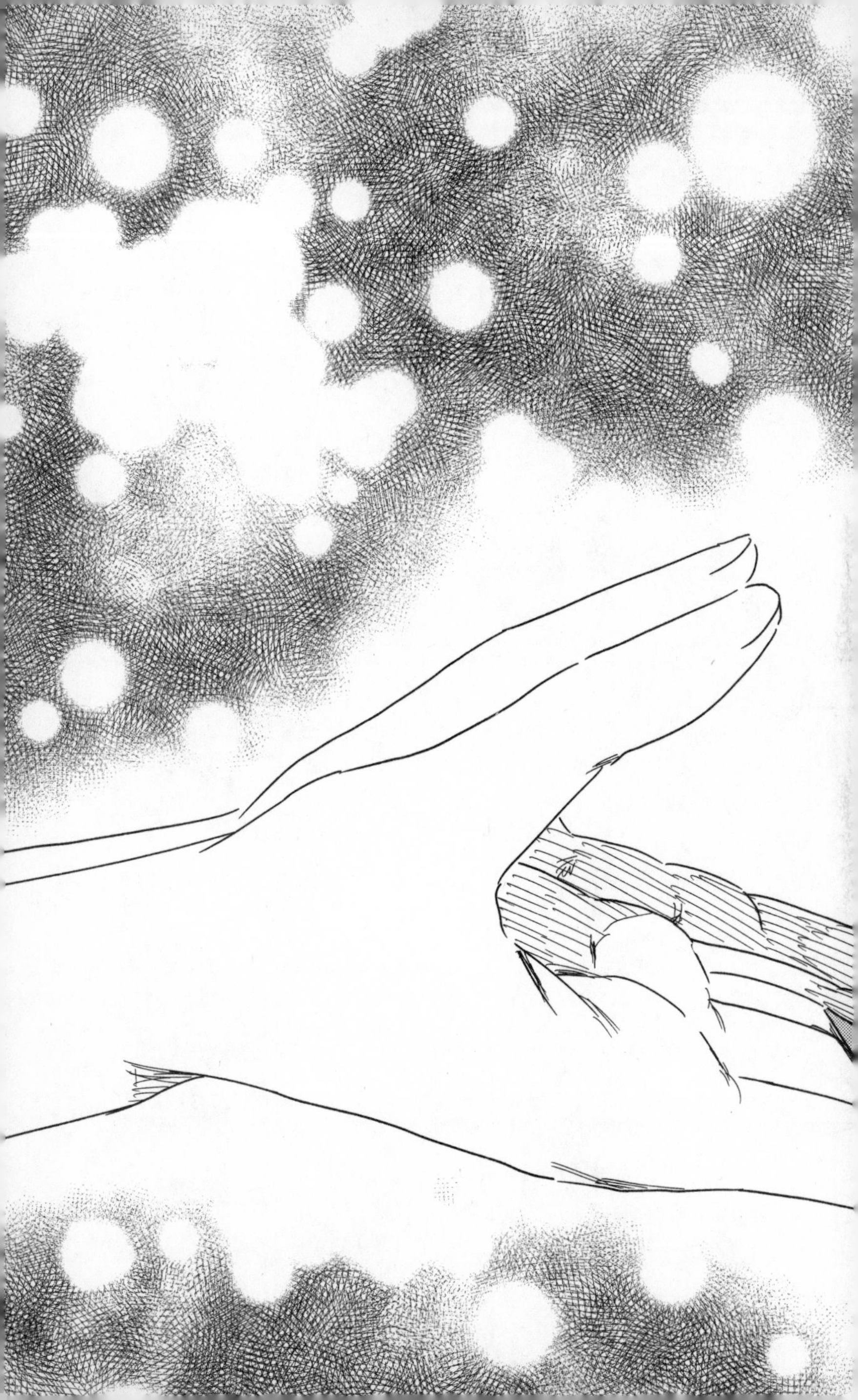

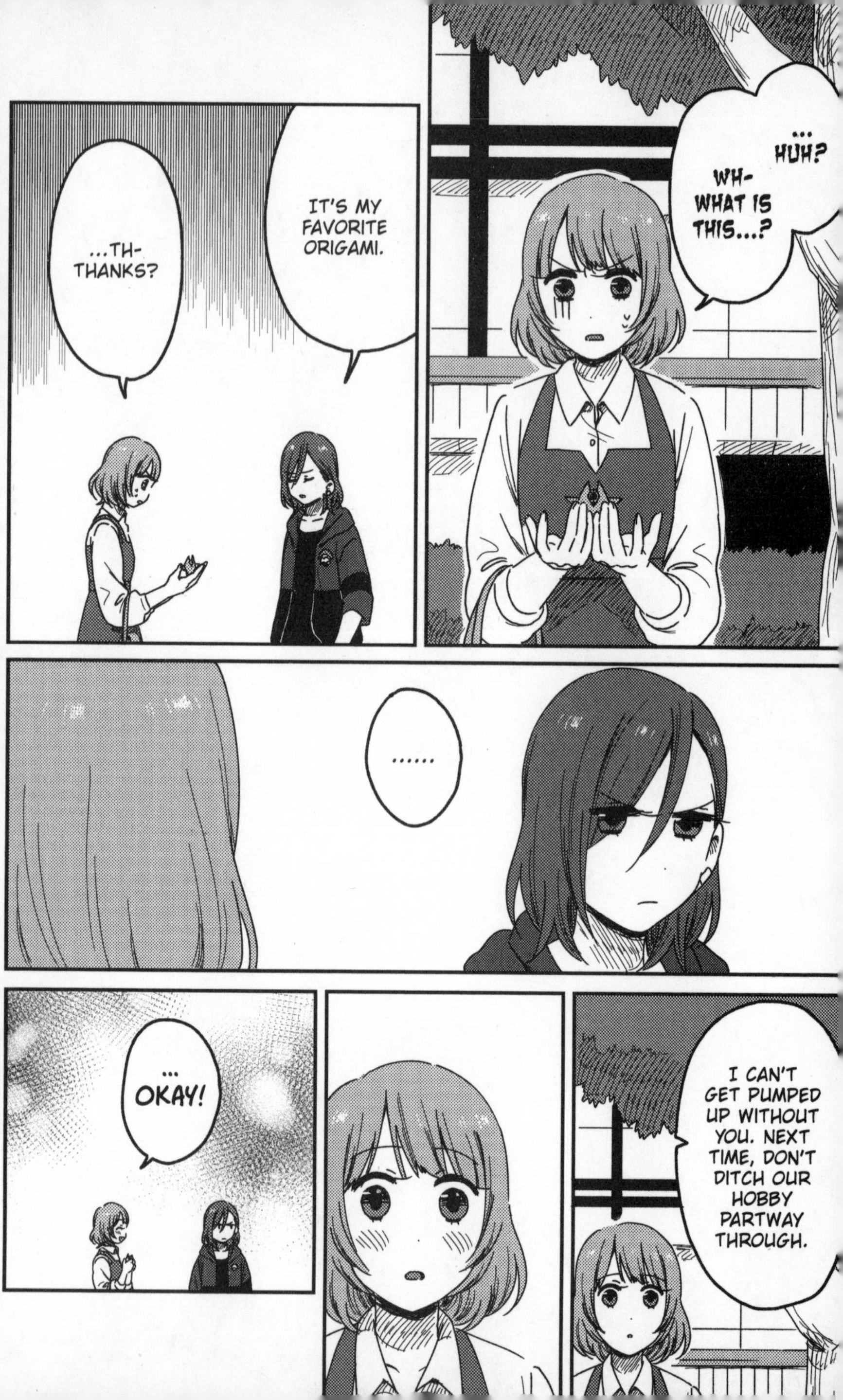
... HUH?
WH- WHAT IS THIS...?
IT'S MY FAVORITE ORIGAMI.
...TH- THANKS?
......
I CAN'T GET PUMPED UP WITHOUT YOU. NEXT TIME, DON'T DITCH OUR HOBBY PARTWAY THROUGH.
... OKAY!

Catch
These
Hands!

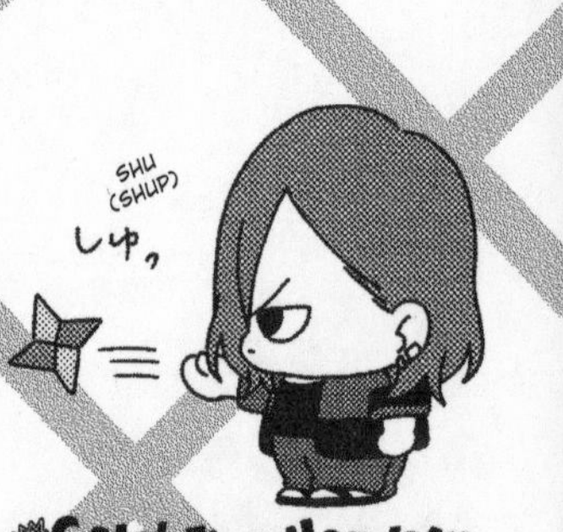
SHU
(SHUP)
しゅっ

Catch These Hands!

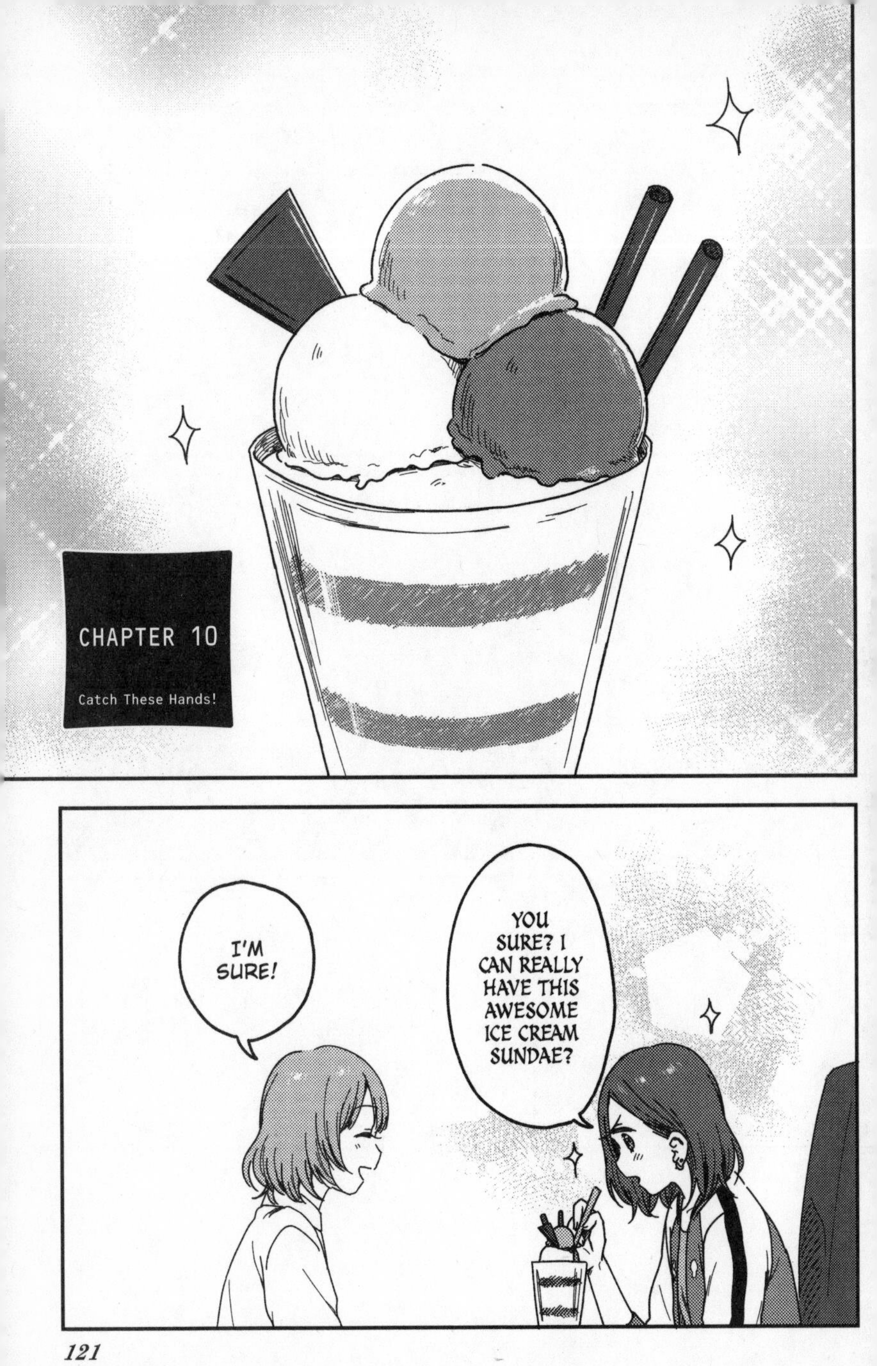
CHAPTER 10
Catch These Hands!
YOU SURE? I CAN REALLY HAVE THIS AWESOME ICE CREAM SUNDAE?
I'M SURE!

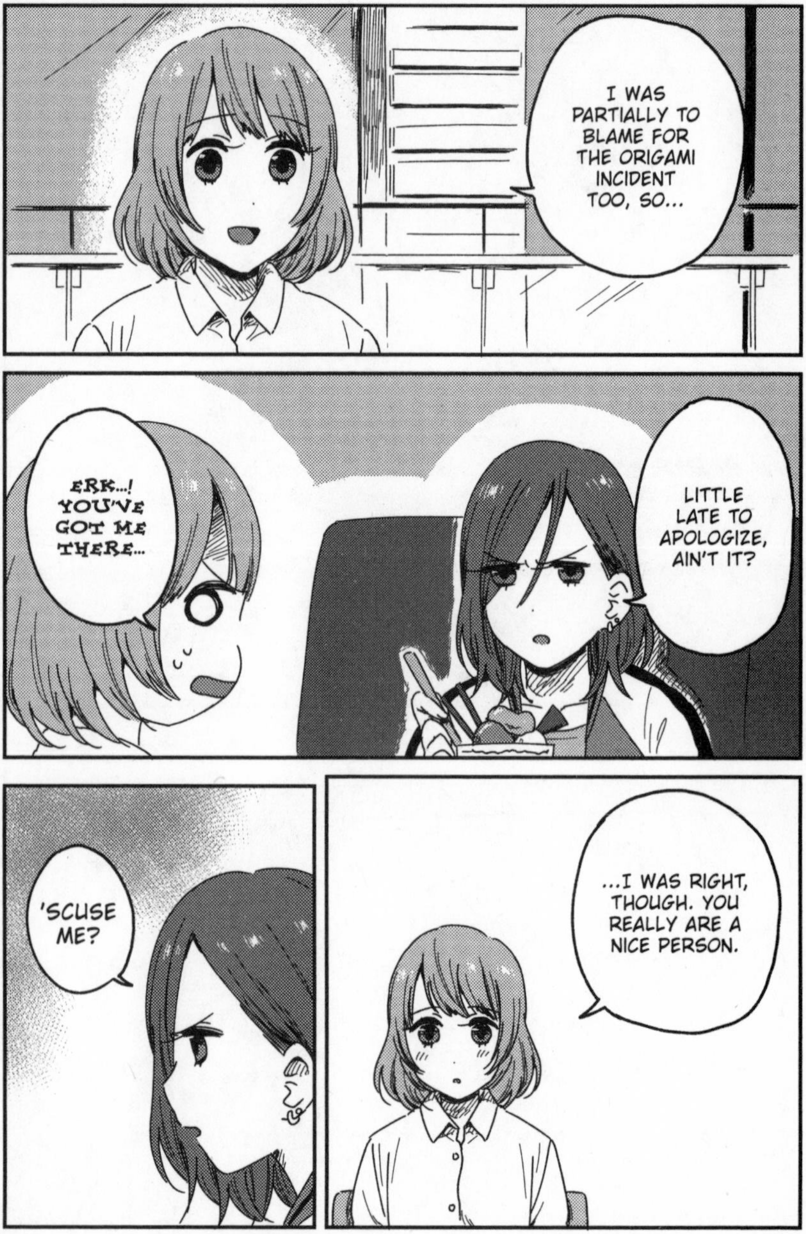
I WAS PARTIALLY TO BLAME FOR THE ORIGAMI INCIDENT TOO, SO...
LITTLE LATE TO APOLOGIZE, AIN'T IT?
ERK...! YOU'VE GOT ME THERE...
...I WAS RIGHT, THOUGH. YOU REALLY ARE A NICE PERSON.
'SCUSE ME?

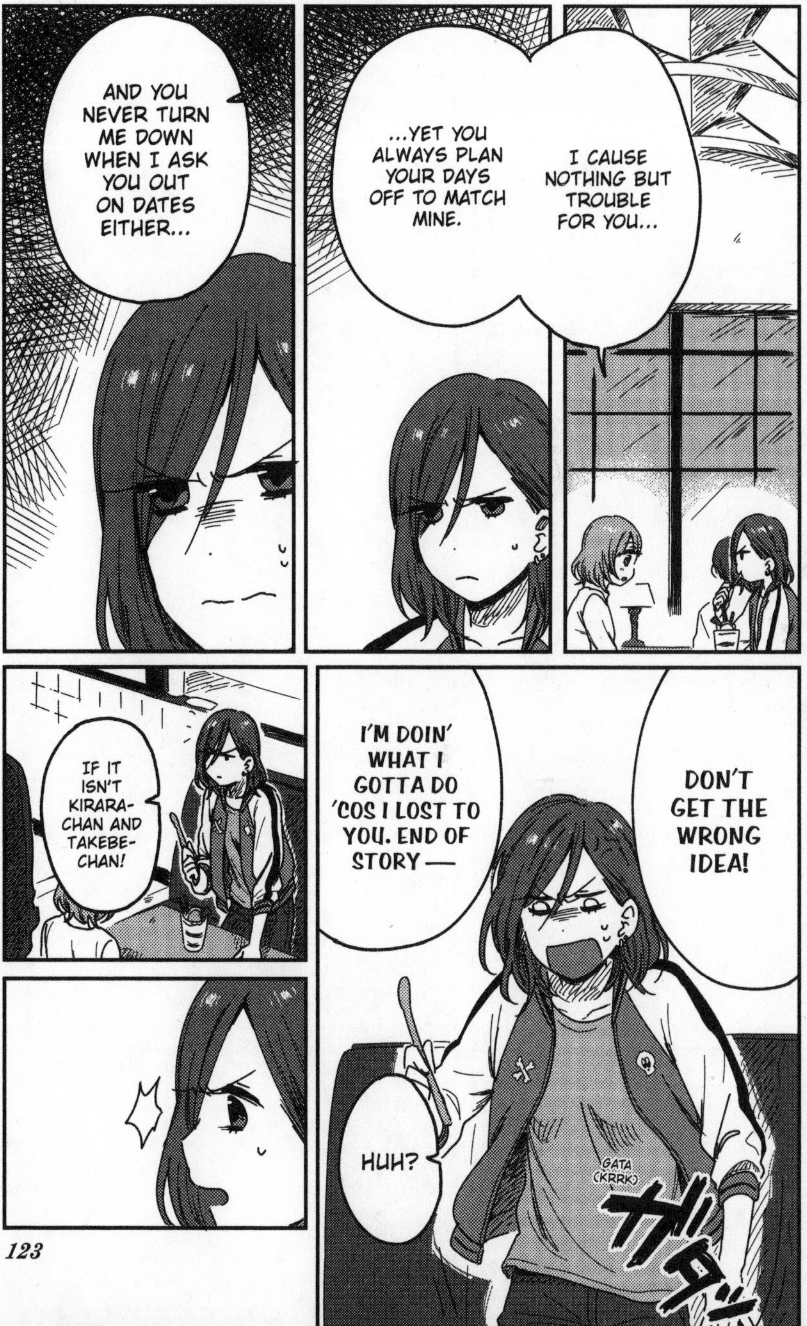
I CAUSE NOTHING BUT TROUBLE FOR YOU...
...YET YOU ALWAYS PLAN YOUR DAYS OFF TO MATCH MINE.
AND YOU NEVER TURN ME DOWN WHEN I ASK YOU OUT ON DATES EITHER...
DON'T GET THE WRONG IDEA!
I'M DOIN' WHAT I GOTTA DO 'COS I LOST TO YOU. END OF STORY—
HUH?
GATA (KRRK)
IF IT ISN'T KIRARA-CHAN AND TAKEBE-CHAN!

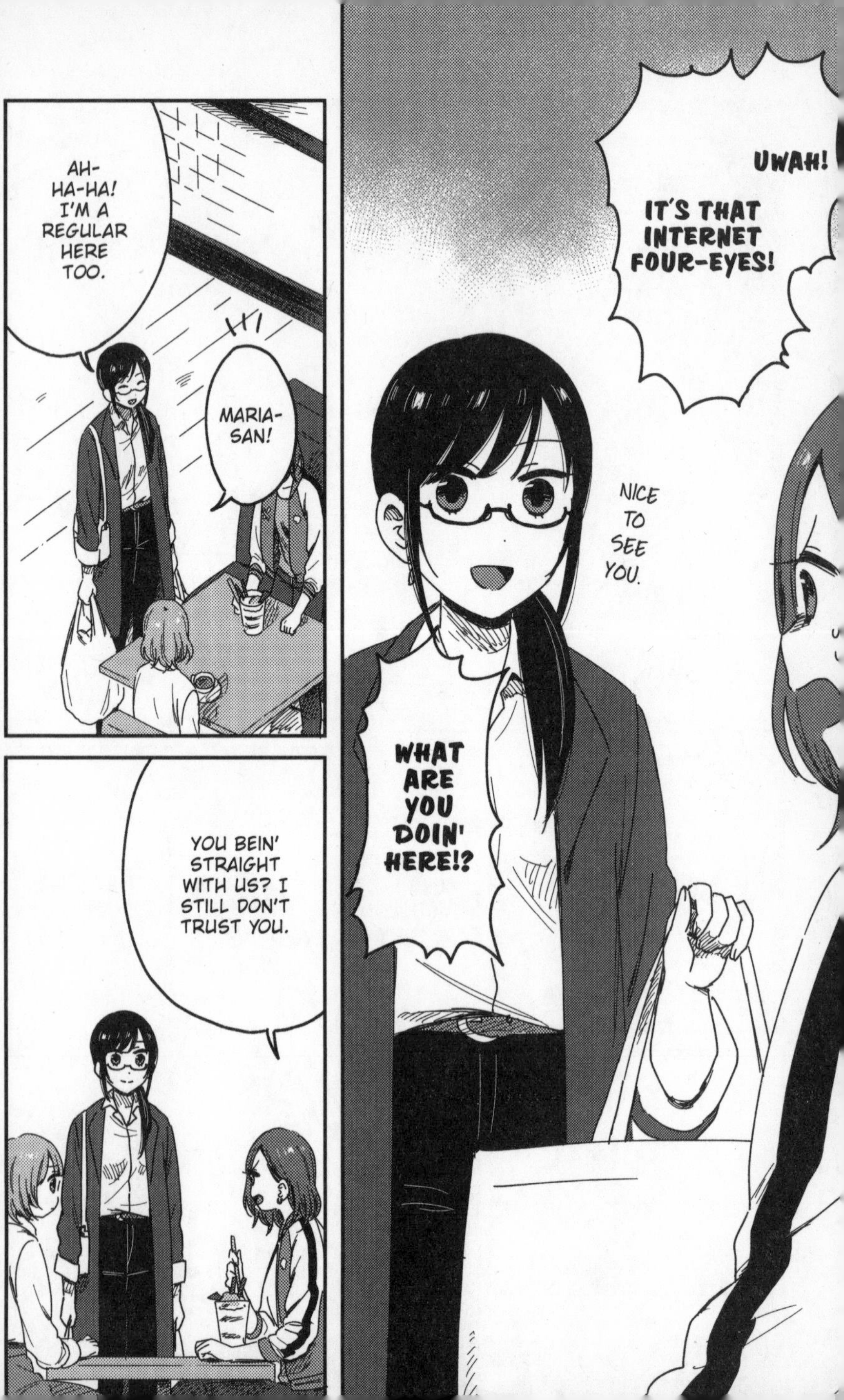
UWAH!
IT'S THAT INTERNET FOUR-EYES!
NICE TO SEE YOU.
WHAT ARE YOU DOIN' HERE!?
AH-HA-HA! I'M A REGULAR HERE TOO.
MARIA-SAN!
YOU BEIN' STRAIGHT WITH US? I STILL DON'T TRUST YOU.

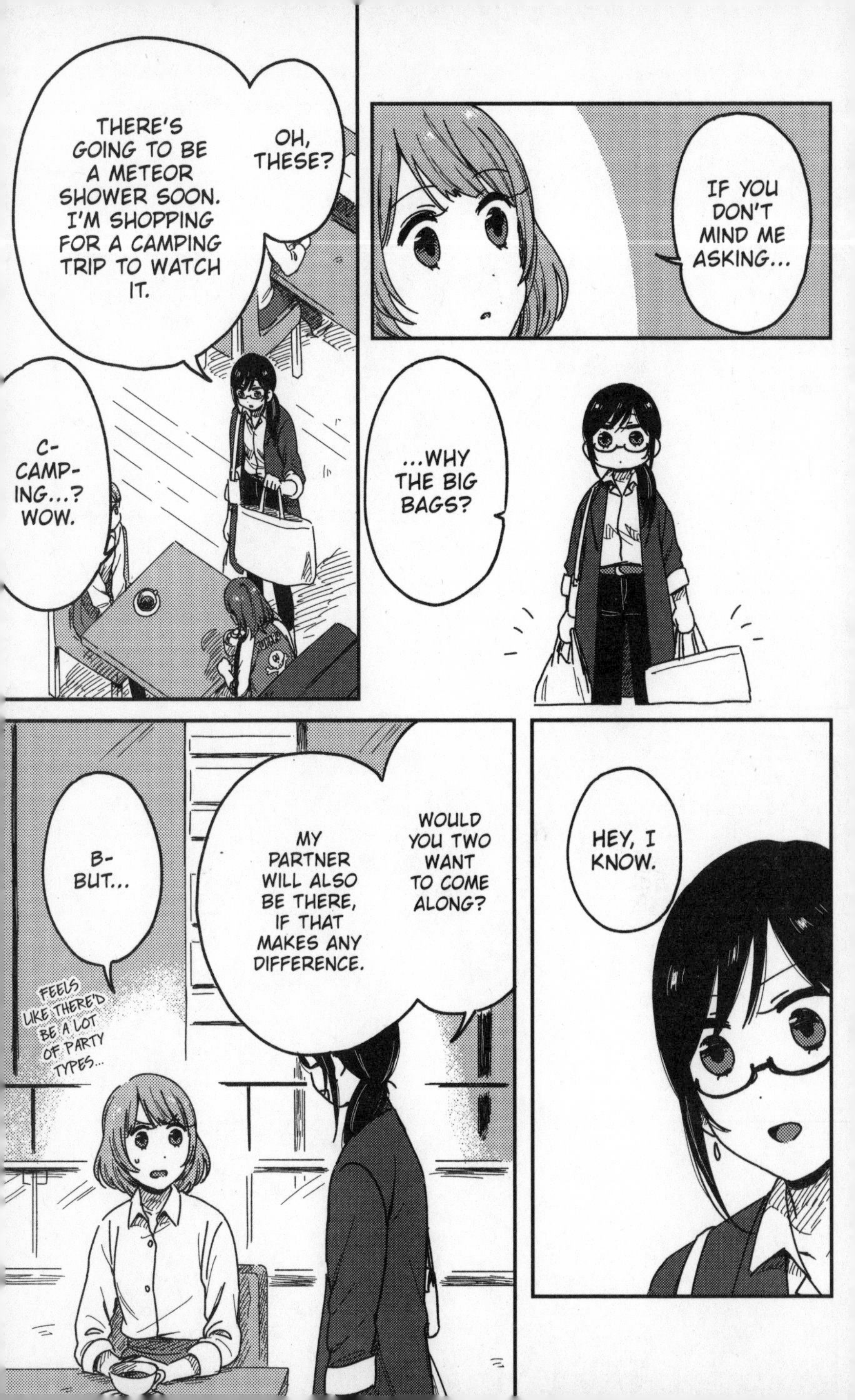
IF YOU DON'T MIND ME ASKING...
...WHY THE BIG BAGS?
OH, THESE?
THERE'S GOING TO BE A METEOR SHOWER SOON. I'M SHOPPING FOR A CAMPING TRIP TO WATCH IT.
C-CAMPING...? WOW.
HEY, I KNOW.
WOULD YOU TWO WANT TO COME ALONG?
MY PARTNER WILL ALSO BE THERE, IF THAT MAKES ANY DIFFERENCE.
B-BUT...
FEELS LIKE THERE'D BE A LOT OF PARTY TYPES...

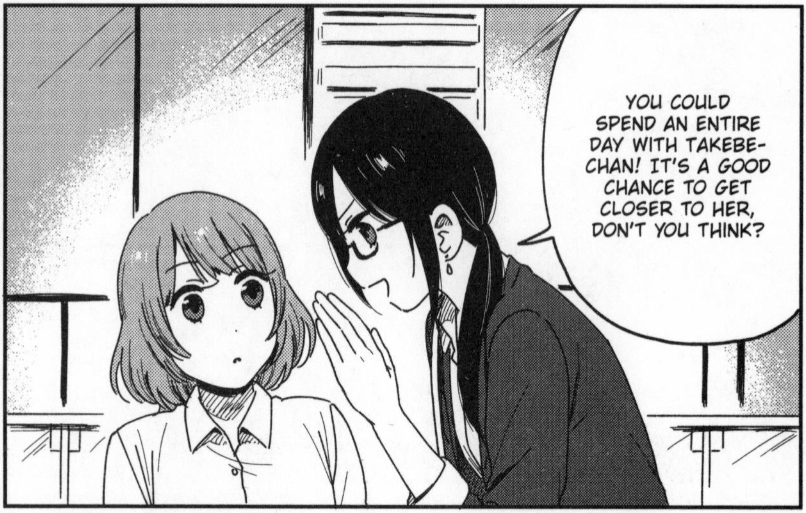
YOU COULD SPEND AN ENTIRE DAY WITH TAKEBE-CHAN! IT'S A GOOD CHANCE TO GET CLOSER TO HER, DON'T YOU THINK?

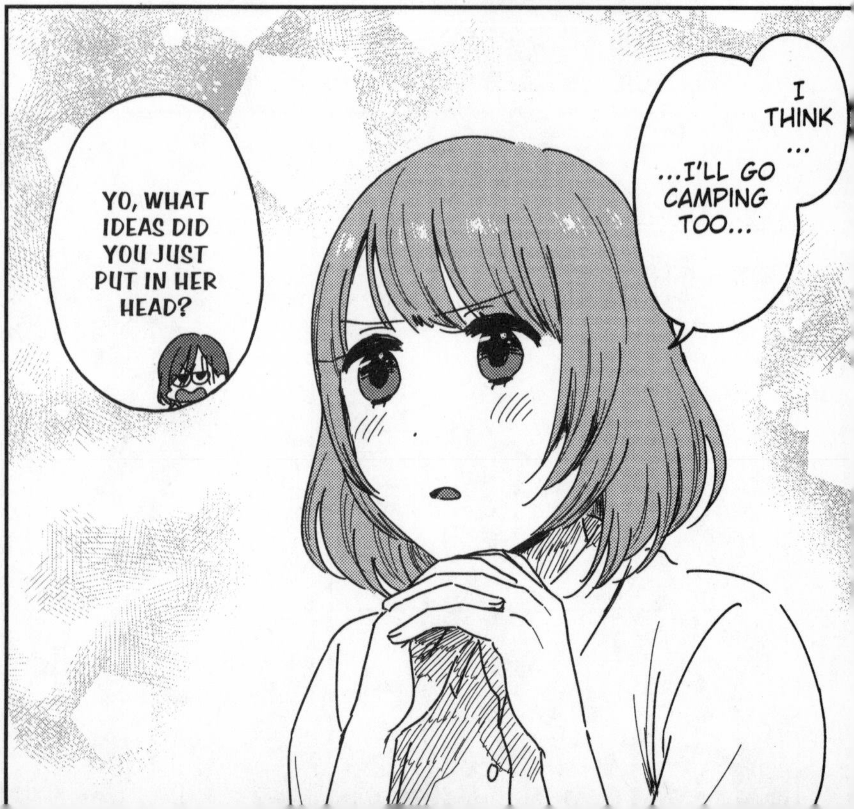
I THINK... ...I'LL GO CAMPING TOO...
YO, WHAT IDEAS DID YOU JUST PUT IN HER HEAD?

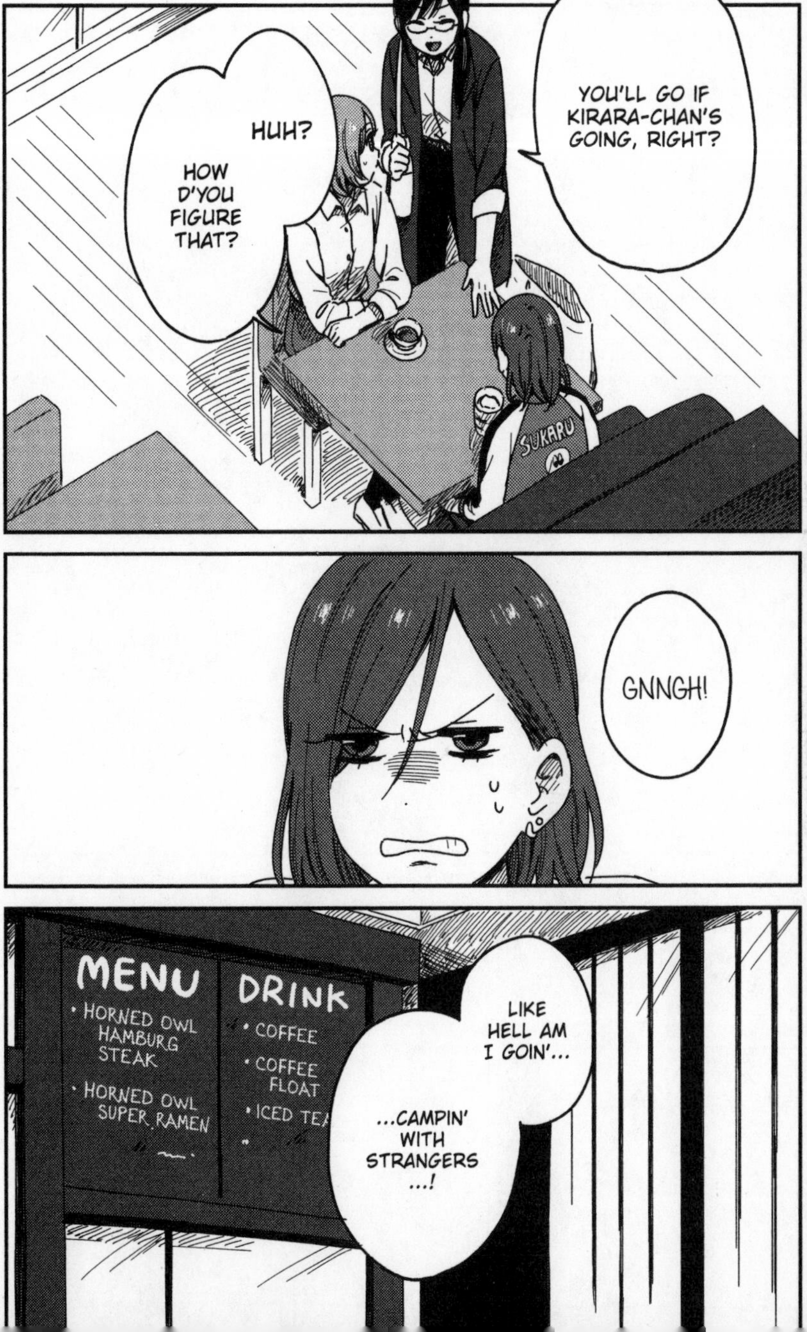
YOU'LL GO IF KIRARA-CHAN'S GOING, RIGHT?
HUH?
HOW D'YOU FIGURE THAT?
GNNGH!
LIKE HELL AM I GOIN'...
...CAMPIN' WITH STRANGERS ...!
DRINK
• COFFEE
• COFFEE FLOAT
• ICED TE
MENU
• HORNED OWL HAMBURG STEAK
• HORNED OWL SUPER RAMEN

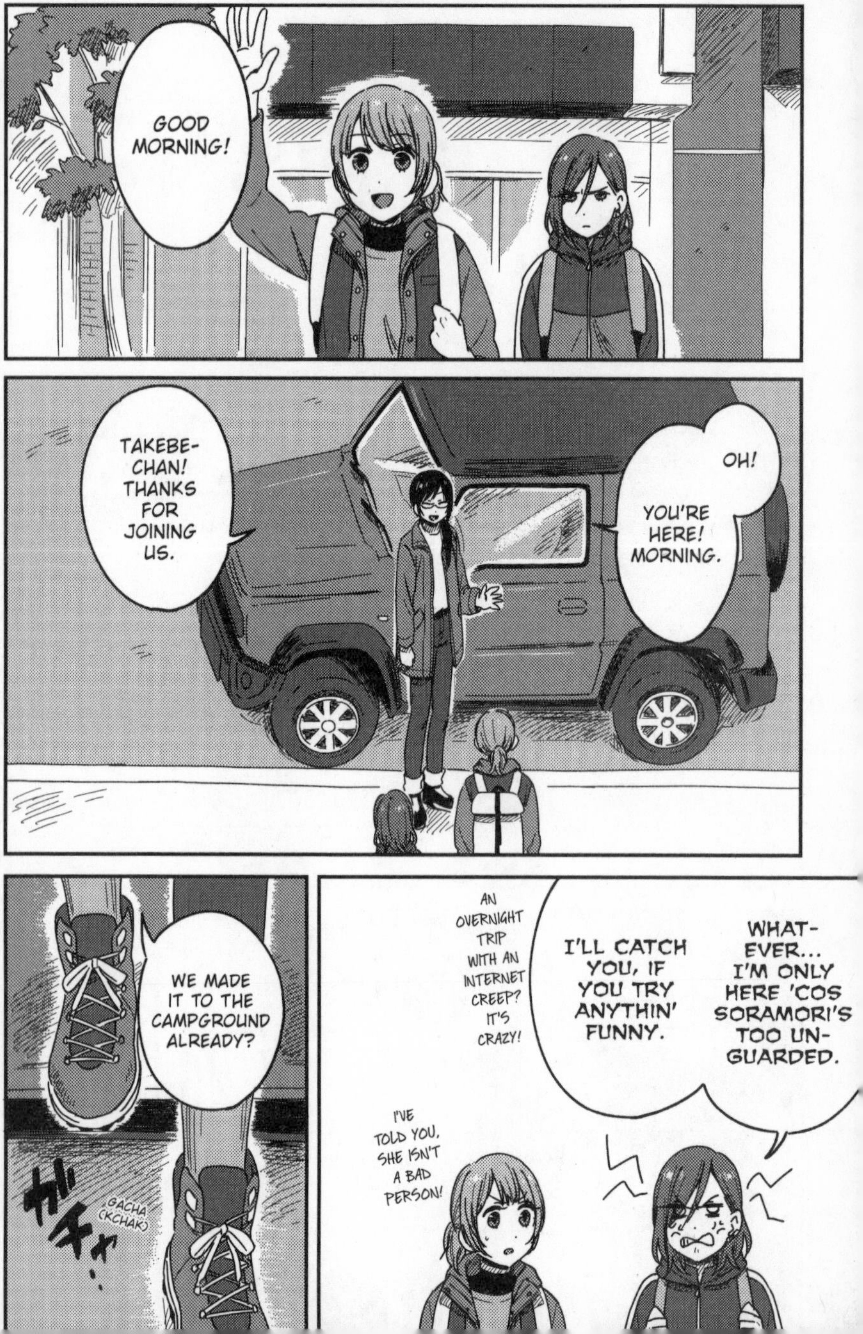
GOOD MORNING!
OH!
YOU'RE HERE! MORNING.
TAKEBE-CHAN! THANKS FOR JOINING US.
WHAT-EVER... I'M ONLY HERE 'COS SORAMORI'S TOO UN-GUARDED.
I'LL CATCH YOU, IF YOU TRY ANYTHIN' FUNNY.
AN OVERNIGHT TRIP WITH AN INTERNET CREEP? IT'S CRAZY!
I'VE TOLD YOU, SHE ISN'T A BAD PERSON!
WE MADE IT TO THE CAMPGROUND ALREADY?
ガチャ
GACHA (KCHAK)

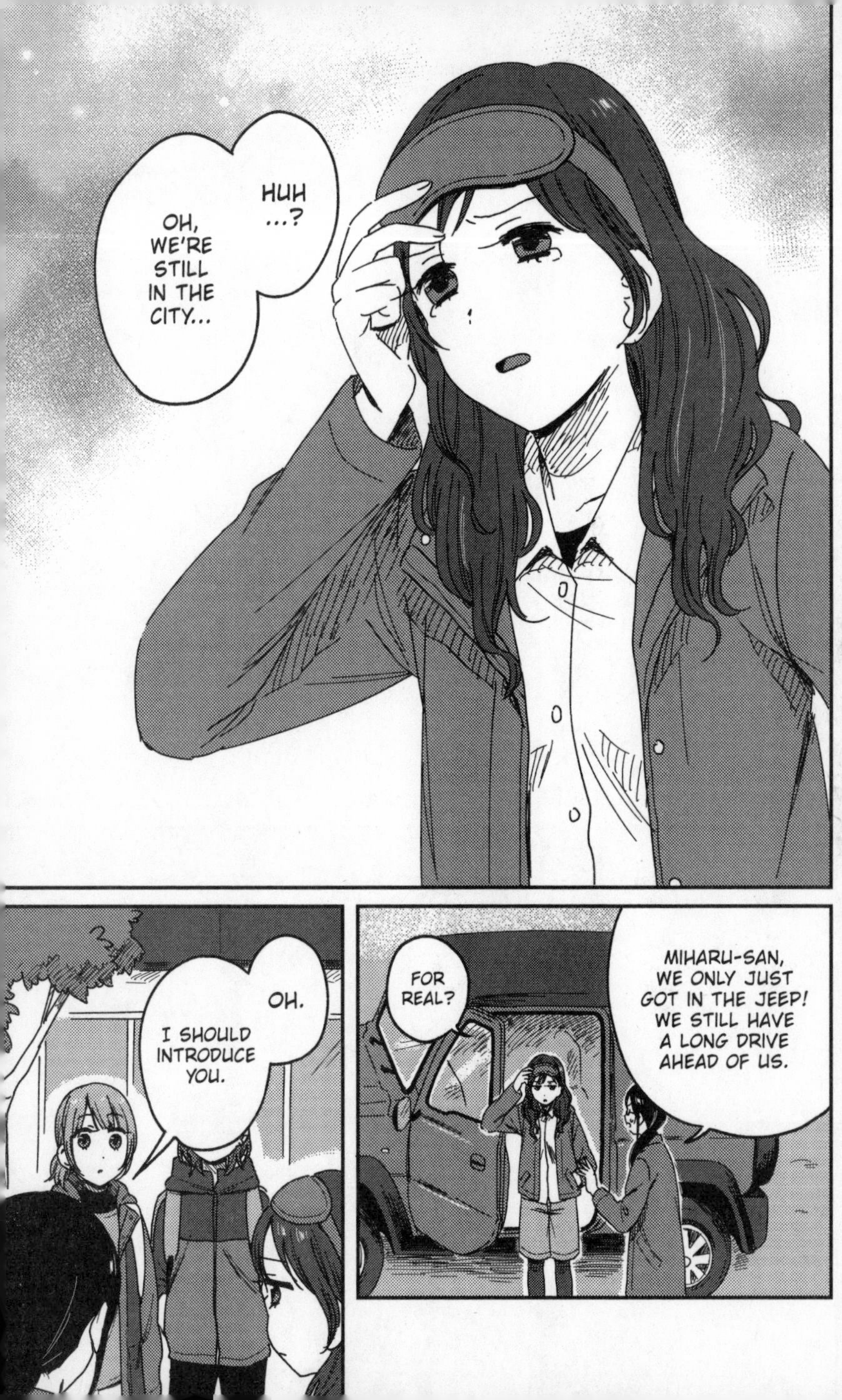
HUH ...?
OH, WE'RE STILL IN THE CITY...
MIHARU-SAN, WE ONLY JUST GOT IN THE JEEP! WE STILL HAVE A LONG DRIVE AHEAD OF US.
FOR REAL?
OH.
I SHOULD INTRODUCE YOU.

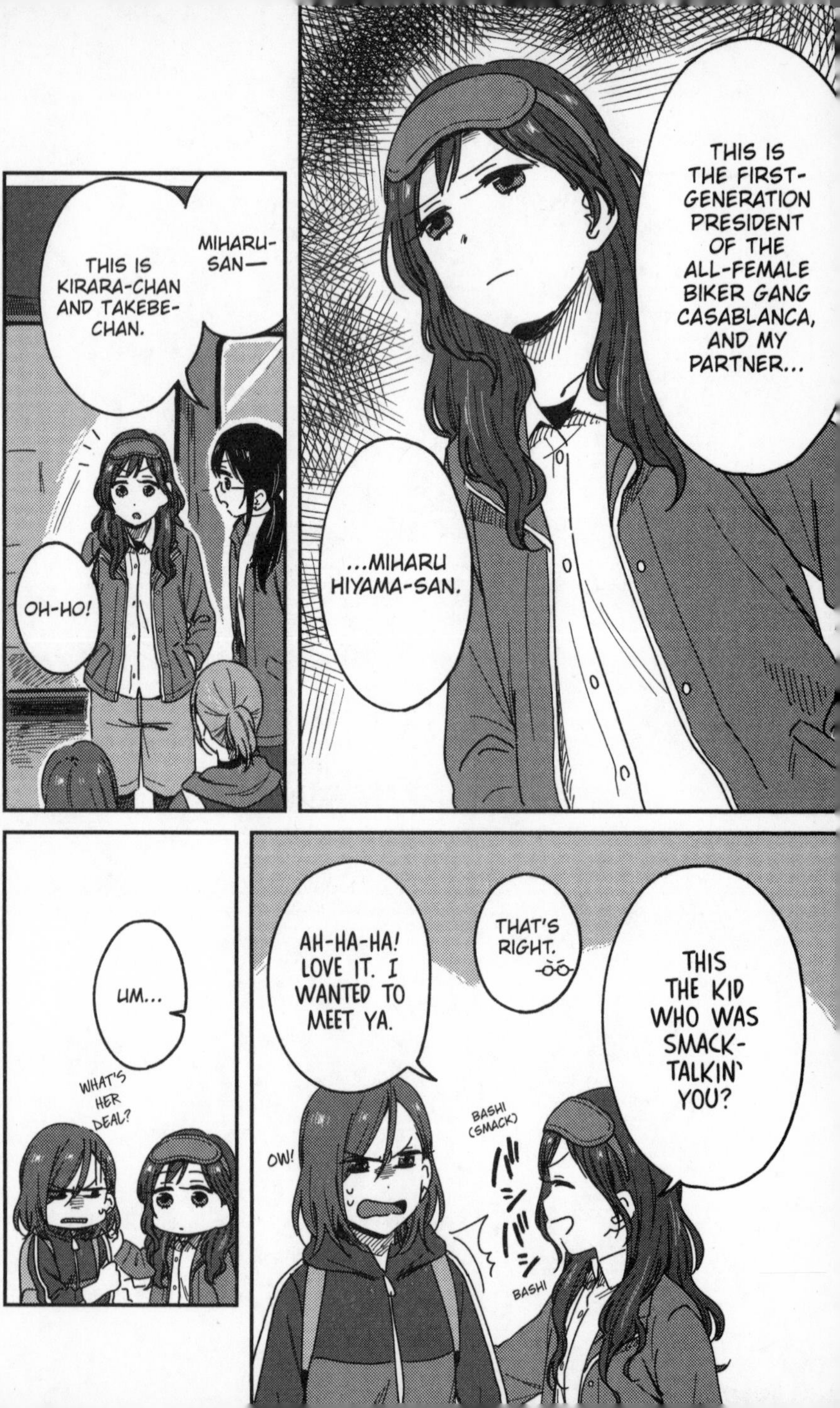
THIS IS THE FIRST-GENERATION PRESIDENT OF THE ALL-FEMALE BIKER GANG CASABLANCA, AND MY PARTNER...
...MIHARU HIYAMA-SAN.
MIHARU-SAN—
THIS IS KIRARA-CHAN AND TAKEBE-CHAN.
OH-HO!
THIS THE KID WHO WAS SMACK-TALKIN' YOU?
THAT'S RIGHT.
AH-HA-HA! LOVE IT. I WANTED TO MEET YA.
BASHI (SMACK)
BASHI
OW!
UM...
WHAT'S HER DEAL?

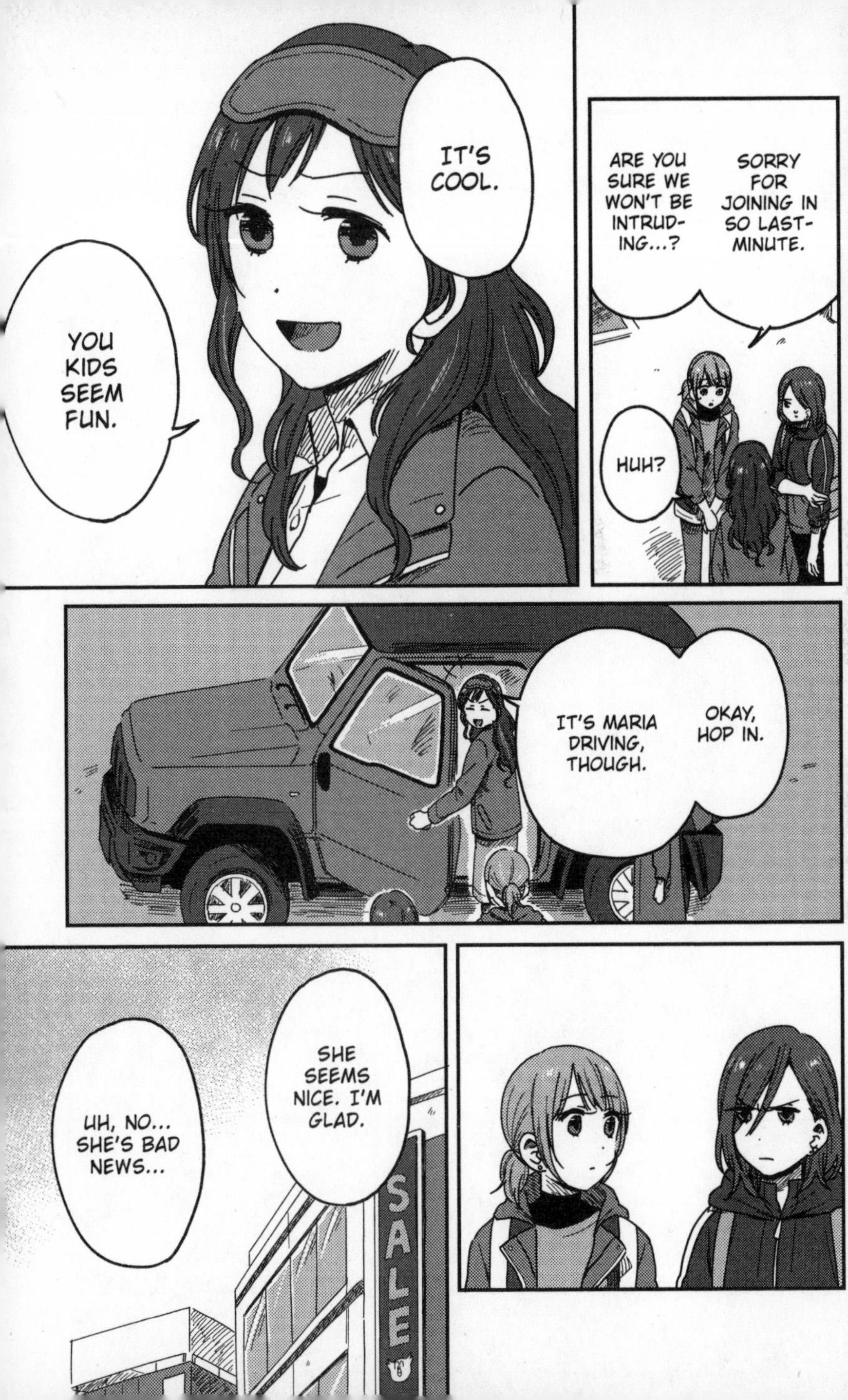
SORRY FOR JOINING IN SO LAST-MINUTE.
ARE YOU SURE WE WON'T BE INTRUD-ING...?
HUH?
IT'S COOL.
YOU KIDS SEEM FUN.
OKAY, HOP IN.
IT'S MARIA DRIVING, THOUGH.
SHE SEEMS NICE. I'M GLAD.
UH, NO... SHE'S BAD NEWS...
SALE

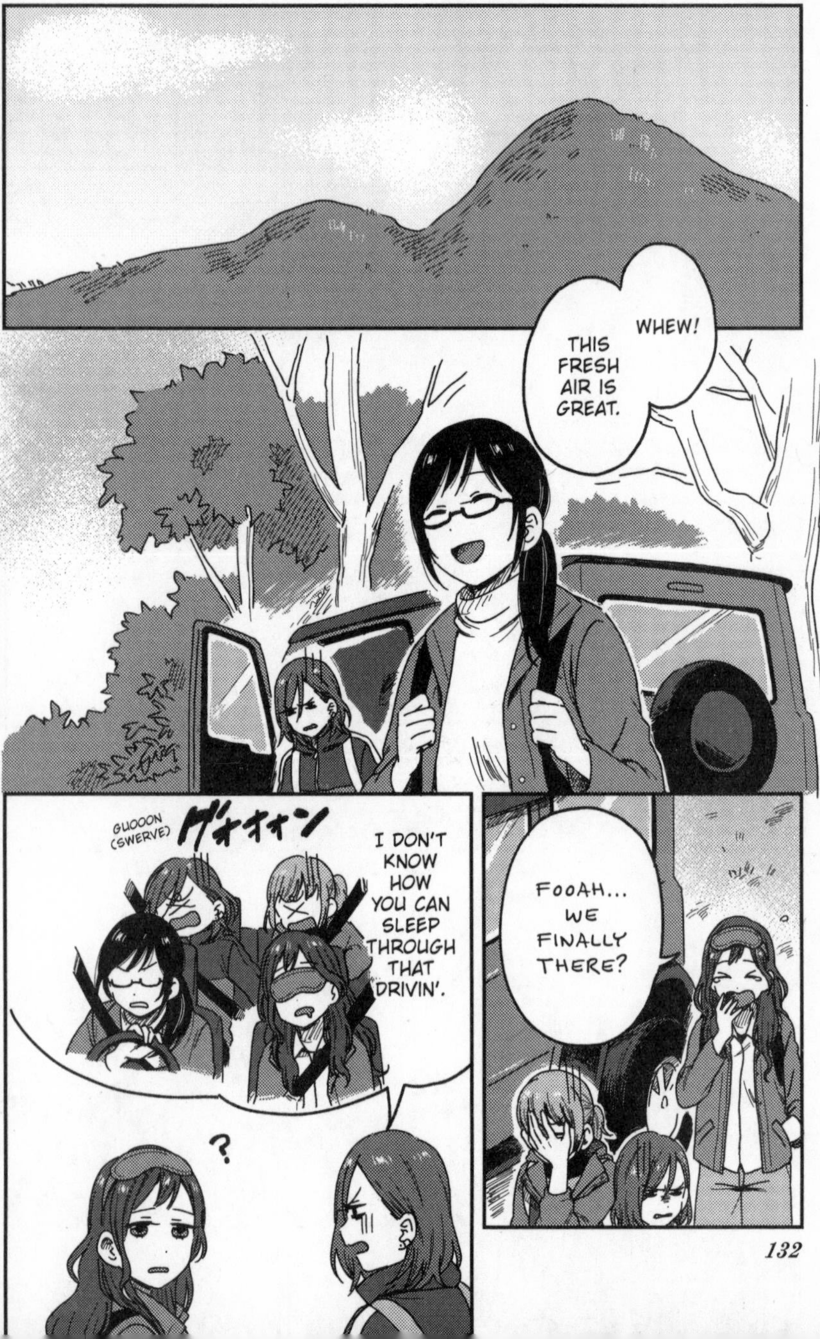
WHEW!
THIS FRESH AIR IS GREAT.
FOOAH... WE FINALLY THERE?
GUOOON (SWERVE)
ヴォオォン
I DON'T KNOW HOW YOU CAN SLEEP THROUGH THAT DRIVIN'.
?

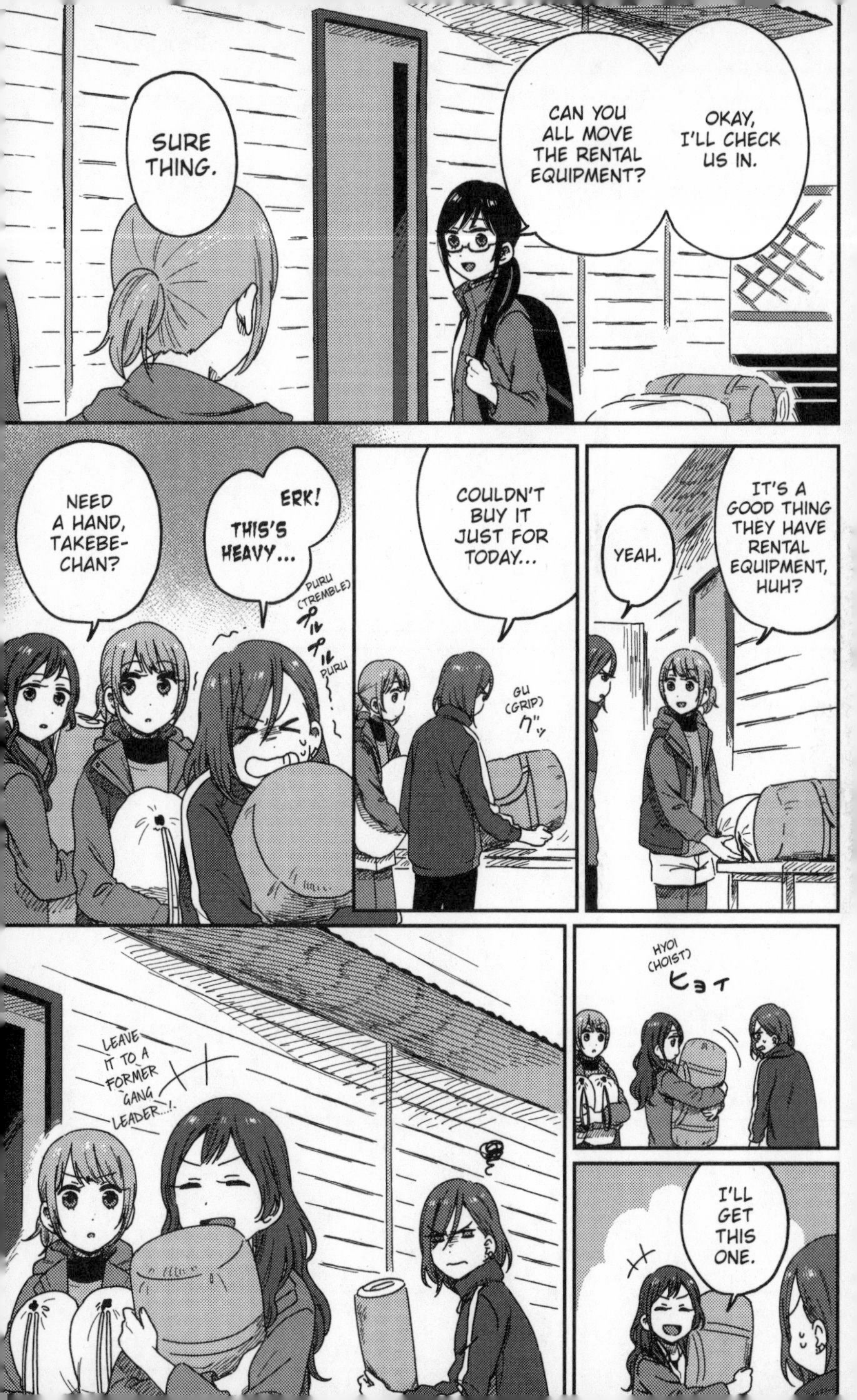
OKAY, I'LL CHECK US IN.
CAN YOU ALL MOVE THE RENTAL EQUIPMENT?
SURE THING.
IT'S A GOOD THING THEY HAVE RENTAL EQUIPMENT, HUH?
YEAH.
COULDN'T BUY IT JUST FOR TODAY...
GU (GRIP) グッ
ERK!
THIS'S HEAVY...
PURU (TREMBLE) プルプル PURU
NEED A HAND, TAKEBE-CHAN?
HYOI (HOIST) ヒョイ
I'LL GET THIS ONE.
LEAVE IT TO A FORMER GANG LEADER...!

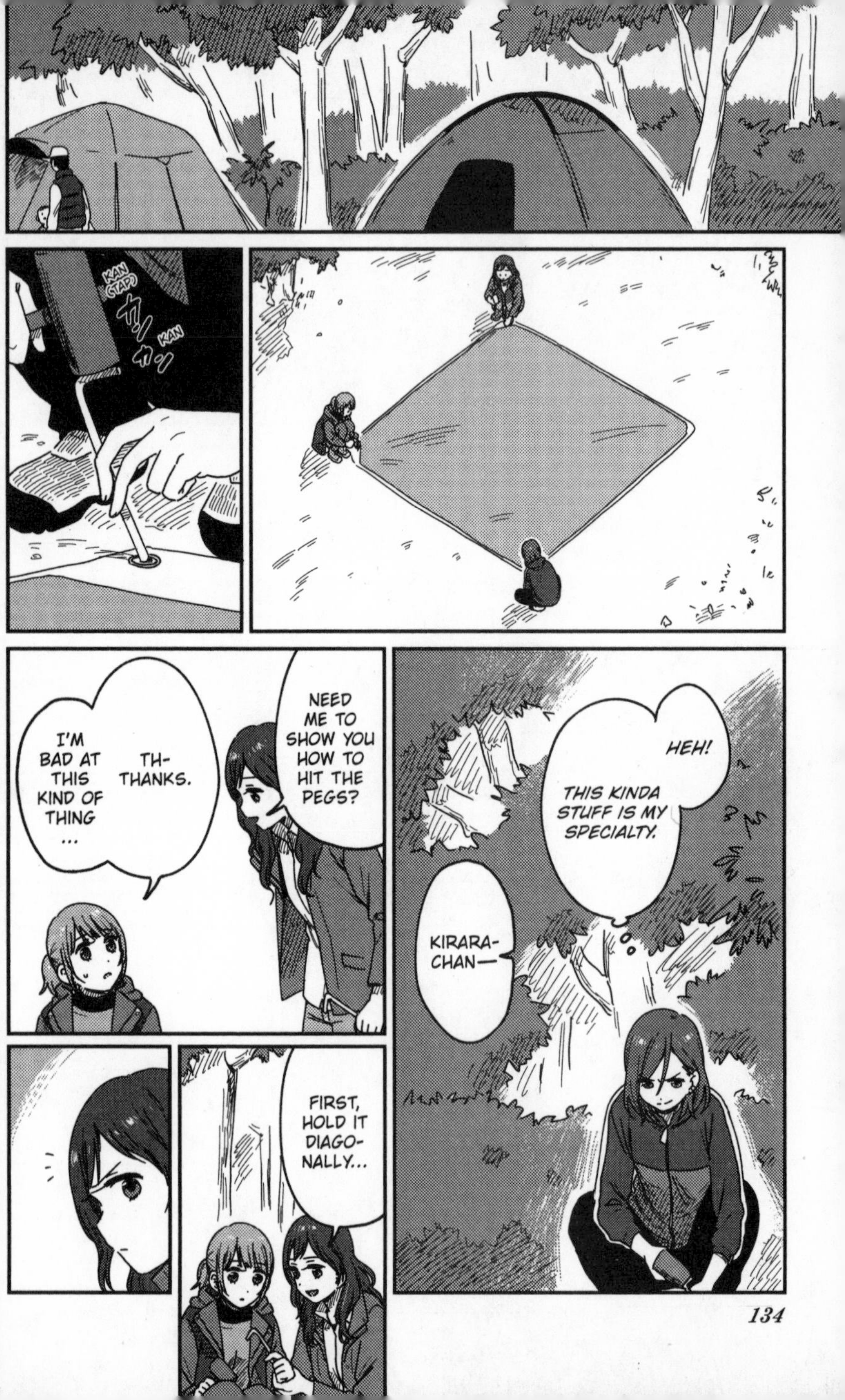
KAN (TAP)
KAN
HEH!
THIS KINDA STUFF IS MY SPECIALTY.
KIRARA-CHAN—
NEED ME TO SHOW YOU HOW TO HIT THE PEGS?
TH-THANKS.
I'M BAD AT THIS KIND OF THING ...
FIRST, HOLD IT DIAGO-NALLY...

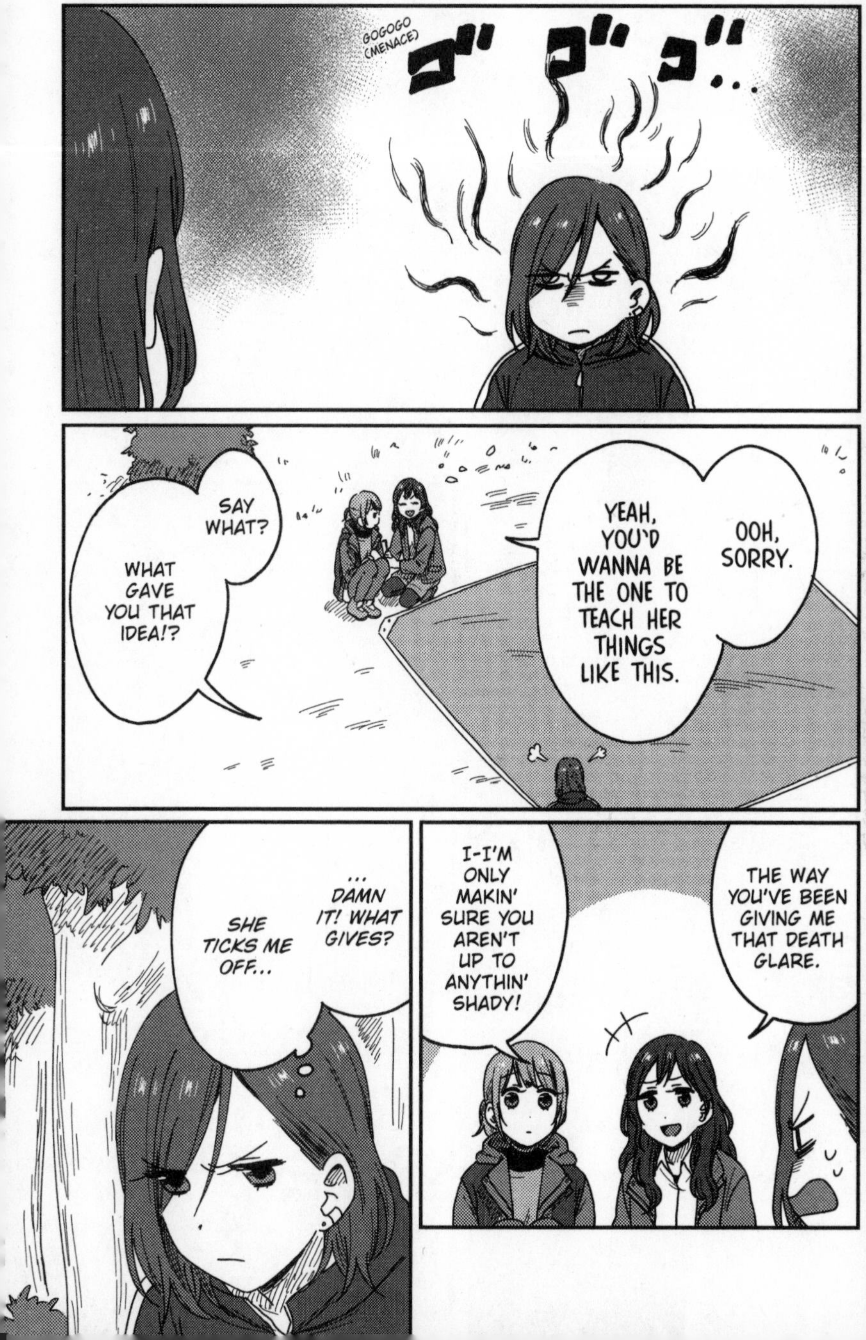
GOGOGO (MENACE)
OOH, SORRY.
YEAH, YOU'D WANNA BE THE ONE TO TEACH HER THINGS LIKE THIS.
SAY WHAT?
WHAT GAVE YOU THAT IDEA!?
THE WAY YOU'VE BEEN GIVING ME THAT DEATH GLARE.
I-I'M ONLY MAKIN' SURE YOU AREN'T UP TO ANYTHIN' SHADY!
... DAMN IT! WHAT GIVES?
SHE TICKS ME OFF...

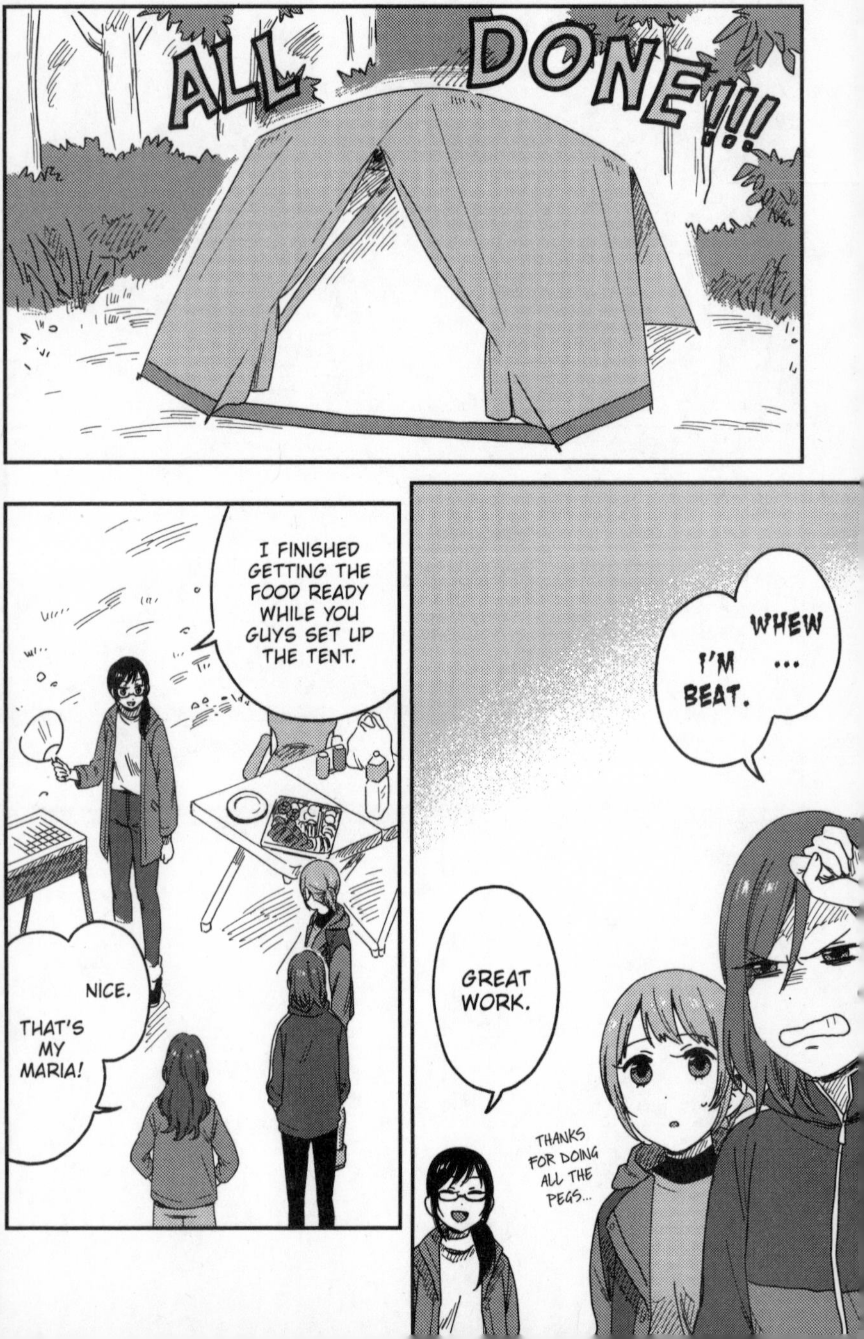
ALL DONE!!!
WHEW... I'M BEAT.
GREAT WORK.
THANKS FOR DOING ALL THE PEGS...
I FINISHED GETTING THE FOOD READY WHILE YOU GUYS SET UP THE TENT.
NICE.
THAT'S MY MARIA!

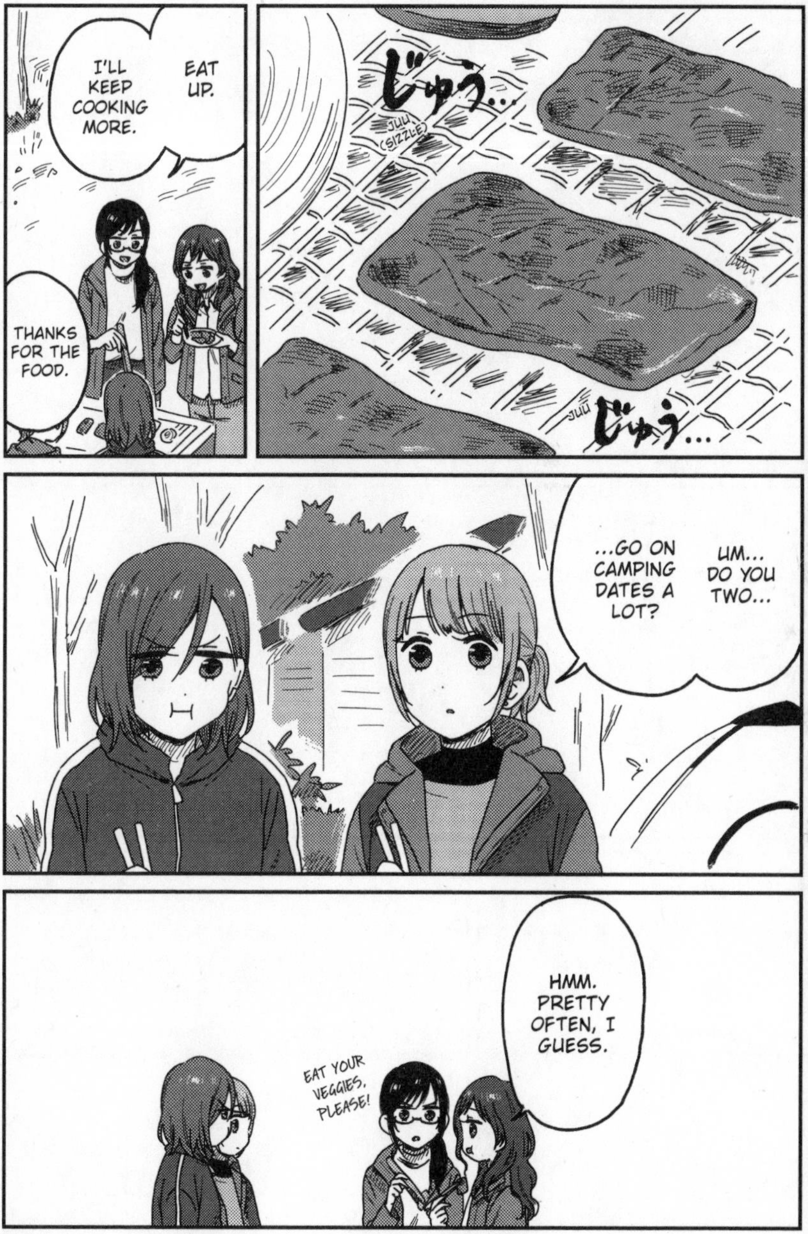
じゅう…
JUU (SIZZLE)
じゅう…
JUU
EAT UP.
I'LL KEEP COOKING MORE.
THANKS FOR THE FOOD.
UM... DO YOU TWO...
...GO ON CAMPING DATES A LOT?
HMM. PRETTY OFTEN, I GUESS.
EAT YOUR VEGGIES, PLEASE!

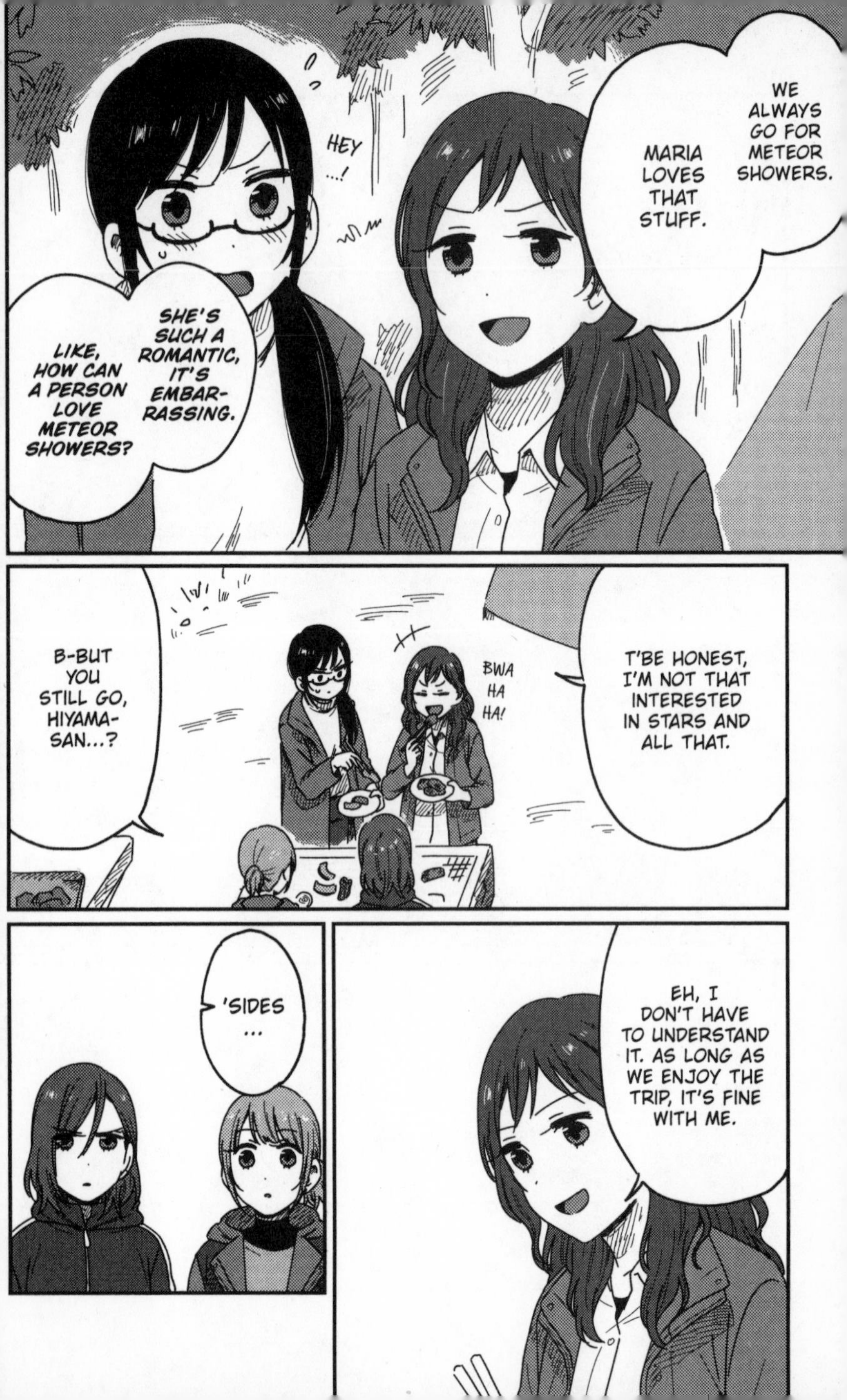
WE ALWAYS GO FOR METEOR SHOWERS.
MARIA LOVES THAT STUFF.
HEY ...!
SHE'S SUCH A ROMANTIC, IT'S EMBARRASSING.
LIKE, HOW CAN A PERSON LOVE METEOR SHOWERS?
T'BE HONEST, I'M NOT THAT INTERESTED IN STARS AND ALL THAT.
BWA HA HA!
B-BUT YOU STILL GO, HIYAMA-SAN...?
EH, I DON'T HAVE TO UNDERSTAND IT. AS LONG AS WE ENJOY THE TRIP, IT'S FINE WITH ME.
'SIDES ...

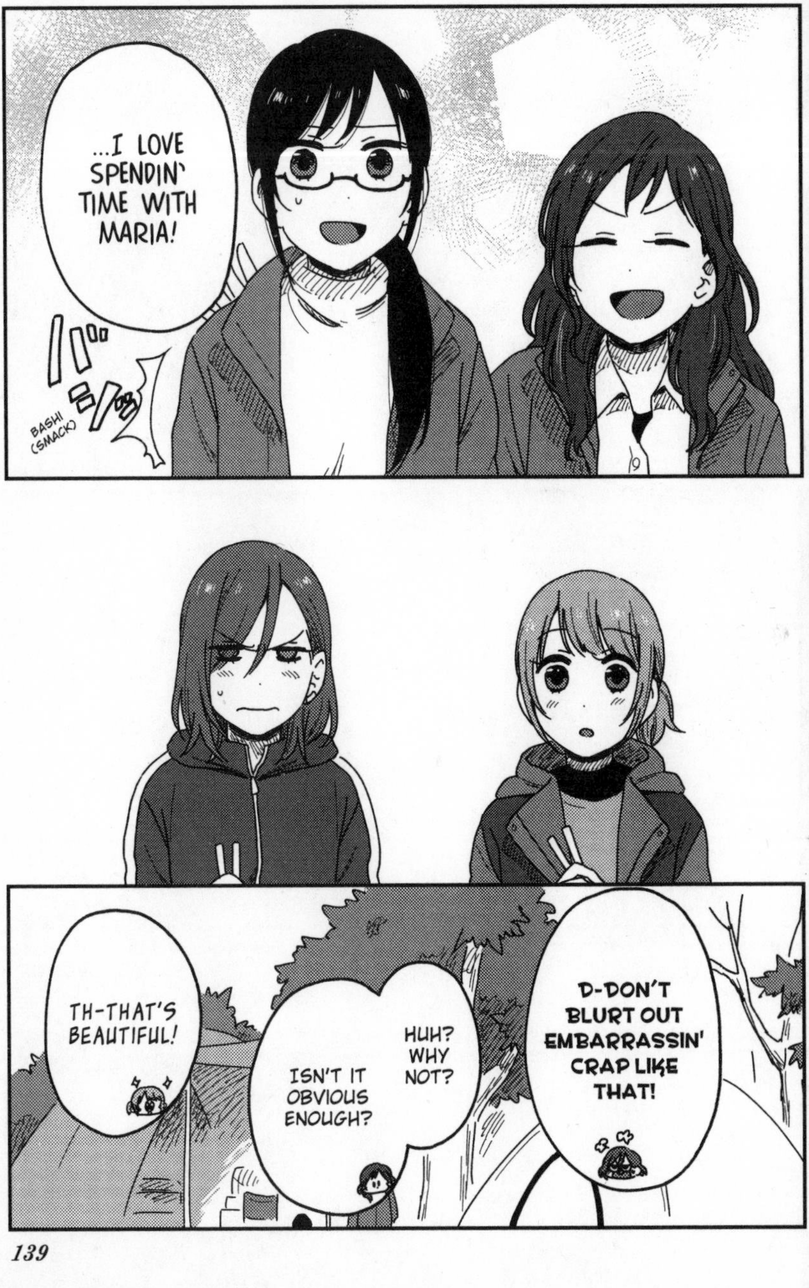
...I LOVE SPENDIN' TIME WITH MARIA!
BASHI (SMACK)
D-DON'T BLURT OUT EMBARRASSIN' CRAP LIKE THAT!
HUH? WHY NOT?
ISN'T IT OBVIOUS ENOUGH?
TH-THAT'S BEAUTIFUL!

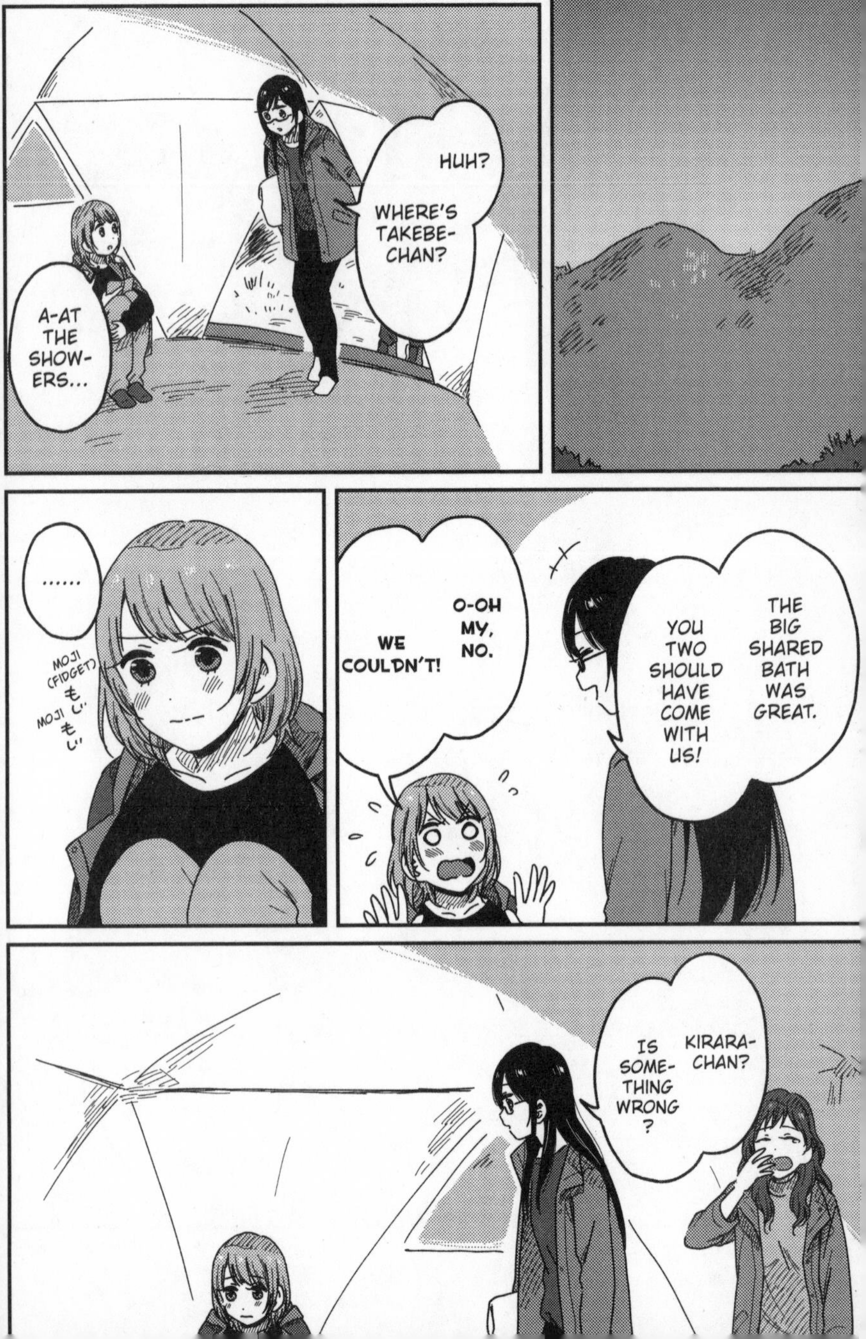
HUH?
WHERE'S TAKEBE-CHAN?
A-AT THE SHOWERS...
THE BIG SHARED BATH WAS GREAT.
YOU TWO SHOULD HAVE COME WITH US!
O-OH MY, NO.
WE COULDN'T!
......
MOJI (FIDGET) もじもじ MOJI
KIRARA-CHAN?
IS SOMETHING WRONG?

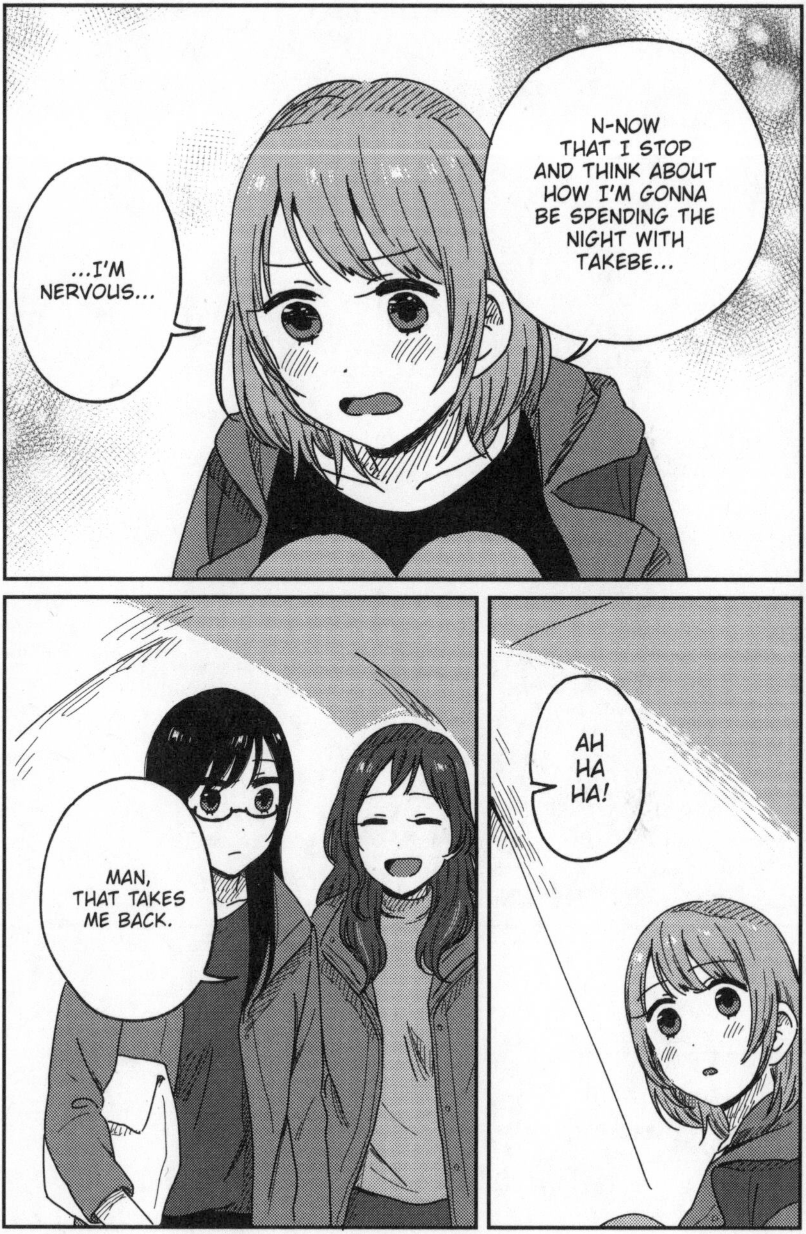
N-NOW THAT I STOP AND THINK ABOUT HOW I'M GONNA BE SPENDING THE NIGHT WITH TAKEBE...
...I'M NERVOUS...
AH HA HA!
MAN, THAT TAKES ME BACK.

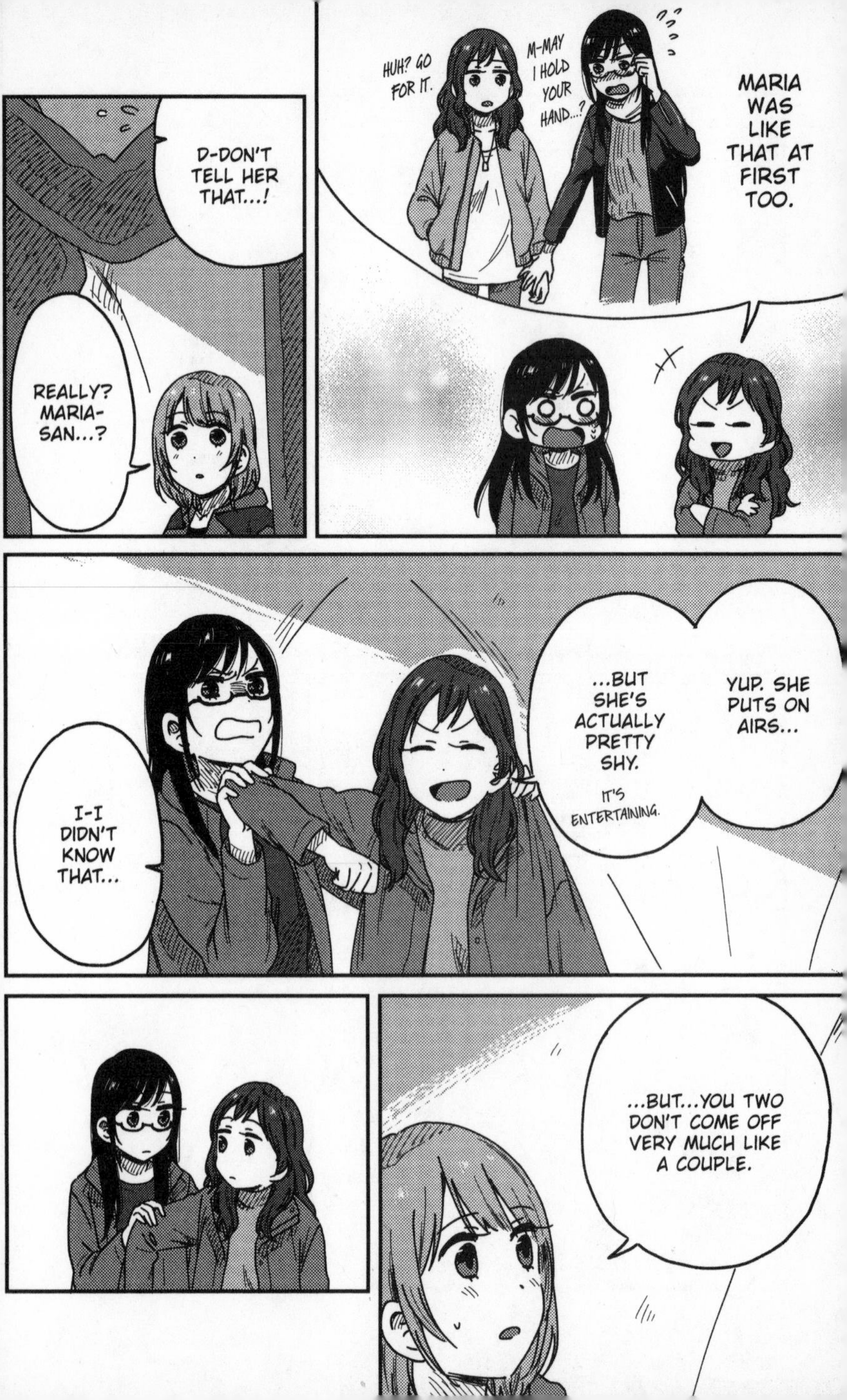
M-MAY I HOLD YOUR HAND...?
HUH? GO FOR IT.
MARIA WAS LIKE THAT AT FIRST TOO.
D-DON'T TELL HER THAT...!
REALLY? MARIA-SAN...?
YUP. SHE PUTS ON AIRS...
...BUT SHE'S ACTUALLY PRETTY SHY.
IT'S ENTERTAINING.
I-I DIDN'T KNOW THAT...
...BUT...YOU TWO DON'T COME OFF VERY MUCH LIKE A COUPLE.

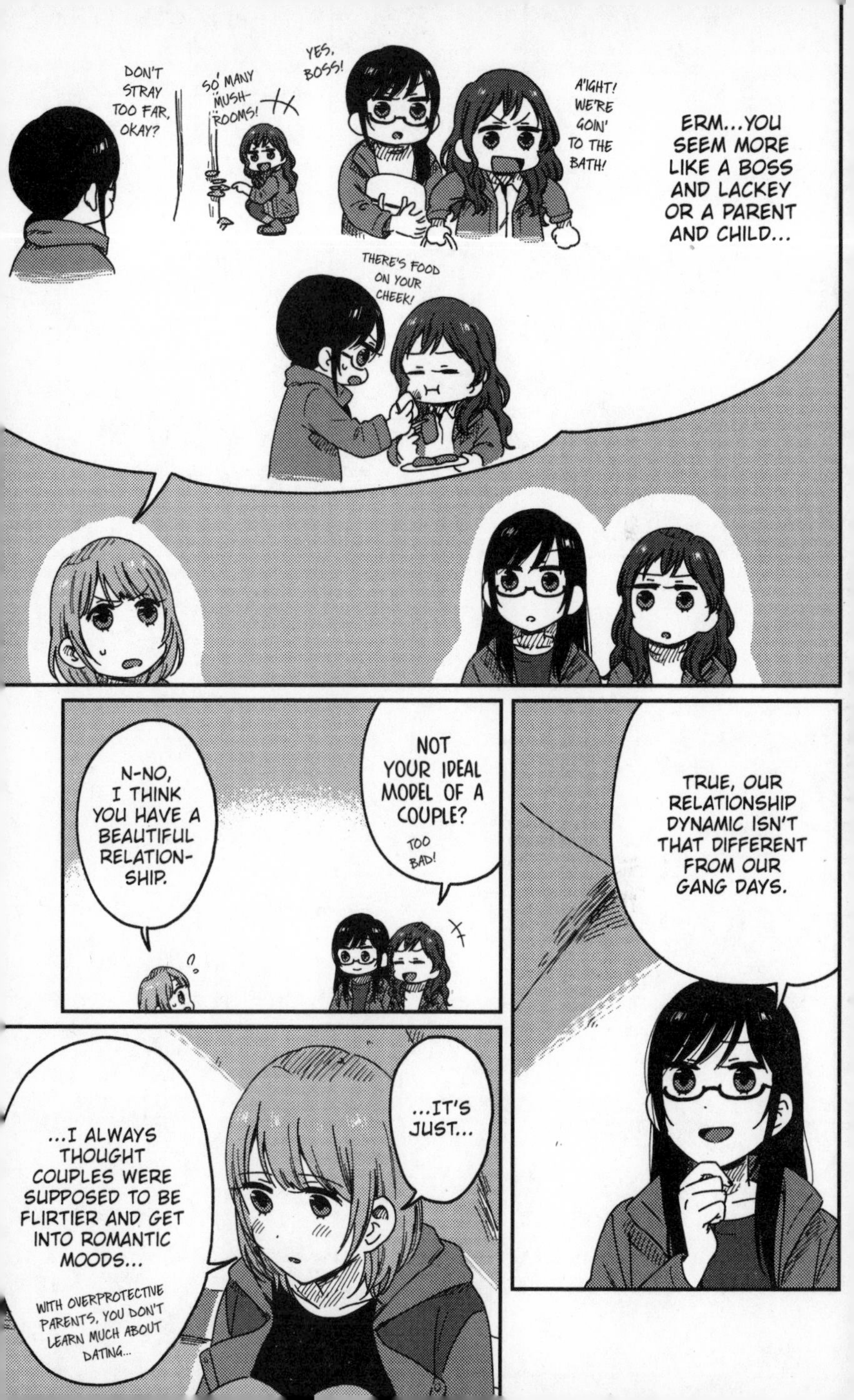
ERM...YOU SEEM MORE LIKE A BOSS AND LACKEY OR A PARENT AND CHILD...
A'IGHT! WE'RE GOIN' TO THE BATH!
YES, BOSS!
SO MANY MUSH-ROOMS!
DON'T STRAY TOO FAR, OKAY?
THERE'S FOOD ON YOUR CHEEK!
TRUE, OUR RELATIONSHIP DYNAMIC ISN'T THAT DIFFERENT FROM OUR GANG DAYS.
NOT YOUR IDEAL MODEL OF A COUPLE?
TOO BAD!
N-NO, I THINK YOU HAVE A BEAUTIFUL RELATION-SHIP.
...IT'S JUST...
...I ALWAYS THOUGHT COUPLES WERE SUPPOSED TO BE FLIRTIER AND GET INTO ROMANTIC MOODS...
WITH OVERPROTECTIVE PARENTS, YOU DON'T LEARN MUCH ABOUT DATING...

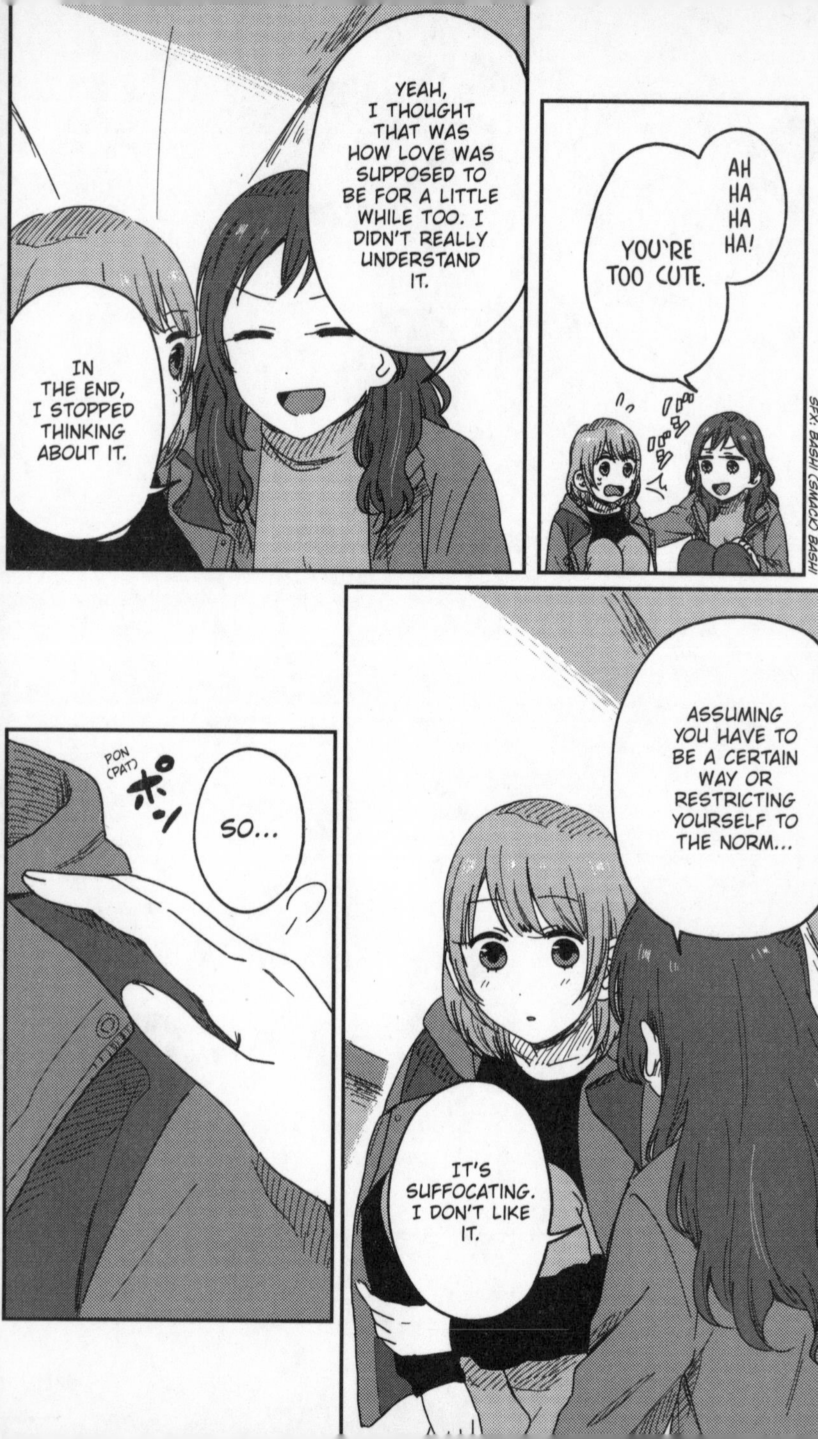
AH HA HA HA!
YOU'RE TOO CUTE.
SFX: BASHI (SMACK) BASHI
YEAH, I THOUGHT THAT WAS HOW LOVE WAS SUPPOSED TO BE FOR A LITTLE WHILE TOO. I DIDN'T REALLY UNDERSTAND IT.
IN THE END, I STOPPED THINKING ABOUT IT.
ASSUMING YOU HAVE TO BE A CERTAIN WAY OR RESTRICTING YOURSELF TO THE NORM...
IT'S SUFFOCATING. I DON'T LIKE IT.
PON (PAT)
SO...

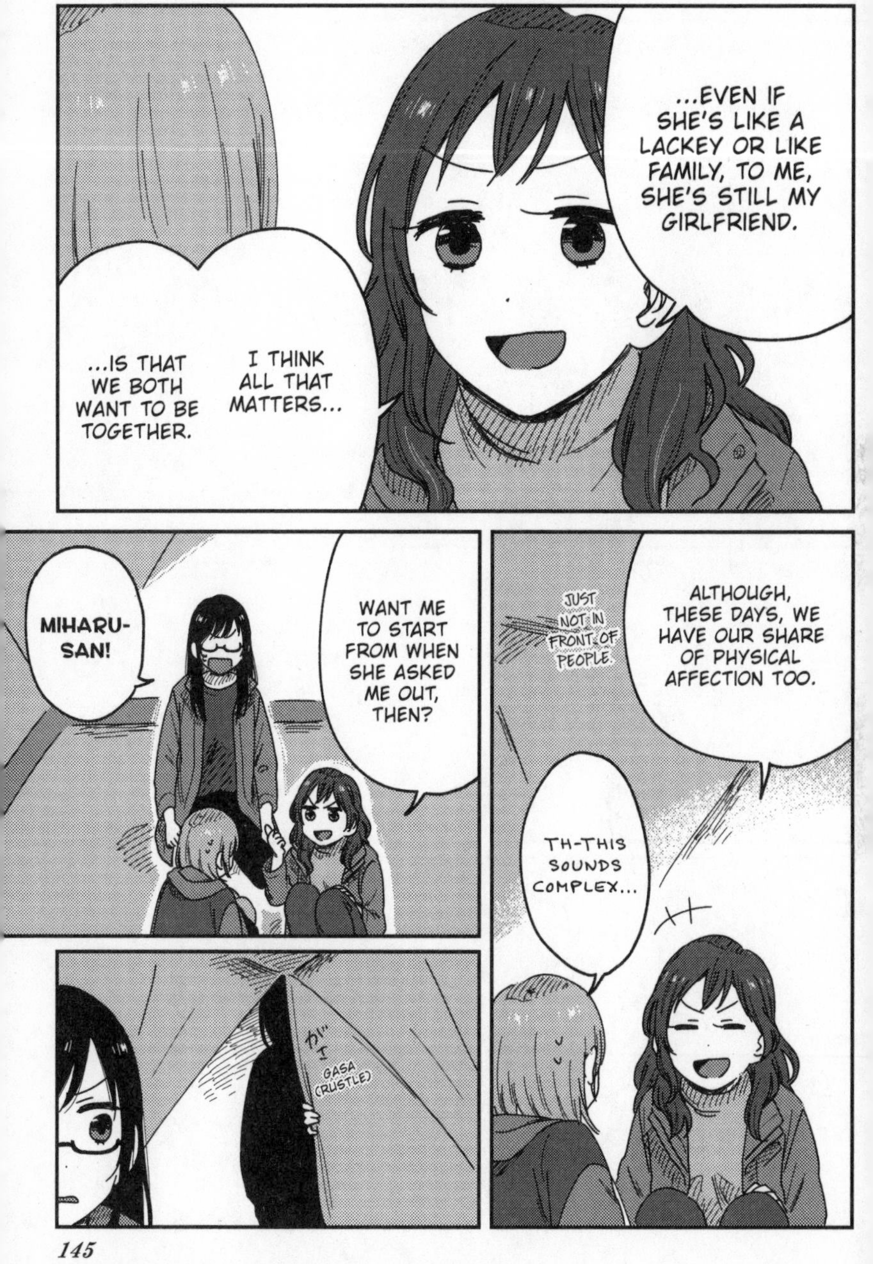
...EVEN IF SHE'S LIKE A LACKEY OR LIKE FAMILY, TO ME, SHE'S STILL MY GIRLFRIEND.
I THINK ALL THAT MATTERS...
...IS THAT WE BOTH WANT TO BE TOGETHER.
ALTHOUGH, THESE DAYS, WE HAVE OUR SHARE OF PHYSICAL AFFECTION TOO.
JUST NOT IN FRONT OF PEOPLE.
TH-THIS SOUNDS COMPLEX...
WANT ME TO START FROM WHEN SHE ASKED ME OUT, THEN?
MIHARU-SAN!
ガサ
GASA (RUSTLE)

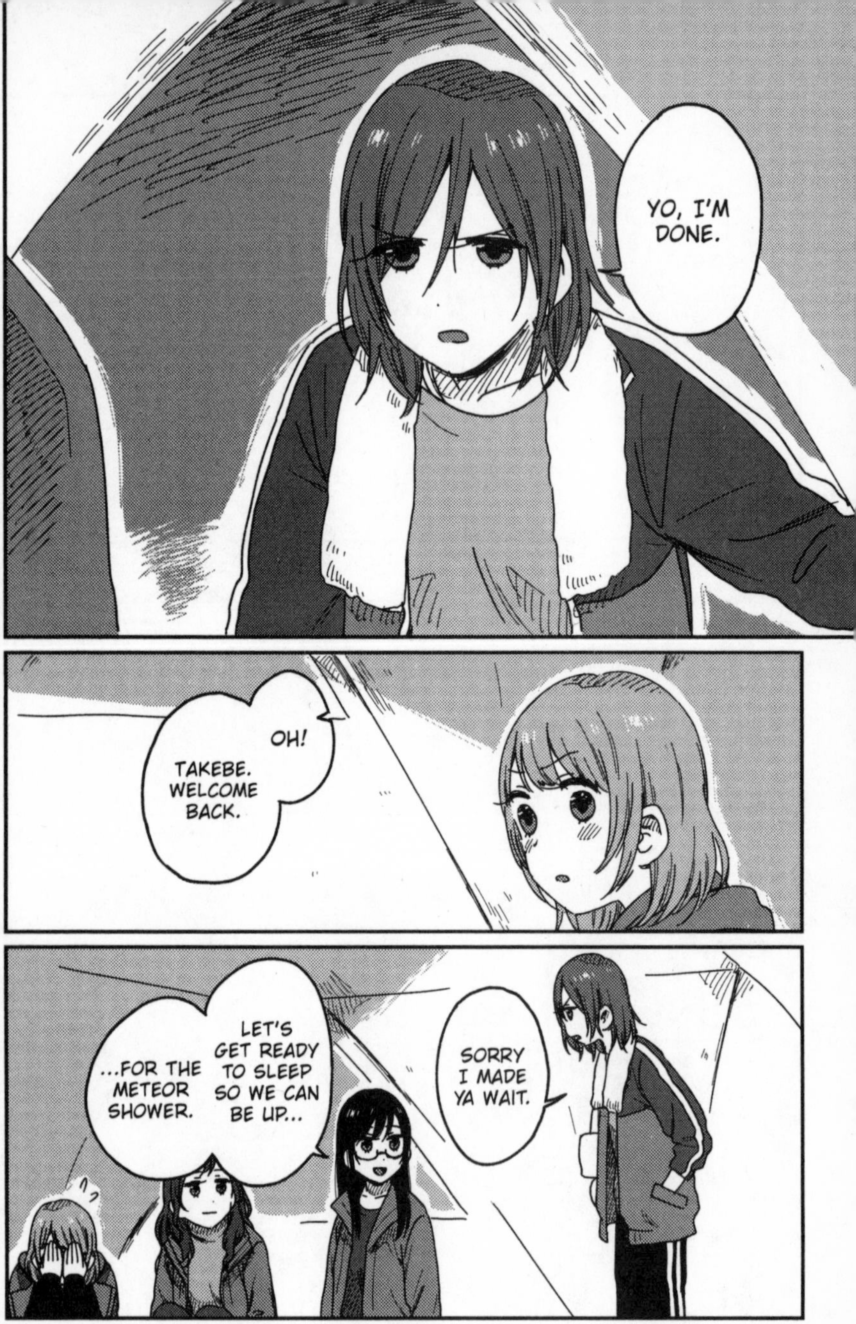
YO, I'M DONE.
OH! TAKEBE. WELCOME BACK.
SORRY I MADE YA WAIT.
LET'S GET READY TO SLEEP SO WE CAN BE UP...
...FOR THE METEOR SHOWER.

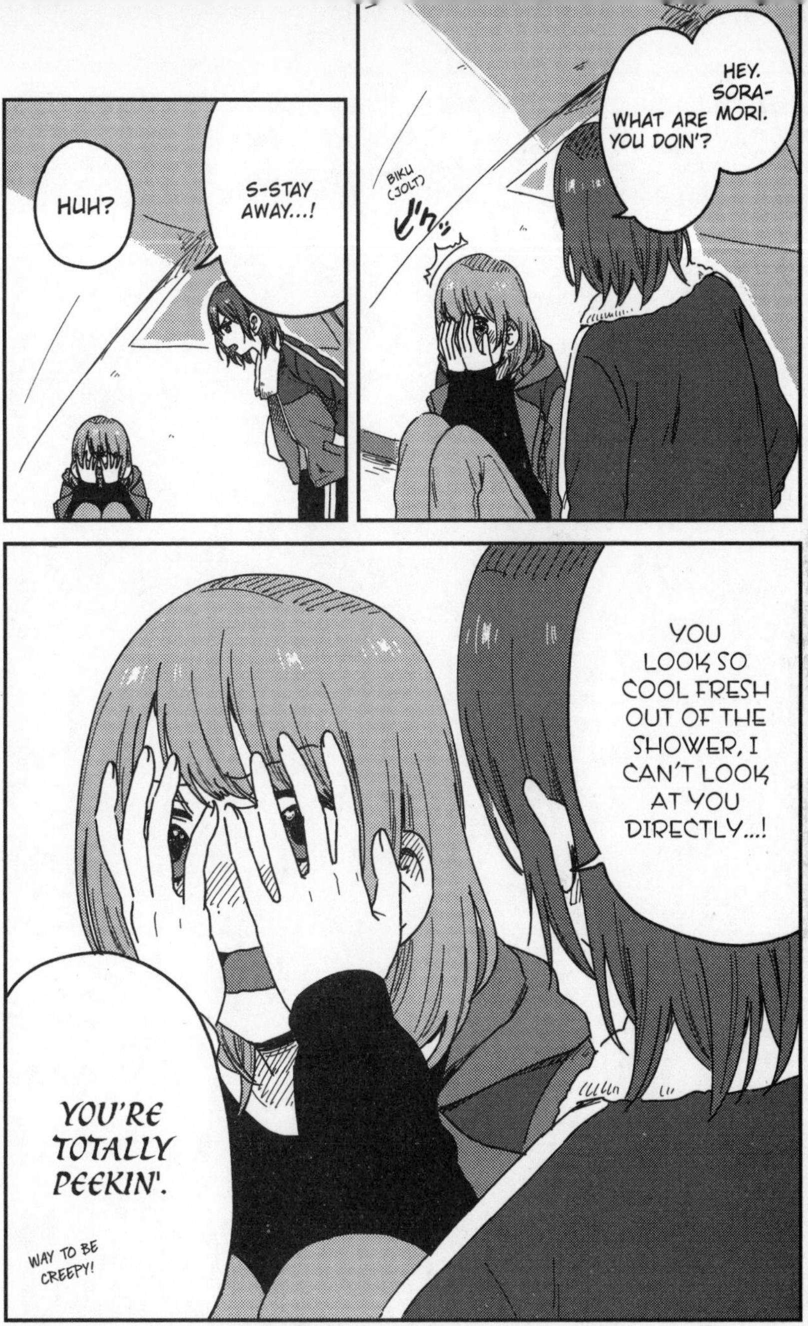
HEY. SORA-MORI. WHAT ARE YOU DOIN'?
BIKU (JOLT)
S-STAY AWAY...!
HUH?
YOU LOOK SO COOL FRESH OUT OF THE SHOWER, I CAN'T LOOK AT YOU DIRECTLY...!
YOU'RE TOTALLY PEEKIN'.
WAY TO BE CREEPY!

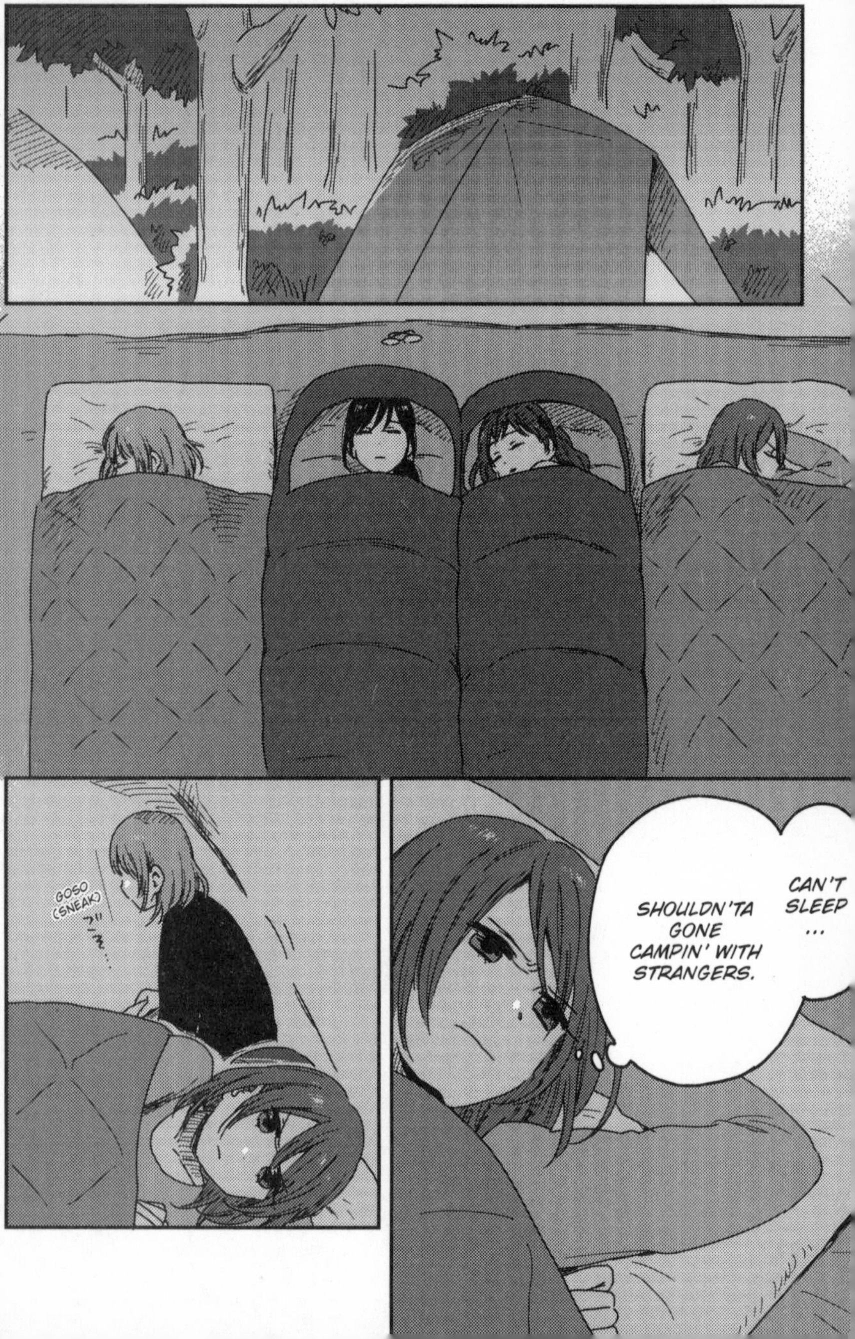
CAN'T SLEEP ...
SHOULDN'TA GONE CAMPIN' WITH STRANGERS.
GOSO (SNEAK)

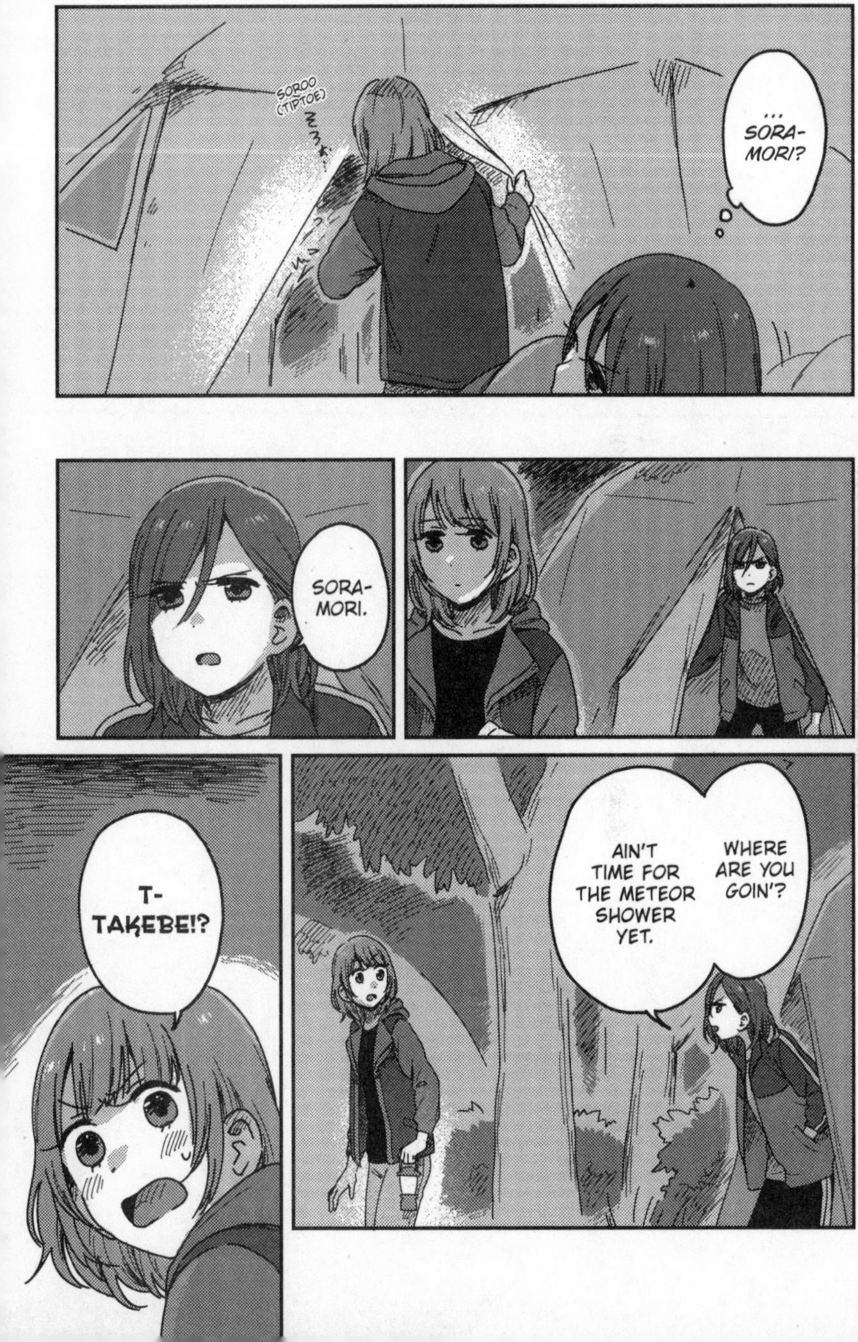
... SORA-MORI?
SOROO (TIPTOE)
SORA-MORI.
WHERE ARE YOU GOIN'?
AIN'T TIME FOR THE METEOR SHOWER YET.
T-TAKEBE!?

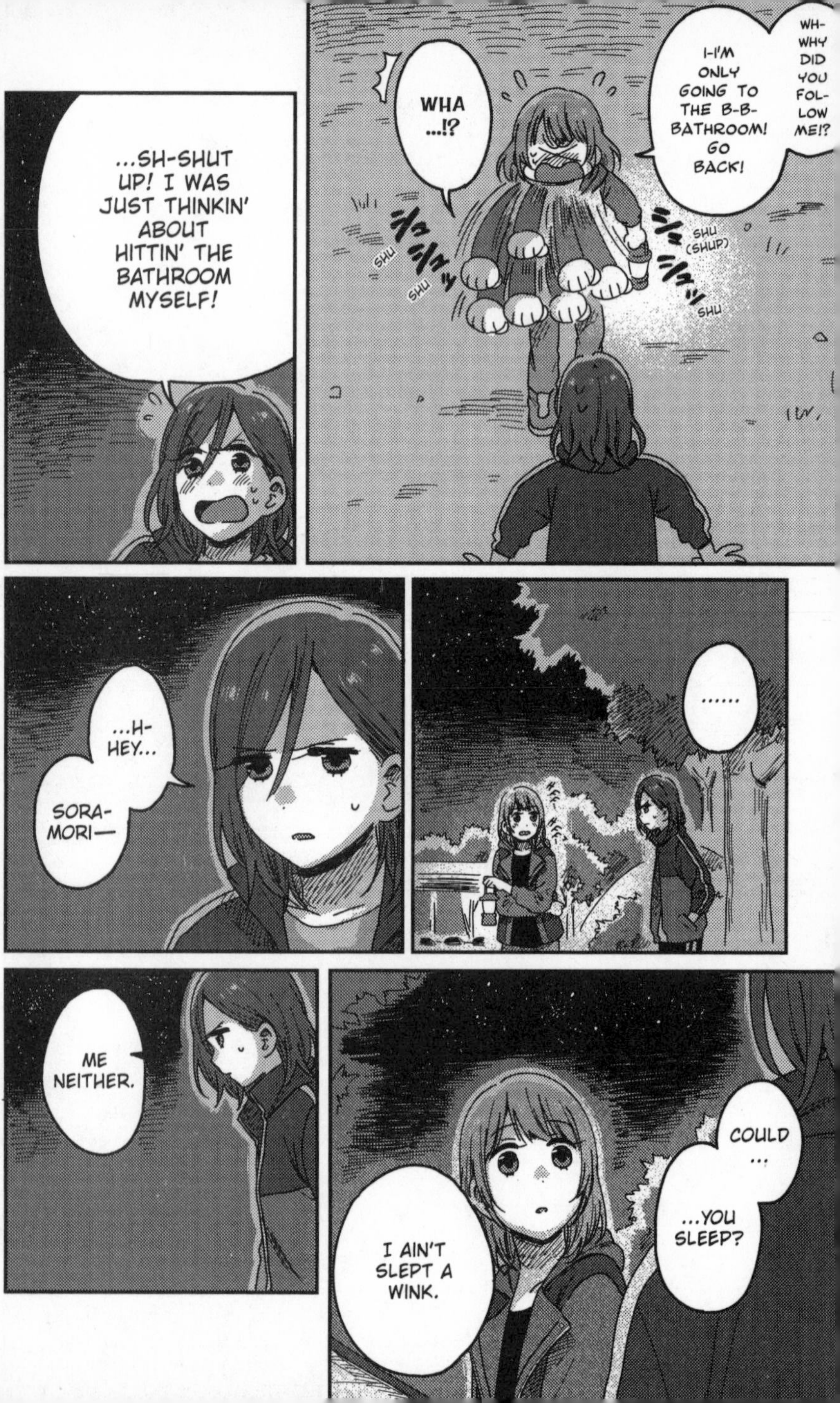
WH-WHY DID YOU FOL-LOW ME!?
I-I'M ONLY GOING TO THE B-B-BATHROOM! GO BACK!
SHU (SHUP)
SHU
WHA ...!?
SHU
SHU
...SH-SHUT UP! I WAS JUST THINKIN' ABOUT HITTIN' THE BATHROOM MYSELF!
......
...H-HEY...
SORA-MORI—
COULD ...
...YOU SLEEP?
I AIN'T SLEPT A WINK.
ME NEITHER.

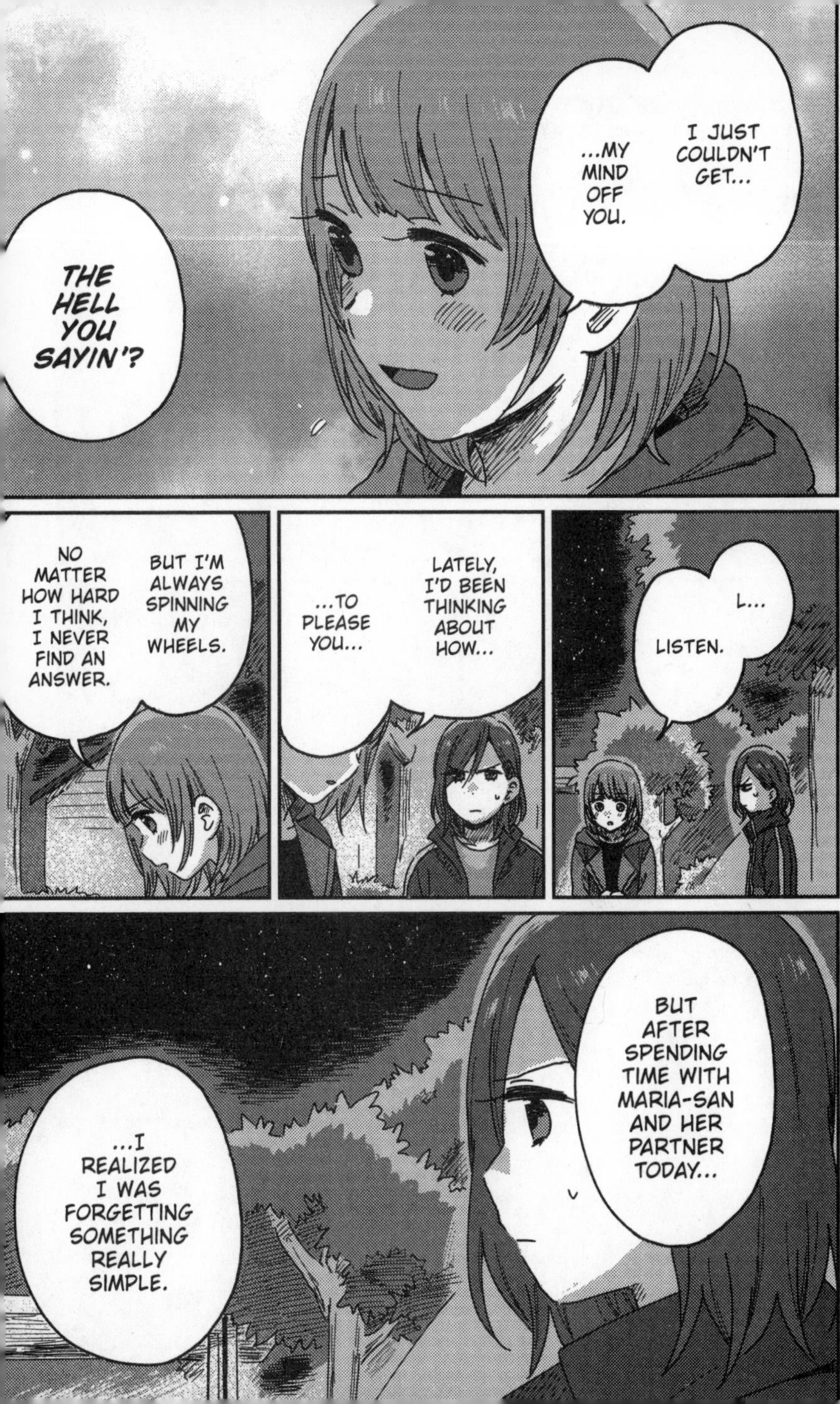
I JUST COULDN'T GET...
...MY MIND OFF YOU.
THE HELL YOU SAYIN'?
I...
LISTEN.
LATELY, I'D BEEN THINKING ABOUT HOW...
...TO PLEASE YOU...
BUT I'M ALWAYS SPINNING MY WHEELS.
NO MATTER HOW HARD I THINK, I NEVER FIND AN ANSWER.
BUT AFTER SPENDING TIME WITH MARIA-SAN AND HER PARTNER TODAY...
...I REALIZED I WAS FORGETTING SOMETHING REALLY SIMPLE.

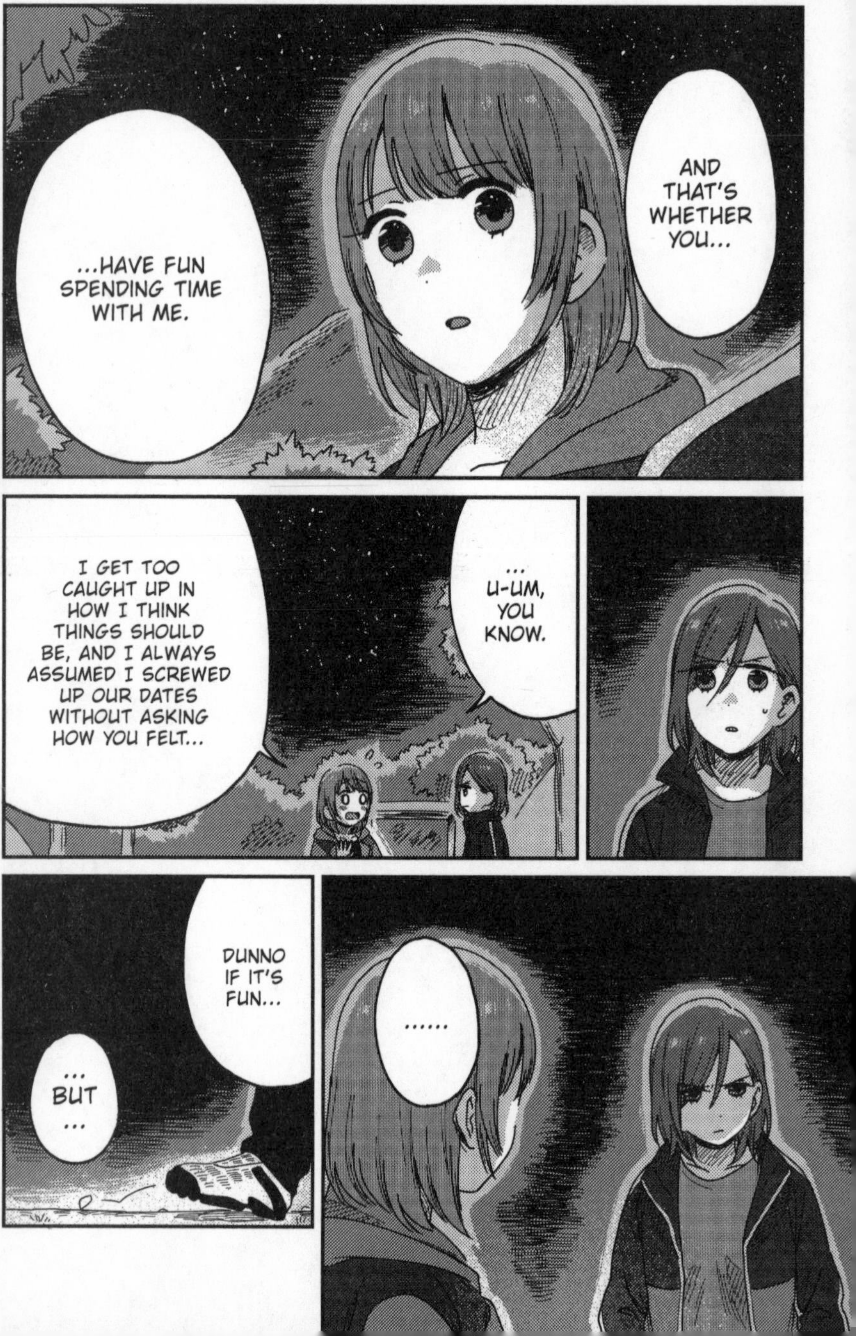
AND THAT'S WHETHER YOU...
...HAVE FUN SPENDING TIME WITH ME.
... U-UM, YOU KNOW.
I GET TOO CAUGHT UP IN HOW I THINK THINGS SHOULD BE, AND I ALWAYS ASSUMED I SCREWED UP OUR DATES WITHOUT ASKING HOW YOU FELT...
......
DUNNO IF IT'S FUN...
... BUT ...

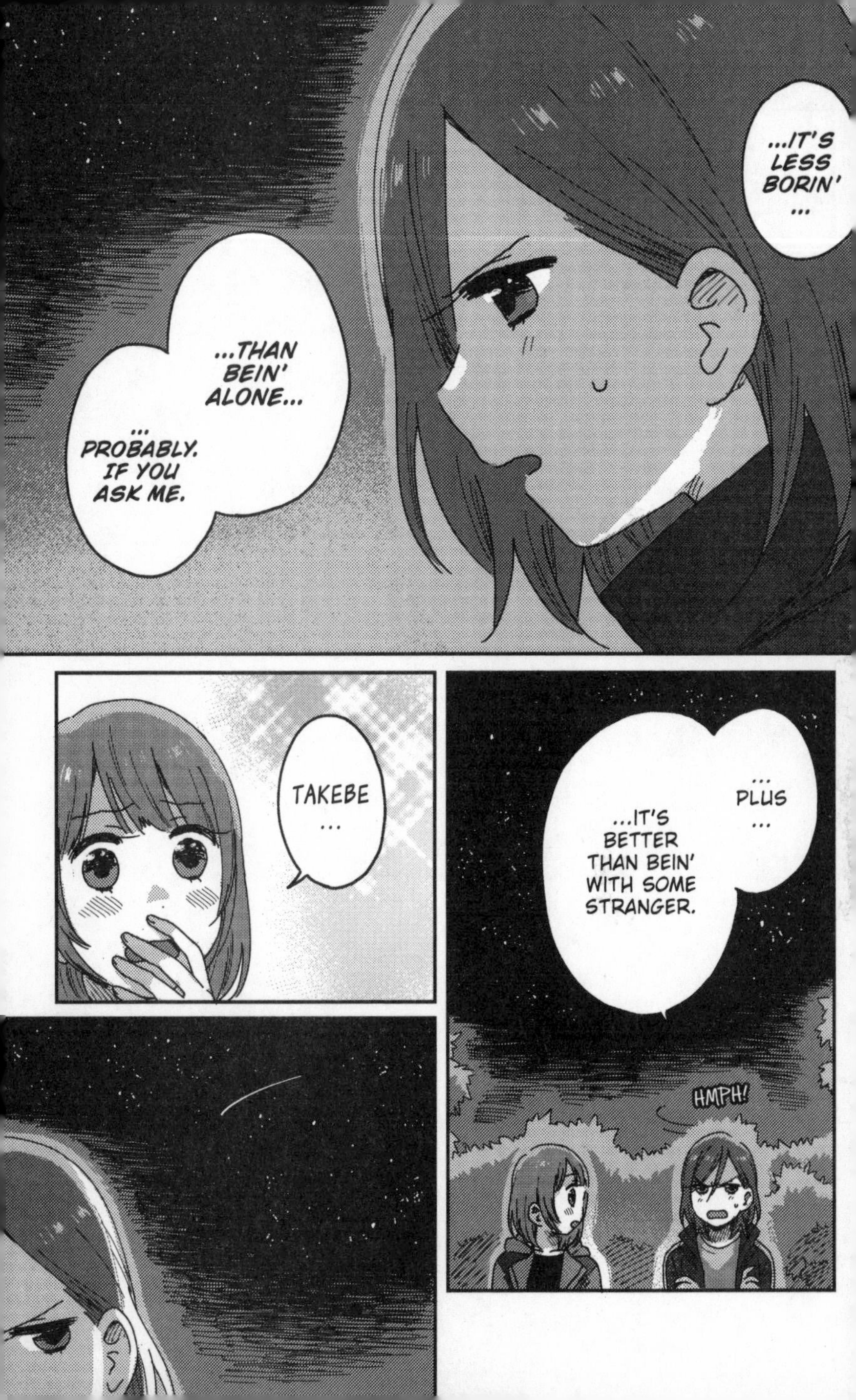
...IT'S LESS BORIN' ...
...THAN BEIN' ALONE...
... PROBABLY. IF YOU ASK ME.
... PLUS ...
...IT'S BETTER THAN BEIN' WITH SOME STRANGER.
HMPH!
TAKEBE ...

...THE METEOR SHOWER!?

IS IT FROM...

LOOK.

A SHOOTIN' STAR.

I-ISN'T THIS THE PERFECT SITUATION...!?

AH!

!?

BIKU (FLINCH)

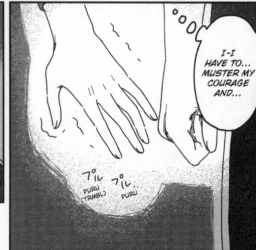

I-I HAVE TO... MUSTER MY COURAGE AND...

ﾌﾟﾙ (TRMBL)

ﾌﾟﾙ PURU

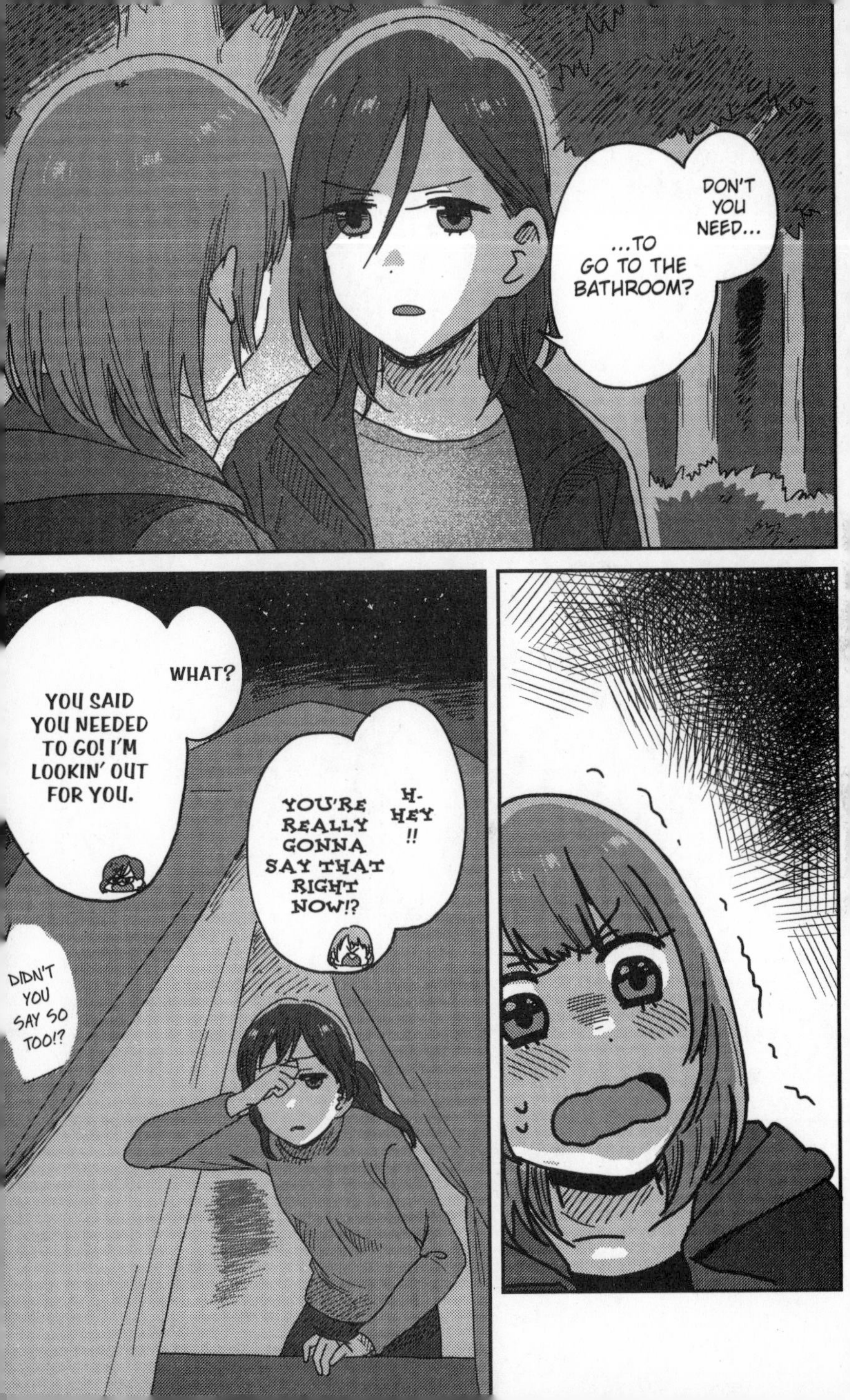
DON'T YOU NEED...
...TO GO TO THE BATHROOM?
WHAT?
YOU SAID YOU NEEDED TO GO! I'M LOOKIN' OUT FOR YOU.
H-HEY!!
YOU'RE REALLY GONNA SAY THAT RIGHT NOW!?
DIDN'T YOU SAY SO TOO!?

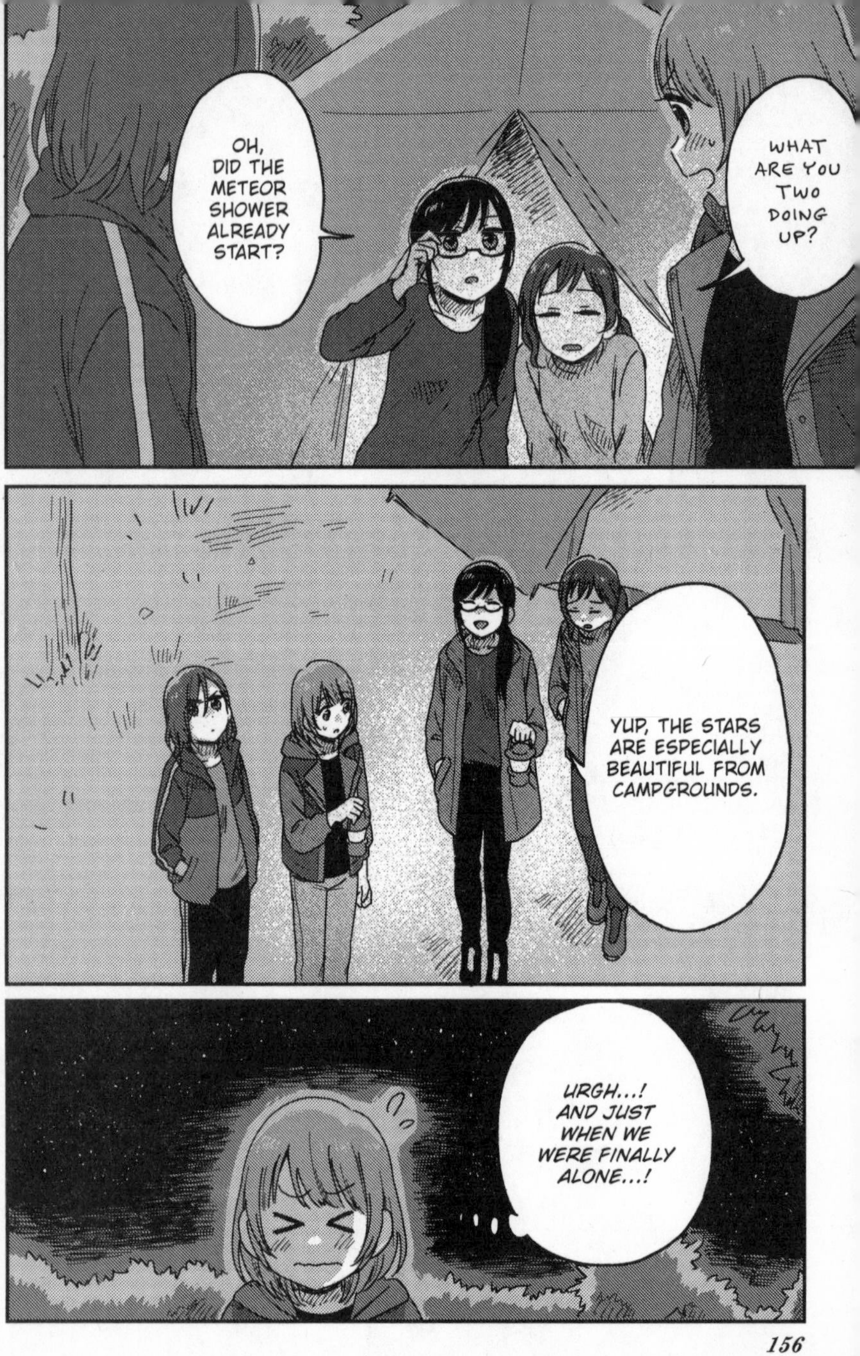
WHAT ARE YOU TWO DOING UP?
OH, DID THE METEOR SHOWER ALREADY START?
YUP, THE STARS ARE ESPECIALLY BEAUTIFUL FROM CAMPGROUNDS.
URGH...! AND JUST WHEN WE WERE FINALLY ALONE...!

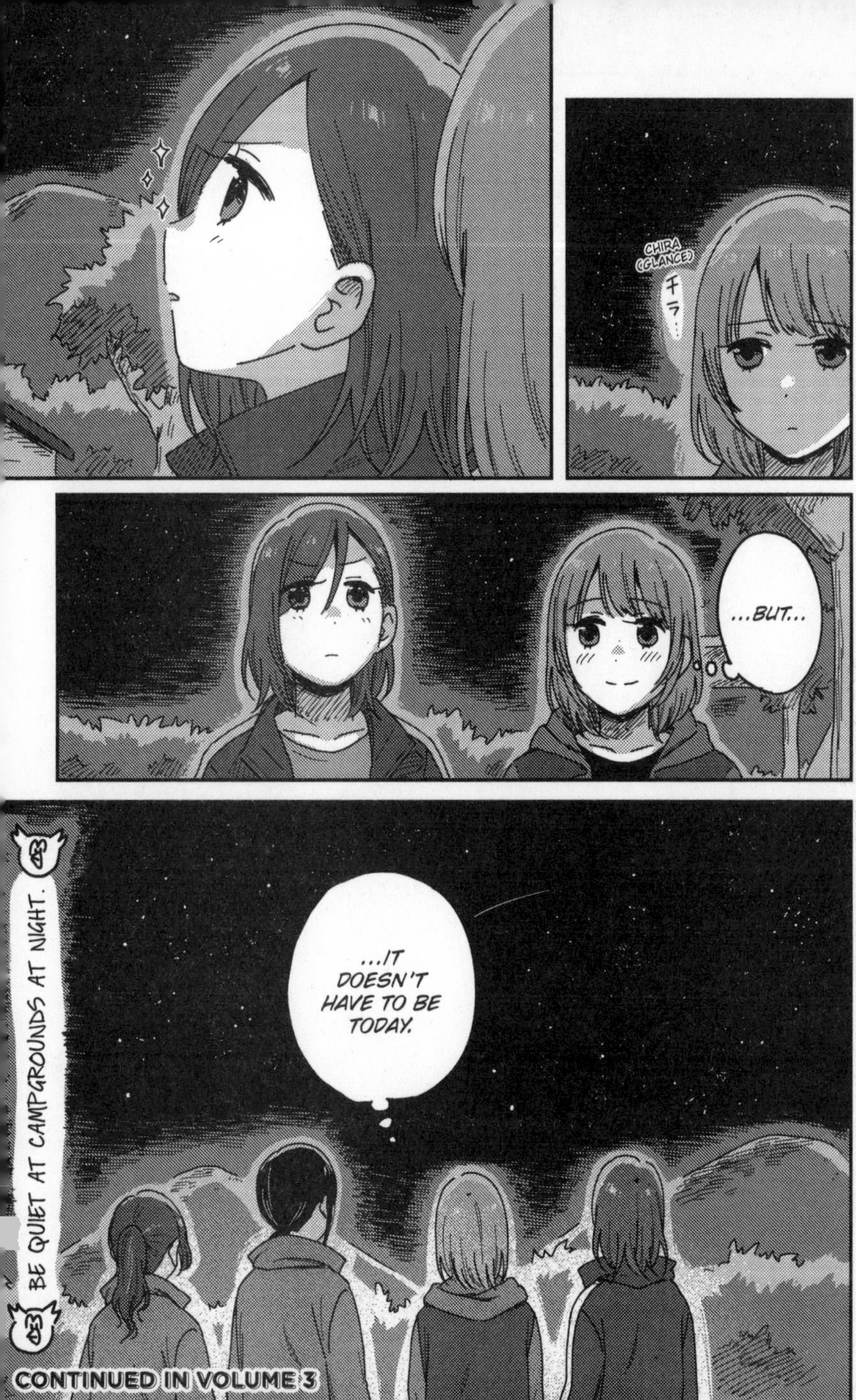
CHIRA (GLANCE)
チラ…
…BUT…
…IT DOESN'T HAVE TO BE TODAY.
BE QUIET AT CAMPGROUNDS AT NIGHT.

CONTINUED IN VOLUME 3

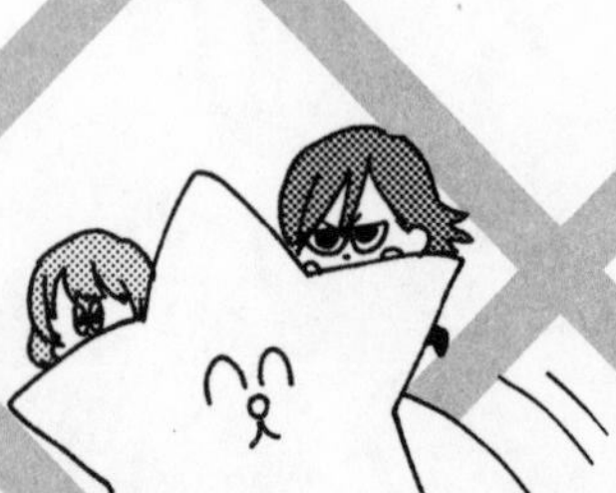

Catch These Hands!

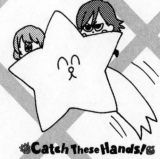

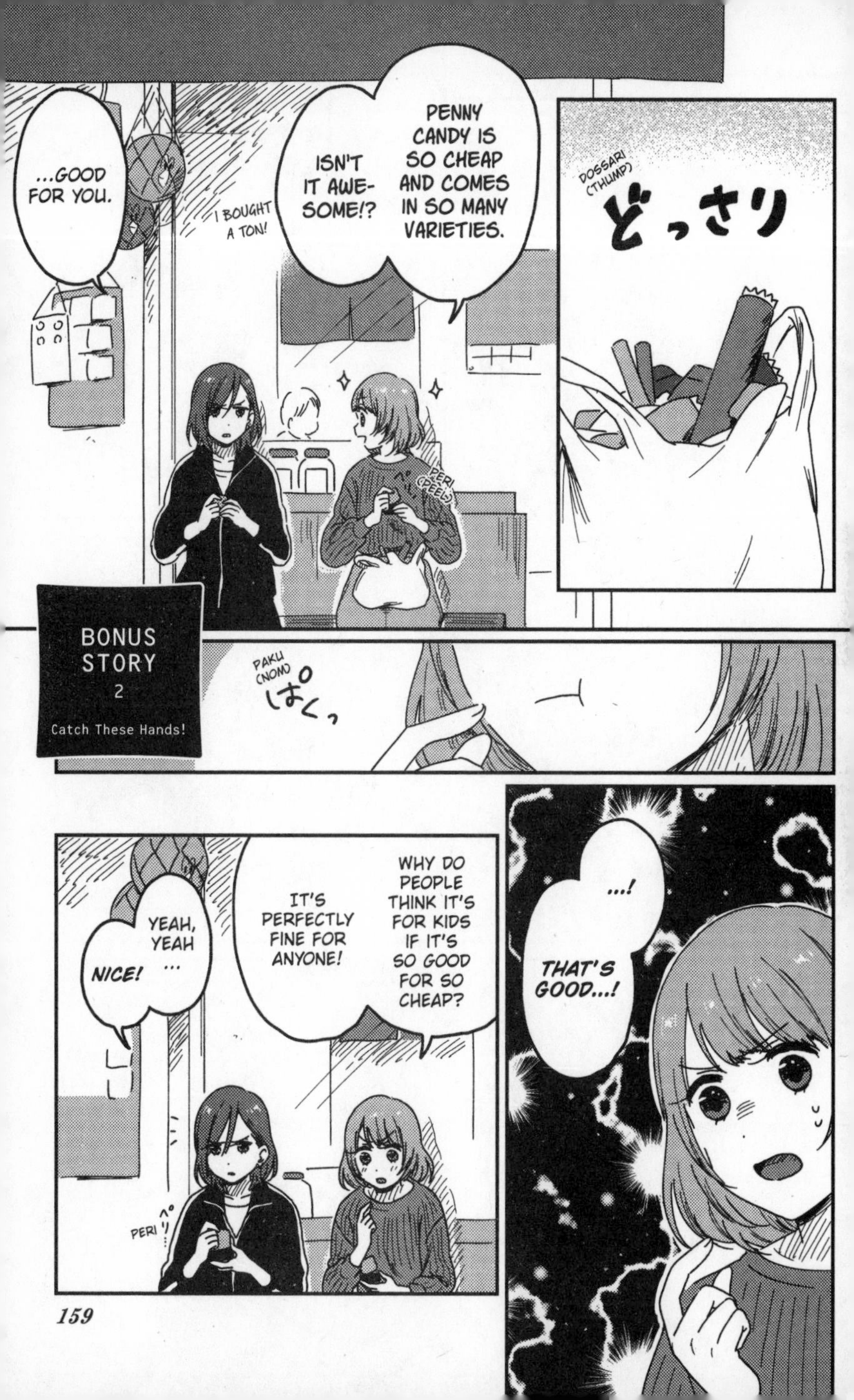
DOSSARI (THUMP)
どっさり
PENNY CANDY IS SO CHEAP AND COMES IN SO MANY VARIETIES.
ISN'T IT AWE-SOME!?
I BOUGHT A TON!
...GOOD FOR YOU.
PERI (PEEL)
BONUS STORY 2
Catch These Hands!
PAKU (NOM)
ぱくっ
...!
THAT'S GOOD...!
WHY DO PEOPLE THINK IT'S FOR KIDS IF IT'S SO GOOD FOR SO CHEAP?
IT'S PERFECTLY FINE FOR ANYONE!
YEAH, YEAH ...
NICE!
PERI
ペリ

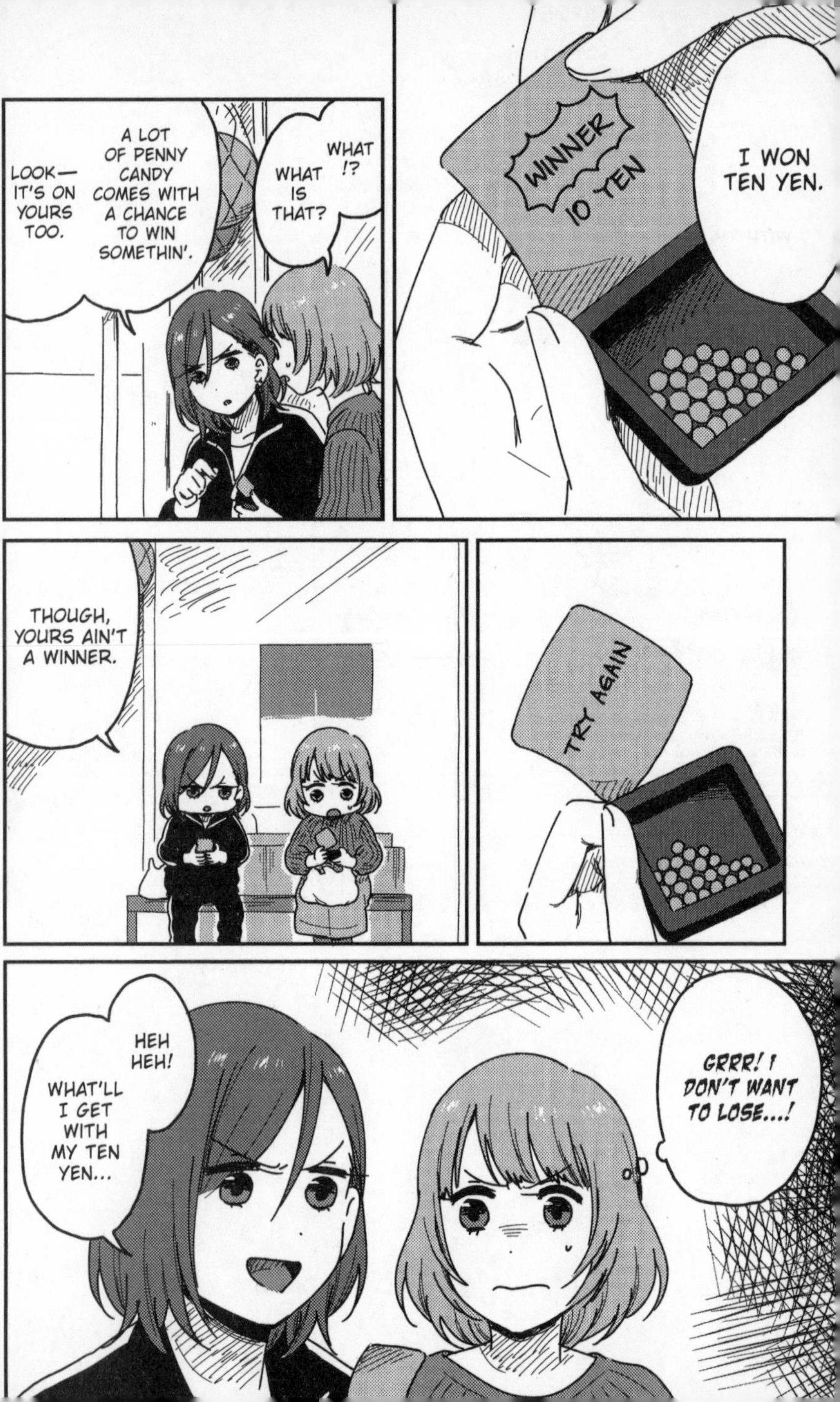
I WON TEN YEN.
WINNER 10 YEN
WHAT !?
WHAT IS THAT?
A LOT OF PENNY CANDY COMES WITH A CHANCE TO WIN SOMETHIN'.
LOOK— IT'S ON YOURS TOO.
TRY AGAIN
THOUGH, YOURS AIN'T A WINNER.
GRRR! I DON'T WANT TO LOSE...!
HEH HEH! WHAT'LL I GET WITH MY TEN YEN...

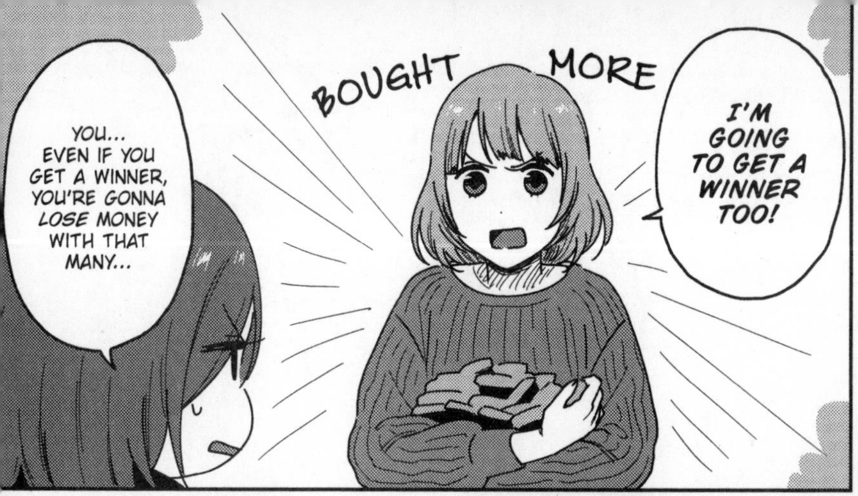
BOUGHT MORE
I'M GOING TO GET A WINNER TOO!
YOU... EVEN IF YOU GET A WINNER, YOU'RE GONNA LOSE MONEY WITH THAT MANY...
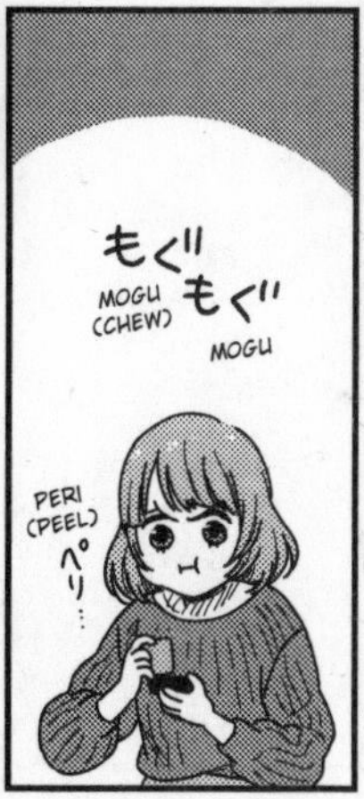
もぐ MOGU (CHEW) もぐ MOGU
ぺり… PERI (PEEL)
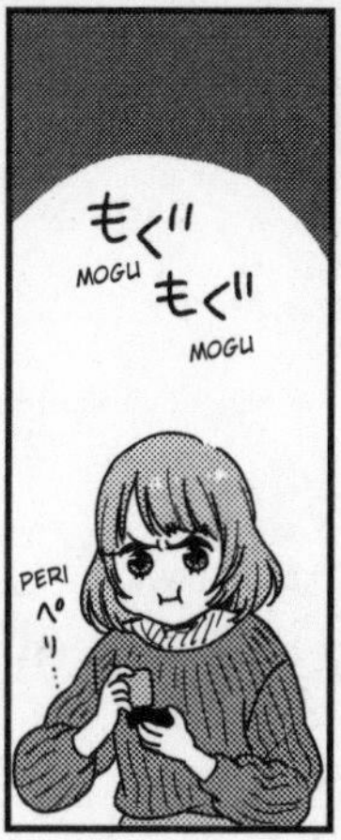
もぐ MOGU もぐ MOGU
ぺり… PERI
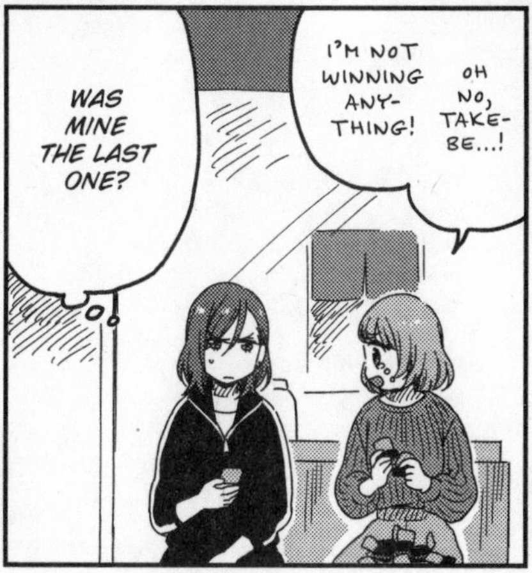
OH NO, TAKE-BE...!
I'M NOT WINNING ANY-THING!
WAS MINE THE LAST ONE?

END

Catch These Hands! 2

murata

Translation: AMANDA HALEY ✖ Lettering: BIANCA PISTILLO

WATASHI NO KOBUSHI WO UKETOMETE!
Vol. 2
©murata 2019
First published in Japan in 2019 by KADOKAWA CORPORATION, Tokyo.
English translation rights arranged with KADOKAWA CORPORATION, Tokyo through TUTTLE-MORI AGENCY, INC., Tokyo.

English translation © 2022 by Yen Press, LLC

Yen Press
150 West 30th Street, 19th Floor
New York, NY 10001

Visit us at yenpress.com
facebook.com/yenpress
twitter.com/yenpress
yenpress.tumblr.com
instagram.com/yenpress

First Yen Press Edition: June 2022
Edited by Yen Press Editorial:
Leilah Labossiere, Carl Li
Designed by Yen Press Design:
Wendy Chan

Yen Press is an imprint of Yen Press, LLC. The Yen Press name and logo are trademarks of Yen Press, LLC.

The publisher is not responsible for websites (or their content) that are not owned by the publisher.

Library of Congress Control Number: 2021950487

ISBNs: 978-1-9753-4015-5 (paperback)
978-1-9753-4016-2 (ebook)

10 9 8 7 6 5 4 3 2 1

WOR
Printed in the
United States of America